APPROACHES TO LIFESPAN WRITING RESEARCH: GENERATING AN ACTIONABLE COHERENCE

PERSPECTIVES ON WRITING

Series Editors, Rich Rice, Heather MacNeill Falconer, and J. Michael Rifenburg
Consulting Editor, Susan H. McLeod | Associate Series Editor, Jonathan P. Hunt

The Perspectives on Writing series addresses writing studies in a broad sense. Consistent with the wide ranging approaches characteristic of teaching and scholarship in writing across the curriculum, the series presents works that take divergent perspectives on working as a writer, teaching writing, administering writing programs, and studying writing in its various forms.

The WAC Clearinghouse, Colorado State University Open Press, and University Press of Colorado are collaborating so that these books will be widely available through free digital distribution and low-cost print editions. The publishers and the Series editors are committed to the principle that knowledge should freely circulate. We see the opportunities that new technologies have for further democratizing knowledge. And we see that to share the power of writing is to share the means for all to articulate their needs, interest, and learning into the great experiment of literacy.

Recent Books in the Series

Lesley Erin Bartlett, Sandra L. Tarabochia, Andrea R. Olinger, and Margaret J. Marshall (Eds.), *Diverse Approaches to Teaching, Learning, and Writing Across the Curriculum: IWAC at 25* (2020)

Hannah J. Rule, *Situating Writing Processes* (2019)

Asao B. Inoue, *Labor-Based Grading Contracts: Building Equity and Inclusion in the Compassionate Writing Classroom* (2019)

Mark Sutton and Sally Chandler (Eds.), *The Writing Studio Sampler: Stories About Change* (2018)

Kristine L. Blair and Lee Nickoson (Eds.), *Composing Feminist Interventions: Activism, Engagement, Praxis* (2018)

Mya Poe, Asao B. Inoue, and Norbert Elliot (Eds.), *Writing Assessment, Social Justice, and the Advancement of Opportunity* (2018)

Patricia Portanova, J. Michael Rifenburg, and Duane Roen (Eds.), *Contemporary Perspectives on Cognition and Writing* (2017)

Douglas M. Walls and Stephanie Vie (Eds.), *Social Writing/Social Media: Publics, Presentations, and Pedagogies* (2017)

Laura R. Micciche, *Acknowledging Writing Partners* (2017)

Susan H. McLeod, Dave Stock, and Bradley T. Hughes (Eds.), *Two WPA Pioneers: Ednah Shepherd Thomas and Joyce Steward* (2017)

APPROACHES TO LIFESPAN WRITING RESEARCH: GENERATING AN ACTIONABLE COHERENCE

Edited by Ryan J. Dippre and Talinn Phillips

The WAC Clearinghouse
wac.colostate.edu
Fort Collins, Colorado

University Press of Colorado
upcolorado.com
Louisville, Colorado

The WAC Clearinghouse, Fort Collins, Colorado 80523

University Press of Colorado, Louisville, Colorado 80027

© 2020 by Ryan J. Dippre and Talinn Phillips and the authors of individual chapters. This work is licensed under a Creative Commons Attribution-NonCommercial-NoDerivatives 4.0 International.

ISBN 978-1-64215-105-3 (PDF) | 978-1-64215-106-0 (ePub) | 978-1-64642-145-9 (pbk.)

DOI: 10.37514/PER-B.2020.1053

Library of Congress Cataloging-in-Publication Data

Names: Dippre, Ryan J., editor. | Phillips, Talinn, editor.
Title: Approaches to lifespan writing research : generating an actionable coherence / edited by Ryan J. Dippre and Talinn Phillips.
Description: Fort Collins, Colorado : The WAC Clearinghouse ; Boulder, Colorado : University Press of Colorado, 2020. | Series: Perspectives on writing | Includes bibliographical references.
Identifiers: LCCN 2020033059 (print) | LCCN 2020033060 (ebook) | ISBN 9781646421459 (paperback) | ISBN 9781642151053 (pdf) | ISBN 9781642151060 (epub)
Subjects: LCSH: English language—Rhetoric—Study and teaching—Research. | Interdisciplinary approach in education.
Classification: LCC PE1404 .A68 2020 (print) | LCC PE1404 (ebook) | DDC 428.0071—dc23
LC record available at https://lccn.loc.gov/2020033059
LC ebook record available at https://lccn.loc.gov/2020033060

Copyeditor: Don Donahue
Designer: Mike Palmquist
Series Editors: Rich Rice, Heather MacNeill Falconer, and J. Michael Rifenburg
Consulting Editor: Susan H. McLeod
Associate Editor: Jonathan P. Hunt
Cover Photo: "Starling Murmuration" by Airwolfhound, licensed under the Creative Commons Attribution-Share Alike 2.0 Generic license

The WAC Clearinghouse supports teachers of writing across the disciplines. Hosted by Colorado State University, and supported by the Colorado State University Open Press, it brings together scholarly journals and book series as well as resources for teachers who use writing in their courses. This book is available in digital formats for free download at wac.colostate.edu.

Founded in 1965, the University Press of Colorado is a nonprofit cooperative publishing enterprise supported, in part, by Adams State University, Colorado State University, Fort Lewis College, Metropolitan State University of Denver, Regis University, University of Colorado, University of Northern Colorado, Utah State University, and Western Colorado University. For more information, visit upcolorado.com. The Press partners with the Clearinghouse to make its books available in print.

For Chuck Bazerman, with deep gratitude for his tremendous investment in us.

CONTENTS

Acknowledgments ix

Preface xi
    Charles Bazerman

Introduction. Generating Murmurations for an Actionable Coherence. 3
    Ryan J. Dippre and Talinn Phillips

PART 1. EMBRACING THE RADICAL 13

Chapter 1. Across, Through, and With: Ontological Orientations for
Lifespan Writing Research 15
    Anna Smith

Chapter 2. Always Already Relocalized: The Protean Nature of Context
in Lifespan Writing Research 27
    Ryan J. Dippre and Anna Smith

Chapter 3. Quantitative Perspectives to the Study of Writing Across
the Lifespan: A Conceptual Overview and Focus on Structural
Equation Modeling 39
    Matthew C. Zajic and Apryl L. Poch

Chapter 4. Making Sense of a Person's Literate Life: Literacy Narratives
in a 100-Year-Study on Literacy Development 67
    Magdalena Knappik

Chapter 5. A Definition of Everyday Writing: Methods for a Writer-
Informed Approach to Lifespan Writing. 81
    Jeff Naftzinger

Chapter 6. Revisiting Participants After Publication: Continuing
Writing Partnerships. 97
    Lauren Rosenberg

PART 2. LEVERAGING OUR TRADITIONS .109

Chapter 7. Literacy Tours and Material Matters: Principles for
Studying the Literate Lives of Older Adults 111
    Lauren Marshall Bowen

Chapter 8. Toward an Understanding of the Multidirectional Nature of Family Literacy Development. 127
    Yvonne Lee

Chapter 9. Writing as a Matter of Life and Death: Writing Through the Transition Between Employment and Retirement in the USA 143
    James T. Zebroski

Chapter 10. The Relations Among the Development of Written Language and Executive Functions for Children in Elementary School . . . 159
    Lara-Jeane C. Costa, Jeffrey A. Greene, and Stephen R. Hooper

Chapter 11. Interpreting and Explaining Data Representations: A Comparison Across Grades 1–7 177
    Diana J. Arya, Anthony Clairmont, and Sarah Hirsch

Chapter 12. Informing Inquiry into Writing Across the Lifespan from Perspectives on Students with Learning Disabilities or Autism Spectrum Disorder. 195
    Apryl L. Poch, Matthew C. Zajic, and Steve Graham

Chapter 13. Visualizing Writing Development: Mapping Writers' Conceptions of Writing through the Lifespan. 211
    Erin Workman

Chapter 14. Addressing the Futurity of Literate Action: Tracing the Enduring Consequences of Acting with Inscriptions throughout the Lifeworld 225
    Kevin Roozen

Conclusion as Prolegomena: From Points of Convergence to Murmurations across Sites, Researchers, and Methods 247
    Ryan J. Dippre and Talinn Phillips

Epilogue. 255
    Deborah Brandt

Contributors 261

ACKNOWLEDGMENTS

This project truly stands on the shoulders of giants and we are so grateful for the foundation they built for us. Many thanks to the original Lifespan Writing Development Group for their decades of individual research and for their work as a collective that makes it possible for us to move forward. We're especially grateful to Deb Brandt and Steve Graham for their ongoing support of our work and the expertise they've offered. Thank you to Christiane Donahue and the other folks at Dartmouth for the gift to the field that is the Dartmouth Summer Seminar. The Writing Through the Lifespan Collaboration probably wouldn't exist without the incredible work they do every year to professionalize composition researchers and to create the intellectual environment where this kind of project could take root. We also want to thank our contributors and the Writing Through the Lifespan Collaboration for their enthusiasm and commitment to the lifespan writing research project. Finally, it will no doubt quickly become clear to readers that none of this exists without Chuck Bazerman. Thank you, Chuck, for all of the work you've done to make this impossible dream start to look possible and for the many, many ways that you've supported us.

PREFACE

Charles Bazerman
University of California, Santa Barbara

Lifespan development of writing has an intuitive obviousness. Of course it takes a long time to develop as a writer! Of course even famous writers keep working at it and learning new things! Of course the five year old struggling with a pencil to form letters may thirty years later be the same person struggling with a plot outline or a corporate report! Of course students had writing experiences before getting to our classes and will have others after!

Yet in that obviousness we are tempted to a naiveté—that we know what skilled writing is and what an idealized developmental pathway to it might look like. Our idealized model might come from the writing life we have known or the writing life we wish we had known. Our idealized model might come from whatever school curriculum we were familiar with or might reflect individualistic rebellion against school values and practices. Wherever our ideas about development came from, they likely would be allied with our beliefs about knowing what writing is and what counts as skilled writers.

Even though I had spent many years researching the variety of writing, the history and distinctiveness of genres within evolving social conditions, the contingences and situatedness of writing choices, and the creative ingenuity of writers forging new paths, I was still tempted to think we could draw something of a coherent picture of development. Somehow I had projected the fortunate writing experiences I had as a middle-class, suburban child passing through elite universities into a normalized picture—as though my complex development would somehow define endpoints of writing development, if not the exact way stations. How egocentric! How arrogant! How persistently naive!

But we all tend to be egocentric in our understanding of writing because we know largely what we have learned, or the imagined trajectories and idealized accounts of icons we cannot measure up to. There is no large, realistic picture available to us at this time, only the neighborhoods we have passed through. From that journey into a world that has become normal to us we make generalizations and idealizations about writing and writing development. Even if curiosity or scholarship or happenstance have introduced us to different writing worlds, we still carry with us our deeply naturalized understandings of writing. These understandings become reinforced every time we sit down to write because we activate the resources and visions we know as we strive to follow our best lights in creating our best next text. This creative and determined growth in successive problem-solving increases the intensity and scope of our best lights, as we incorporate new tricks, strategies, and deeper understandings. Yet our vision remains limited to the space illuminated by those best lights.

Under such illusions I initially brought together a panel of wonderful scholars that engaged in four years of illuminating discussion—Arthur N. Applebee, Virginia W. Berninger, Deborah Brandt, Steve Graham, Paul Kei Matsuda, Sandra Murphy, Deborah Wells Rowe, and Mary Schleppegrell. The group, in their collective wisdom, moved the discussion to a broader and more comprehensive vision of principles of investigation that would make visible the great diversity of writing development trajectories (see Bazerman et al., 2017, 2018). We got far, but it remained only the invitation to a beginning.

The Writing Through the Lifespan Collaboration and this, their first volume, take up that invitation, cutting us loose from our moorings of normalization into the great varieties of experience, the great varieties of trajectories that look so different. Even more challenging, writing itself is constantly evolving, growing through the creative inventions of writers who constantly remake writing and themselves in addressing the challenges in front of them. The Writing Through the Lifespan Collaboration also started from hopes of coherence of a great study that would contain multitudes, yet could be comprehended in a single large frame, like a Breughel painting. But bringing the inquiries together rather than adding up pulls us in many directions. We have yet to find the practices, themes, processes, principles that can draw it all together with some clarifying structure. Some methods proposed here try to aggregate quantitatively or at least follow similar paths by proposing repeated methods for following the writers, but they are only bets to lead us into the obscure. If we are now finding uncontainable multitudes, we must first get lost within the multitudes to know its vastness and variety. At some point exploratory knowledge may, we trust, emerge in orders—not predetermined orders or orders forced by our lassoing various wild pieces and trying to tie them down. We trust that order will reveal itself within the material we find.

The leaders of the collaboration and editors of this volume, Ryan Dippre and Talinn Phillips, draw on the metaphor of bird murmurations to express a trust in emergent order. The order that emerges and coordinates motion in a flock forms not because any of the birds have a spatial sense of the whole or a plan for coordinated movement. The order emerges because each is attuned to the movement of a few of its close neighbors. To take this metaphor seriously is to hope that somehow the inquiry will be self-organizing as studies will position themselves in relation to neighboring studies and soon observable patterns will emerge. This is a plausible hope, a plausible strategy, rather than imposing a dominant theory or frame to organize a normal science, or an incremental adding of facts that will somehow add up to a great structure. In this particular case it is a strategy befitting the complex variety of writing development—responsive to so many variables and constantly inspired by human invention and creativity in protean and evolving situations. But as of the moment we are still seeing the birds flying in different directions, not sure whether self-organization will occur or whether some groups will start to identify some pattern at some level that will attract them to align with each other and form coherent clusters moving in coordinated harmony.

The metaphor of murmurations has a further implication that defines our current naiveté. The patterned fluid beauty of the murmurations of birds is perceivable only by those that stand apart and view it from a distance. The ones that participate in the flock sense only what is immediately around them. Now we do not yet have that distance to see even if any patterns are emerging. We can see only those studies around us that attract us to align ourselves with. So now the first task is to watch in wonder at the rich variety they display, to see what we can point out to each other, to appreciate the vastness of how people find their separate paths to grow into writing creatures. In so doing we can expand our sights and see more that we can align ourselves with and move in response to each other.

While it is uncomfortable to venture forth on journeys where we don't know where we are headed, yet it is a journey filled with inspirations. Writing evolves, textual worlds evolve, the social worlds that writing is part of evolve, people evolve as writers, and our research to understand this emergent world itself evolves perhaps in turn to change practice. What a broad and deep sky to explore together! How many best lights to follow and enjoy! What unknown orders for us to bring into awareness!

REFERENCES

Bazerman, C., Applebee, A. N., Berninger, V. W., Brandt, D., Graham, S., Jeffrey, J. V., Matsuda, P. K., Murphy, S., Rowe, D. W., Schleppegrell, M. & Wilcox, K. C. (2017). Taking the long view on writing development. *Research in the Teaching of English, 51*(3), 351–360.

Bazerman, C., Applebee, A. N., Berninger, V. W., Brandt, D., Graham, S., Jeffery, J. V., Matsuda, P. K., Murphy, S., Rowe, D. W., Schleppegrell, M. & Wilcox, K. C. (Eds.). (2018). *The lifespan development of writing*. National Council of Teachers of English.

APPROACHES TO LIFESPAN WRITING RESEARCH: GENERATING AN ACTIONABLE COHERENCE

INTRODUCTION.
GENERATING MURMURATIONS FOR AN ACTIONABLE COHERENCE

Ryan J. Dippre
University of Maine

Talinn Phillips
Ohio University

Increasing numbers of researchers in writing studies, literacy, and education are recognizing that studying literacy development over wider segments of time yields new and exciting insights that we cannot achieve through more traditional methods. Recent special issues (e.g., *Writing and Pedagogy*, 2018 and *Literacy and Composition Studies*, 2018) and edited collections (Bazerman et al., 2018; Fishman & Kimme-Hea, in press) that draw on longitudinal approaches are coinciding with the production of impressive longitudinal work (e.g., Compton-Lilly, 2014). Combined, this recent research suggests a growing interest in longitudinal and lifespan writing research. This volume calls for more lifespan writing research while also working to operationalize that research agenda. We examine methodological challenges and opportunities in lifespan research and suggest that a range of new insights and understandings about writing and literacy await us when we shift our perspective to how writing changes throughout the entire lifespan.

When Bazerman (2018) subtitled his recent chapter "A Heuristic for an Impossible Dream," he did not exaggerate the difficulties of developing radically longitudinal studies of writing development—studies that might even follow writers throughout the course of their lives. Building the kind of multi-site, multi-generational study Bazerman proposes is indeed a daunting task. He asks, "how can we understand people's varied pathways into writing and their varied pathways to achievement" (2018, p. 327)? He suggests that in order to trace these widely varying pathways of writing development—what Dippre (2019) has referred to as "rambling pathways" of development (p. 14)—that writing studies researchers could build "a rich body of longitudinal studies of writing development across the entire span of many people of many backgrounds and experiences" (p. 327).

Bazerman notes that a project such as this "may seem quixotic and perhaps impossible in its magnitude, expense, and logistical complexity" (2018, p. 327), but he works through this complexity to trace the broad outlines of such a project.

Approaches to Lifespan Writing Research works to flesh out that outline as a next step toward aligned, integrated, multi-site longitudinal studies of writing. In each of these chapters our authors attempt to explicate their epistemological stances, methodological choices, and theoretical reasoning so that resonance across research sites, methods, and findings can begin to be articulated, followed up, and built upon. If Bazerman's initial challenge to the field requires a disregard for what is easy—even, perhaps, for what is possible—the very complexity embraced by the project has also generated an embrace of collaboration and of joint attention to a difficult problem.

The complexity of researching writing through the lifespan emerges, in large part, from the fact that writing is itself complex (Bazerman et al., 2017, 2018). Writing is caught up in all facets of our lives, whether explicitly attended to or not. Whether we are writing to our senators or our child's school, making a list of groceries, completing taxes, or writing a report for our employers, we are engaged in various spheres of social and material engagement, working with various audiences, and attending to various demands on our own and others' time. But through it all, we are writing. Attending to writing through the lifespan needs to attend to all of this complexity *somehow*. The task of this volume is to present potential "hows" and begin to render the impossible slightly more possible for future research on writing through the lifespan.

Yet our aims for this volume are not just that it coheres in these ways, but that it actively *generates murmurations*, or a path forward for those engaged in lifespan writing research. *Murmurations* describes the coordinated movements of flocks of birds (especially starlings—footage is readily available online) and may involve up to thousands of birds moving together while also easily able to change directions and goals. Murmurations are simultaneously chaotic and deeply ordered—chaotic in that a murmuration changes continuously in shape and direction through time, yet deeply ordered in that the movement is seamless and unified and displays a common goal. Fluidity and unified purpose through chaos seem to us a plausible strategy for tackling such a complex research problem, a claim we unpack more fully in our conclusion.

WRITING THROUGH THE LIFESPAN COLLABORATION: A BRIEF AND PARTIAL HISTORY

The Writing through the Lifespan Collaboration had its start at the 2016 Dartmouth Summer Seminar for Composition Research and Conference. Charles

Bazerman, a Summer Seminar leader and a plenary speaker at the accompanying conference, gave both a workshop and a closing address in which he shared about the lifespan work he'd initiated among senior writing studies scholars from multiple disciplines—the Lifespan Writing Development Group. Bazerman's Dartmouth presentations encouraged researchers to turn their attention to the lifespan by "think[ing] longitudinally" about the work of studying writing. In response to Bazerman's call, we, as participants in the Seminar and Conference, wrote a call for interested researchers to take up this challenge of longitudinal writing research that would truly capture lifespans. Our call yielded over forty researchers in over half a dozen different countries.

These initial participants met online in early 2017, followed by a face-to-face meeting at the Conference on College Composition and Communication in Portland, Oregon. In these meetings, the Collaboration decided to focus our attention on shared language and understandings that we might bring to bear on research across a range of theoretical and empirical approaches, as well as participant age groups. The group turned to the earlier work of Bazerman's Lifespan Writing Development Group and their principles for lifespan writing development, as articulated in abbreviated form in *Research in the Teaching of English* and in greater detail in *The Lifespan Development of Writing* edited collection (Bazerman et al., 2017, 2018). Participants explored their understandings of these principles in blog posts at www.lifespanwriting.org. These online discussions triggered further waves of online meetings about the themes emerging across the blog posts.

Through these online discussions, the Collaboration identified three themes to shape our inaugural conference on lifespan writing research in May 2018: theory, identity, and society. These themes led to over two dozen presentations and plenary talks during the conference from May 31–June 2, 2018, which in turn have led to this book.

In this volume, we build upon that conference, drawing in other voices from the diverse fields that research writing, to chart a course for future lifespan writing research. Part of this work involves developing a sense of what it means to take a lifespan perspective on writing research. Is there a meaningful distinction between *lifespan* writing research and longitudinal research? Is lifespan writing research a method? A methodology? A theoretical framework? A philosophical orientation?

Drawing on the work and insight of the Collaboration as a whole over several months, we arrived at a working definition of *lifespan writing research*, beginning with an independent definition of each term:

> *Lifespan*: Refers to the entirety of a lifetime—both chronologically (i.e., cradle to grave) and across the many social

spheres that writers participate in (the term "life-wide" has also been used to reference this). To orient something to the lifespan is to locate change within a life-long and life-wide perspective, up to and including multiple lifespans (i.e., across generations).

Writing: Refers to acts of inscribed meaning-making. Any act of this sort necessarily involves multiple modes of semiotic engagement and multiple dimensions of human activity.

Research: Refers to the accountable collection and study of records, or evidence of writing broadly construed (i.e., retrospective examination of lived experience, textual artifacts, video capture of inscription, and so on). Different research traditions determine what counts as "accountable," and different research questions will direct what records to collect and analyze.

From these individual definitions, we developed this working definition of the lifespan writing research concept:

Lifespan Writing Research examines acts of inscribed meaning-making, the products of it, and the multiple dimensions of human activity that relate to it in order to build accounts of whether and how writers and writing change throughout the duration and breadth of the lifespan. (Writing through the Lifespan Collaboration, 2019)

This definition, as we will see in this collection, allows for studies with a wide range of methodological approaches, theoretical orientations, and subpopulations to inform our study of writing through the lifespan, while also orienting all research toward a common goal (that is, a holistic understanding of writing from cradle to grave).

Thus, while lifespan writing research is often longitudinal and qualitative, it is not exclusively so. We will likely also find that focused studies on particular age groups and populations that are under-studied in writing research generally (e.g., Lee; Rosenberg; Bowen; Arya et al., this volume) may offer useful insights for a lifespan perspective on writing, as will some quantitative methods (e.g., Zajic & Poch or Costa et al., this volume). As the chapters in this collection show, our approach to lifespan writing research is methodologically expansive, embracing any method that promises to contribute to our understanding of writing development. We also suggest that when lifespan research *is* longitudinal and qualitative, it is still distinct in that it recursively, intentionally, and methodically looks forward, backward, and across in time as it works to understand the causes, triggers, and impacts on writing development in an individual's life. Thus, the work of the Collaboration, from its inception to the chapters in this volume, suggest that the term lifespan refers to research oriented to both a lifelong and life-wide understanding of how writers write and of how they change as writers in their lifeworlds. Lifespan writing research as an area of inquiry must then endeavor to run across lifeworlds, across ages, across technologies, across social strata, and across populations, but always with the intention of attending to writing in all of its complexity from cradle to grave.

Readers may have also noticed the conspicuous absence of the term "development" from the definition above. This was a deliberate choice on the part of the Collaboration to further our broader aims of disrupting the writing normativities that proliferate, especially during formal schooling. And while, by definition, members of the Collaboration are highly invested in the value of writing, we don't wish to suggest that a life without writing is somehow a failure. Thus, it is not that we are uninterested in *development* but that we are equally interested in *change*, in *stasis*, even in *decline* in one's abilities. In short, we want to understand what happens in people's writing lives and why, regardless of whether what happens could be understood as "development" or not. Moreover, we argue that investigating writing lives—period—can enable those of us in writing studies to support more people becoming more versatile and capable writers.

GENERATING MURMURATIONS FOR AN ACTIONABLE COHERENCE

Since the beginning of the Collaboration, and perhaps because of the complexity that the Collaboration has tried to embrace, there has been a keenly felt need for a unified path forward in lifespan writing research. That is, the members of the Collaboration were not interested in merely developing studies that looked across wide swaths of time at different sites. These swaths of time, these sites, had to speak to one another in some way. It quickly became clear that we were unlikely to get these sites to synergize through a shared methodology, though methodology was certainly one avenue through which coherence could be built. Instead, we've focused on aligning sets of methods so that epistemological foundations, methodological choices, and the conceptualizing of results could resonate across studies.

Within this volume, our approach to coherence can be explained by a family of terms. First, the following chapters cohere through a shared *phenomenon of interest*. Each chapter draws on a range of methods, populations, and theoretical orientations to understand, in some way, lifespan writing in all of its complexity. But a phenomenon of interest, even one as capacious as lifespan writing, still has limits since, at this point, lifespan writing is still largely an unknown. As Bazerman et al. (2018) note, many questions remain about the ways in which writers (and their writing) change throughout the course of a lifetime. The uncertainties of our phenomenon of interest call for openness in our embrace of theories and methods. Will phenomenological hermeneutics provide insight to lifespan writing? Will structural equation modeling? Would it be productive to align sociohistoric theory with large-scale data collection? These questions, and many others, are worth considering as the field's understanding of what it means to write through the lifespan continues to grow. Even while we attend to a phenomenon of interest, then, we are careful to remain open to new approaches for examining that phenomenon.

Openness, as a concept, keeps lifespan writing a "big tent" research activity—it encourages new approaches and new understandings that can contribute to a growing understanding of this phenomenon of interest. But openness alone does not wholly capture the inherent interdisciplinarity of lifespan writing research or the value of a big tent. The pursuit of coherence not only embraces openness but also actively *resists regimentation*. If, as Haswell (2012) suggests, "the true enemy is people's love of regimentation," then the nebulous nature of lifespan writing will regularly run the risk of being simplified, flattened, and rendered easy to measure via regimentation. Any attempt at coherence across methods, methodologies, theories, and orientations needs to actively deny regimentation in order to ensure that we're researching the whole massive research object—the entire elephant, not just its parts. By attending to the phenomenon of interest of lifespan writing with openness while actively resisting regimentation, the Collaboration—and, by extension, this collection—seeks to develop a coherence across theoretical frameworks, methods, and findings.

The chapters in this collection explore new framings, methods, and approaches for lifespan writing research, propose new sites of study, identify provocative findings, and do so while both looking inward, toward a coherent series of connections across studies, and looking outward, toward future research questions, sites, and methods. Like all effective research, the work of the next fourteen chapters both presents answers to pressing questions and uses those answers to develop new questions that future research —more informed, more responsive to other methods, more tied into a growing and coherent understanding of lifespan writing—can follow.

OVERVIEW OF APPROACHES TO LIFESPAN WRITING RESEARCH

This volume is organized into two parts that provide a detailed but coherent vision of the ongoing development of lifespan writing research, its limits, and its possibilities. It is our hope that subsequent lifespan writing researchers will keep this robust multidimensionality in mind as they continue to expand our knowledge of what it looks like to write through the lifespan. One of the ongoing risks of working with such a massive research object is the too-human tendency for simplicity. While simplicity certainly has its value, we argue that the multidimensionality of lifespan writing needs to be valued and carefully attended to so that our understandings of it do not flatten over time. To that end, we've drawn together authors from diverse fields invested in writing research and asked those authors to give special attention to methodology throughout so that we can both learn from each other and develop a deeper appreciation for bringing diverse methods to bear on lifespan writing. Our authors employ the diverse disciplinary discourses of fields including rhetoric & composition, education, sociology, psychology, medicine, and more. Their diversity begins to uncover the range of expertise needed for lifespan writing research and it is our sincere hope that the interconnected work of this volume encourages similar tendencies in future work.

We begin as we mean to go on: boldly. "Part 1: Embracing the Radical" collects innovative and even radical frameworks and methodologies from different disciplines that have been developed in order to give writing studies the tools to tackle lifespan writing. With this section we demonstrate that, to capture the complexity of the lifespan, we must engage in ongoing methodological reflection and, in many cases, substantial innovation. In Chapter 1, Anna Smith proposes three orientations to lifespan writing research that would enable researchers to reflexively engage with their selection of methods and theory in conducting this kind of radical longitudinal research. Next, Ryan J. Dippre and Anna Smith (Chapter 2) suggest that treating context as protean and responsive to the ongoing use of practices in context is a vital consideration for future lifespan writing research. Then Matthew C. Zajic and Apryl L. Poch (Chapter 3) draw our attention to the importance of quantitative research for lifespan research, introducing us to the possibilities that structural equation modeling offers lifespan writing researchers when set along a broad enough time frame. In Chapter 4, Magdalena Knappik provides a rigorous assessment of the affordances of the literacy autobiography as lifespan research data while Jeff Naftzinger (Chapter 5) urges lifespan writing researchers to include *everyday writing* in their work. Drawing on time-use diaries and interviews, Naftzinger uncovers the power of everyday writing as a concept for both researchers and participants at all stages of the lifespan. Lauren Rosenberg (Chapter 6) concludes "Embracing the Radical" by diving more deeply into the realities of interacting with qualitative research participants longitudinally. She also considers the ways in which revisiting participants might provide new insights for researcher and participant alike.

But just as lifespan writing research needs radical departures from disciplinary confines (as exemplified in Part 1), "Part 2: Leveraging Our Traditions" capitalizes on what writing studies already offers by exemplifying targeted innovations to well established theories, methods, and frameworks. In Chapter 7, Lauren Bowen adapts sociohistoric methods to study the literate action of one older writer but does so with an innovative *literacy tour* approach. Yvonne Lee's (Chapter 8) qualitative project suggests the possibilities of radically longitudinal work by attending to intergenerational connections in one family and James T. Zebroski (Chapter 9) offers autoethnographic examinations of the intersecting spaces of the social and the personal. In Chapter 10, Lara-Jeane C. Costa, Jeffrey A. Greene, and Stephen R. Hooper draw on structural equation modeling to trace the relationship of executive function and written language from first through fourth grade.

The remaining chapters give particular attention to semiosis. Diana Arya, Anthony Clairmont, and Sarah Hirsch (Chapter 11) draw on students of varying ages, backgrounds, and socioeconomic statuses to examine critical meaning-making and data representation, thereby bringing new modalities to our attention as we think about how writers grow and change over time.

Apryl L. Poch, Matthew C. Zajic, and Steve Graham (Chapter 12) take a lifespan perspective on understanding the writing skills of individuals with learning disabilities or with autism spectrum disorder, highlighting what is currently known about these two groups of writers and where research needs to go. Erin Workman (Chapter 13) then transforms the research tradition of concept maps for unpacking the psychological complexity of the literate lives that our research participants engage in. Finally, Kevin Roozen (Chapter 14) explores the continual becoming of people, practices, and social worlds through a longitudinal case study of one undergraduate throughout his college experience. By attending to the range of everyday inscription that his subject engages in, Roozen identifies the ways in which lifeworlds are integrated, laminated, and developed throughout the lifespan.

We conclude by demonstrating how these seemingly disconnected individual studies together suggest patterns of inquiry. We outline how the points of convergence in some of these chapters can be developed into *lines of inquiry*—a rigorous investigation of a concept or set of concepts that can be traced through the lifespan and scaled from a case study to a large data set—and posit that those lines of inquiry can generate the kinds of murmurations needed to keep such a diverse set of researchers, projects, and sites moving forward, together.

With these chapters we argue for the richness and diversity inherent to lifespan writing research and for the serendipities it creates. We hope that this wide-ranging volume encourages lifespan writing researchers to maintain an openness and generosity to the unique contributions that diverse methods, research traditions, and disciplinary perspectives offer up as we jointly pursue lifespan writing.

REFERENCES

Bazerman, C. (2018). Lifespan longitudinal studies of writing development: A heuristic for an impossible dream. In Bazerman et al. (Eds.), *The lifespan development of writing* (pp. 326–365). National Council of Teachers of English.

Bazerman, C. (Ed.). (2018). Writing across the lifespan [Special issue]. *Writing and Pedagogy, 10*(3).

Bazerman, C., Applebee, A. N., Berninger, V. W., Brandt, D., Graham, S., Jeffrey, J. V., Matsuda, P. K., Murphy, S., Rowe, D. W., Schleppegrell, M. & Wilcox, K. C. (2017). Taking the long view on writing development. *Research in the Teaching of English, 51*(3), 351–360.

Bazerman, C., Applebee, A. N., Berninger, V. W., Brandt, D., Graham, S., Jeffery, J. V., Matsuda, P. K., Murphy, S., Rowe, D. W., Schleppegrell, M. & Wilcox, K. C. (Eds.). (2018). *The lifespan development of writing*. National Council of Teachers of English.

Bowen, L. M. & Rumsey, S. K. (Eds.). (2018). Composing a further life [Special issue]. *Literacy in Composition Studies, 6*(2).

Compton-Lilly, C. (2014). The development of writing habitus: A ten-year case study of a young writer. *Written Communication, 31*(4), 371–403.

Dippre, R. J. (2019). *Talk, Tools, and Texts: A Logic-in-Use for Studying Lifespan Literate Action Development*. The WAC Clearinghouse; University Press of Colorado. https://doi.org/10.37514/PRA-B.2019.0384 https://wac.colostate.edu/books/practice/talk/.

Fishman J. & Hea, A. K. (Eds.). (in press). *Telling Stories: Perspectives on Longitudinal Writing Research*. Utah State University Press.

Haswell, R. (2012, Aug 26). Re: Re: Trusting Teachers. Was: Digital Faculty: Professors and Technology, 2012 | *Inside Higher Ed* [Electronic mailing list message]. https://lists.asu.edu/cgi-bin/wa?A2=WPA-L;811419ef.1208&S=.

PART 1.
EMBRACING THE RADICAL

Deepening our understanding of how writing changes across the lifespan is, on its face, a herculean task. Having named our massive research object, what now? The work of the Lifespan Writing Development Group (Bazerman et al., 2018) made clear that a diverse array of expertise is needed in order to fully grasp the complexity of writing across the lifespan. The authors in Part 1 take up that torch, articulating some radical new ways that diverse and evolving research traditions can provide important understandings and methodological approaches for lifespan writing researchers. These six chapters call on us to build exciting new frames for our work and to rethink research commonplaces such as "context" and "informing participants" so that our methods might more fully capture lifespan writing.

Anna Smith opens the collection by asking researchers how we orient ourselves ontologically to our work. She asks us to avoid traditional comparative frameworks and instead to consider orientations *through* which writing development is realized instead of just how, *across* times, spaces, and materials instead of in them, and *with* developing writers instead of simply about them. The second chapter, co-authored by Anna Smith and Ryan Dippre, argues for a much more complicated understanding of context as protean and always being constructed by writers and their communities. They suggest that when researchers treat context as protean instead of static, we are encouraged to focus on the "moment-to-moment work of literate action" and to approach that work from an actor-oriented perspective. Apryl L. Poch and Matthew C. Zajic then provide an overview of what quantitative approaches can contribute to the study of writing development, focusing in particular on the uses of Structural Equation Modeling and its uses for lifespan writing research. In the next chapter, Magdalena Knappik takes us on a deep dive into the "literacy autobiography," arguing for its unique value for lifespan writing research. Drawing on sociological research, including German-language research that monolingual English readers wouldn't otherwise be able to access, Knappik shows us how a richer understanding of the literacy autobiography as a constructed artifact reveals how writers are making sense of their own literacy development. Jeff Naftzinger's chapter explores the work of "everyday writers," or writers who don't really consider themselves writers but, like most of us, engage in various quotidian writing tasks. Naftzinger argues that by asking everyday writers to define the tasks of writing in their lives, that researchers can gain a richer understanding of writing throughout the lifespan. Finally, Lauren Rosenberg explores the powerful, generative capacity of revisiting research participants. Expanding upon feminist research traditions, Rosenberg argues that by revisiting our participants, researchers can foster participants' agency, even leading to new and more deeply collaborative research projects.

The underlying premise of this section (and this book) is that we can't bring something as large, diverse, and complicated as lifespan writing research to heel by simply doing the same old things. Taken together, these chapters nudge us out of our comfort zones methodologically and disciplinarily, asking us to reassess our work and retool it to capture *more*. While other chapters in the book, at least in part, report findings from studies that are currently under way or that have already concluded, these first chapters especially aim to help those who are just undertaking lifespan writing research or who are beginning new projects by urging us towards richer, more multi-faceted work.

CHAPTER 1.

ACROSS, THROUGH, AND WITH: ONTOLOGICAL ORIENTATIONS FOR LIFESPAN WRITING RESEARCH

Anna Smith
Illinois State University

ORIENTING OURSELVES TO WRITING DEVELOPMENT

An *orientation* is consequential. The angle from which we witness an encounter like a car crash heavily influences our perception of what occurred. Did the blue car pull out first? Did the red one slow down? The answers to these questions are not just dependent on empirical evidence, but are also based on the relative perspective from which the accident was experienced. Conceptual and ideological orientations operate similarly. When reading the methodologies of a research report, for instance, the findings can often be anticipated. As part of the inherent bias in any research study, the perspective from which the researcher took on the project focused and constrained her field of vision theoretically and methodologically. For these reasons, when it comes to understanding a person's writing over the lifespan, it matters—or rather, it's consequential—what ontological orientations the researcher brings.

Orientation often refers to a person's attitude, beliefs, or feelings in relation to a particular subject or issue—in the case of lifespan writing, their perspectives on aspects of writing development. Do they emphasize product over process? Where do they look for signs of development? How do they feel about composing themselves, and how does that influence what they anticipate seeing and hearing from others? In this chapter, I also want to invoke a second meaning: *orientation* as the relative position of an entity in reference to another. An orientation is a positional and relational construct. Orientation's synonyms—location, position, and situation—are similarly theoretically consequential for understanding literacies activity (cf. Vandenberg et al., 2006). It's consequential, then, how writing researchers are angled ontologically toward lifespan writing and development in research approaches: What is assumed about writing and its development and how does that play into how we position ourselves relative to the activity in lifespan research? What do these ontological orientations allow writing researchers to see, support, and sustain, and what is obstructed by these perspectives?

In this chapter, I suggest three ontological orientations for lifespan writing research. As a positional question, these orientations are named with prepositions: *across*, *through*, and *with*. For each preposition, I provide theoretical groundings for the orientation and illustrate possible methodological ways forward with examples from long-term, longitudinal, and lifewide writing research to illuminate what comes into the frame with these perspectival orientations. These theoretical and methodological moves, I suggest, assist in embracing the complexity of writing (see Smith, 2018) in lifespan research approaches as they attune writing researchers to mobilities, scaling, and answerability across the lifespan.

Across, *through*, and *with*, as ontological orientations, are presented with the provocation that comparative frameworks have historically dominated methodological approaches in large-scale studies of writing development. Commonly used comparative research designs include setting the work of a cohort of younger writers, say 8-year-olds, alongside that of an older cohort of 12-year-olds, or looking across individuals' development before and after an instructional intervention or school grade promotion. When oriented to the comparative *only* within these designs, however, chronological time, age, or curricular sequence can play an *a priori* determining role in findings (see Smith, Hall et al., 2011); meaning, the later writing or older or more experienced writer is *predetermined* to be the more developed subject. The earlier writing or younger or less experienced writer is then compared against the other, positioning the younger writer and earlier writing in perpetual deficit in relation to the other regardless of the writing practices at play or features of the writing. Across methodological approaches in large-scale writing development studies, from the experiments of Flower and Hayes (1981), to the taxonomy of audiences and functions written by students in high school by the Britton et al. (1975) team, to process studies in writing workshop interventions (e.g., Calkins, 1983), writers' development has been predetermined by being associated with the older student or later writing (see Andrews & Smith, 2011).

Comparative frameworks work well to answer questions regarding *what* is developing—such as differences in the degree of sentence complexity, the number of genres written, or the types of rhetorical approaches tried. If the later, older, and more experienced are assumed to be further developed, however, and analytic attention is focused solely on the comparative points in the design of research, the contours of change in the writing and writer's activity *between* the two comparative points can become occluded. The complex relations of intervening variables, indirect influences, co-emerging life stories, and individuated pathways of development (Bazerman et al., 2017) can be left unexamined. If we merely compare point A to point B on a writer's timeline, we miss the middle. I might go so far as to say we miss the developing writing altogether. A power of lifespan studies is that not only are time and space points A and B within the scope of the research, but so too are points C, D, E, F, G, etc. The lifespan—both radically longitudinal and radically contextual (Dippre & Phillips, this volume)—is a much needed focus in writing studies, because, as argued by Bazerman et al. (2017), research centering writing development that crosses times and spaces are rare and often occur across sub-disciplines, making them difficult to connect with each other. However, a lifespan writing study could still miss the in-betweens and the means or mechanisms of change and stasis in a writer's development, if only oriented to compare points in time and space.

I suggest that one way to work *both* with and beyond comparison is to reflexively consider how writing researchers are oriented ontologically toward the methods and theories taken up in lifespan writing research even, or perhaps especially, when those are comparative. Writing researchers who have been engaged in longitudinal and lifewide studies of writing have most likely grappled with many of the concepts discussed in this chapter. Rather than presenting these orientations as new ways of ontologically positioning ourselves, my intention for this chapter is to present these prepositions as language that can be used to articulate ontological orientations to each other in ways that help us as writing researchers articulate the, at times, unstated assumptions of our research interests. It is a hope of mine that across disciplinary and methodological difference, as orientations are articulated, we may find common ground from which to build collective understandings of writing across the lifespan.

THREE ONTOLOGICAL ORIENTATIONS

How do writing researchers ensure "development" is not predetermined by chronological time or an existing curricular sequence? How do writing researchers study the dynamic in-betweens and embrace the complexity of writing across the lifespan? How do we as writing researchers account for and attune ourselves to the emergent, multidimensional, and dynamic speeds and rhythms of change and stasis? One way to orient writing research to the in-betweens is to draw focus to the means and mechanisms *through* which writing development is realized. This is not just a question of research methods, however. Rather, it is one regarding what writing development is considered to be, or in other words, our ontologies of writing. Seeing writing development as a continual, dynamic, lifewide becoming (Prior & Smith, 2020), for instance, is an ontological perspective that orients the researcher to consider not just what is developing *in* a locale, piece of writing, or time, but *across* times, spaces, and materials. Finally, I suggest we consider lifespan writing research as an activity not just *about* a developing writer, but research conducted *with* developing writers that can draw the writing researcher nearer to the contours of writing development by enabling intimate perspectives on writers' lifespans. Each of these ontological orientations can position researchers toward the in-betweens of development across a lifespan, helping us to embrace the complexity of writing development.

MOBILIZING RESEARCH *ACROSS* THE SPANS OF LIFE

When ontologically oriented to the social and situated nature of literacy practice, writing studies is very good at characterizing writing *in*—in a site, community, workplace, home, etc. In addition to an *in* orientation, I suggest writing researchers purposefully orient their work to studying *across*. An across orientation assumes writing—its writers, artifacts, practices, etc.—are in constant motion (Kell, 2009), and that writing in one location and time is not tethered or isolated to that context; rather, writing is a widely distributed, highly complex phenomenon (Prior, 1998; Shipka, 2011). The concept of *across* seems at the heart of life*span* writing research. Looking across the span of life—be it locations, genres, times, etc.—orients the researcher to how writers become across contexts, across practices, across identities, across modalities, etc. (Prior & Smith, 2020), as well as how those becomings are enabled and constrained as writers move across life. Orienting ontologically to writing's crossings mobilizes the researcher's gaze and methods. For instance, a mobilized gaze on writing is one that is always looking for writing's next crossing, following its lead where it wends its way Nordquist, 2017. Such a gaze is inclusive of lifewide writing across the lifespan. Everyday writing across contexts—lists, text messages, social media posts—are brought into the frame of interest. Naftzinger (this volume) argues that taking this type of orientation with methods such as time-use diaries not only accounts for writing across the life, but also serves to broaden conceptions of writing and who is a writer.

One way to orient methods toward how writing is mobilized across is by taking up a transliteracies approach (Hawkins, 2018; Roozen, 2020). A transliteracies approach is a flexible heuristic focused on "tracing connections and boundaries . . . [in] the activity of creating, maintaining, and disassembling associations across space times" (Stornaiuolo et al., 2017, p. 73). In my work with colleagues Amy Stornaiuolo and Nathan Phillips in developing a transliteracies framework, we highlight that the modifier *trans-* signals attention to mobilities or how things are enabled or acted on to move across, as well as the interrelationships of people, material, and power on the move through social, political, and material networks built into everyday life. We offer four "thinking devices" (Gee, 2014) or moves researchers can make to attend to change and stasis across phenomena—emergence, uptake, scale, and resonance (or the nonlinear, non-causal, and indirect relationships across time-spaces). To think about the (im)mobilities of literacies (inclusive of writing) we suggest questions for each of these moves. Derived from these questions, I suggest that an ontological orientation to across leads to trans- oriented questions such as: How do the writing, writer, and writing practices shift and travel over time and spaces in relation to differently available resources? What are the developmental pathways that emerge as a writer interacts within and across spaces? What are the developmental trajectories made possible across institutions, situations, and the writer's lifespan? How do writing practices become shared and circulate across spaces and times? Attending to how people make meaning across sociomaterial interactions through such questions, we suggest, can "foreground how people and things are mobilized and paralyzed, facilitated and restricted, in different measure and in relation to institutions and systems with long histories" (Stornaiuolo, Smith & Phillips, 2017, p. 72).

These types of questions are oriented to following the lead of the writer as they make their many life crossings—as they move across grades in school, as their practices travel from home to work, as their writing circulates online, as they compose across modes, etc. This presents a clear challenge for the lifespan writing researcher who, for practical and logistical reasons, can't follow every lead. This is, perhaps, why the emphasis in this chapter is on having an ontological orientation rather than any one particular method or approach. If researchers are anticipating ontologically that writing development is a mobilized phenomenon, then they'll approach each method and study design with this in mind. Take, for instance, the research of Wynhoff Olsen and VanDerHeide (2020), who were studying the development of students' argument writing essentially *within* a single classroom and genre. Oriented to writing's mobilities, however, they introduced an intertextual method of analysis that they used to trace students' writing across curricular opportunities, classroom conversations and interactions, and students' lived histories and potential futures as discussed in interviews. This method entailed a backward mapping from a final written artifact across not just drafts, but observation notes, transcribed interviews, and anecdotal details gathered over the study. By orienting to writing across, they were able to trace the ways a shared curriculum diverged in the uptake across four young people's writing practices, calling into question the fallacy of the standardization of writing. Such analysis does not just paint a picture rich in detail of students' writing, but draws lines of connection across moments, locations, practices, and artifacts that fill the lifespan.

Through: Getting at Means and Mechanisms

In discussing approaches in longitudinal studies Saldaña (2003) shares that he intentionally uses the terms of "through" or "across" time instead of "over time," explaining that "over time . . . suggests a sweeping temporal leap, while 'across or through' suggests a more processual immersion throughout the course of longitudinal research" (p. 8). Saldaña is suggesting that orienting toward *through* and *across* are ways to attend to developmental processes or the *hows* of change and stasis in a phenomenon. Since the preposition "across" was used to mobilize a perspective on writing across the lifespan, here I will employ the preposition "through" to orient us to the "processual immersion throughout" or the means and mechanisms of development. As an incredibly complex activity, just tracing what is changing across time and contexts is daunting. Because of this, many methods have been developed to characterize the "whats" of writing—products, processes, practices, craft techniques, etc. This complexity is increased as attention is angled to how that change is accomplished through time and activity. This goes for stasis as well; writing researchers not only trace what stayed the same, but ask: How did intervening factors through time and spaces influence, support, and sustain particular writing processes or practices or craft techniques across time, genre, writing situation, etc.?

There are many ways to orient toward the throughs of writing development. One particular place to look that has proven to be generative in long-term and longitudinal literacy studies is to sociohistoric and sociogenetic scaling activity (see Compton-Lilly, 2017). Lemke's (2000) notion of temporal or timescales, for instance, is one particularly helpful construct to orient the researcher to consider how one space-time is co-produced through another space-time (or Point A and Point B). Lemke argues that different scales of time—from a moment to a class hour to a lifespan—make up and are made of each other. For example, an elderly woman attends a writing group at a café and brings a poem she wrote as a hymn for church for feedback. This activity is just a moment in time, but the activity is drawn from several histories of practice on longer timescales: writing groups, hymnal writing, schooling feedback practices, and the accumulation of her own writing experiences. Her activity is, at the same time, contributing to what writing means for each of those histories. Thus, paying attention to how writing activity scales through moments to longer timescales can help reveal how a writing practice, process, or pathway takes hold or is sustained or changes across the lifespan.

Long-term and longitudinal studies provide a special perspective as a form of lifespan research. In such studies there are either and/or both sustained embedded study alongside participants, and/or long expanses of time between data gathering. This "long view," to borrow the term from Bazerman et al. (2017), provides an opportunity for researchers to draw connections between events, practices, and artifacts through time to identify mechanisms of change that can be less directly observed at a shorter timescale. Researchers are also positioned to trace scaling activity, change, and stasis through timescales that are typically out of reach. In my work with Paul Prior (Smith & Prior, 2020), for instance, we used the concept of the laminated assemblage as a sociogenetic scaling construct to analyze and articulate the development of writing at Urban Word NYC, a Spoken Word and writing-focused out-of-school organization I was privileged to work with across several years (see Dippre & Smith, this volume, for more on contexts as protean). Orienting to the means and mechanisms through which writing developed at the organization and for four focal young men who frequented the out-of-school organization, I traced through scales of activity—from particular events and moments for the young men (such as a poetry performance that occurred spontaneously inside a Burger King one night) to the practices and participation structures that had become typified chronotopically (like poetry slams and writing workshops)—to reveal chains of writing activity through time resonant with activity that might seem distant in times, spaces, and even tenor.

For the young men with whom I worked over the years, they too engaged in temporal scaling practices to effect change in their writing development. David, an Afro-Latinx young man for example, engaged in recurring temporal practices of reminiscence and anticipation (Smith, 2015) around the idea of "the same" to propel his writing across spaces and time. At the beginning of the study David called his early writing "vague teenage banter," which he described as nonspecific, conceptual messages about what was bothering him. He mimicked the writing as, "Teenagers should speak up and say something." Laughing, he shared in a confessional tone that what teens should say or why they should speak up was not explored. To compose these pieces, he had the practice of writing out loud and in his mind while on trains and at home. He wrote print text as a post-composition transcription practice to keep record of his compositions. David also had a visual aesthetic commitment to transcribing the text as closely to a square shape as possible.

One day he had a seemingly innocuous interaction with a friend in a cafeteria. She told him all his personal writing was "the same." This memory crystallized in his mind, and he reminisced on it several times over the next couple of years in order to counter that depiction of his writing. Starting that very night he went home and composed on the page for one of the very first times. He used both Spanish and English in specific, descriptive language to describe a scene and varied the line lengths—breaking the mold of his previous square texts. Such a drastic change in his writing approach was simple to capture empirically as from one day to the next there was an observable status in writing practice to a triggering event to a different writing approach. However, through the temporal scaling practices of reminiscing on this event and anticipating the characterization of his writing as "the same" in the future, he sustained—or scaled—the moment to having lasting effects years later. Now an award winning writer and teaching artist whose writing spans genres, platforms, and modalities, he still refers to this moment in media interviews and talks about the importance of always looking for the ways to think of writing and lives as hybrid, liminal, and divergent—i.e., not "the same." Orienting to the means through which his writing was developing as it scaled across time drew analytic attention to these temporal practices, just as orienting to the mechanisms through which change was occurring for Urban Word NYC provided access to seeing how the organization's typified practices scaled to other disparate traditions such as both schooling and Hip Hop.

Scales and scaling activity (both timescales and sociolinguistic scaling)—and the converse, what does not scale or is left in ruin (Tsing, 2012)—are just one way that change and stasis can be traced *through* Point A to Point B and beyond, or in other words, how writing researchers could orient attention and approaches to how writing development occurs through time and spaces. The invitation here is to consider how approaches in lifespan writing research can be oriented to both what is changing across time, as well as how changes in practices, processes, participant structures, etc. through long timespans and across spaces come to be.

A *With* Orientation Alongside a Life

The final orientation to consider is how the research endeavor itself is conceived with this key question: Are writing researchers conducting research on, research about, or research with people? Beyond the critically important argument that researching *with* is potentially a more humanizing orientation than researching *about* (Paris & Winn, 2014), there are fundamental implications for the phenomenon of study. Researching with a developing writer and with their families and communities makes writing researchers privy to critical *in vivo* insights and provides proximity to practice that cannot be otherwise articulated. In recognizing participants' impressions, intentions, and affect, writing researchers can better discern how understandings of experiences across contexts inform actions and impact developmental pathways (see also Knappik, this volume). As Wilkinson (1986, p. 67) quipped, "Development obviously takes place, but it does not take place obviously." Indeed, engaging in a *with* orientation can facilitate the orientations of *across* and *through*.

A parallel question can be asked: When conducting lifespan writing research are we studying the written products, writing processes, writing practices, and/or the developing writer? As a question of *life*span, it might seem obvious that the focus is on a developing writer (Dippre, 2016), but this is not a given with some methods or research designs. With a *with* orientation, however, we might imagine how to augment and pair methods, to be reflexive and engage in a responsive praxis to better trace the developing writer across and through comparative points.

One way to orient to researching *with* is to consider Patel's (2016) call for *answerability* in decolonizing educational studies. Being answerable, she explains, "includes aspects of being responsible, accountable, and being part of an exchange" (Patel, 2016, p. 73). In this case, researchers see themselves and their research as part of an exchange wherein they are not just *accounting for* their influence in the study, but act *accountable to* participants. Orienting toward answerability with research partners positions writing researchers to "maintain coming-into-being with, being in conversation with" (Patel, 2016, p. 73) relations that keep researchers answerable to the individual or individuals, and to learning as dynamic, responsive, and constant across contexts. Rosenberg (this volume) suggests the method of revisiting as a way to not only account for participants' perspectives across time, but to elicit the "interconnectedness (or lack thereof) between researcher and participant networks of texts, tools, actors, and activity." Methods of this type position the researcher alongside writers as co-producers of the research by maintaining exchange and continuing in conversation with participants. Likewise Knappik (this volume) argues for an embrace of retrospective interviewing, arguing that a writing life lived is informed by the writing life as told. In this method and others such as the time-use diaries employed by Naftzinger (this volume), writers are made central and partnered with researchers rather than positioned as subjects of the researcher who is, in turn, positioned to define development for the partner.

Patel (2016) suggests a few areas that need attentive care when working to be answerable in research. First, she suggests that writing researchers hold themselves answerable to learning, meaning embracing its complexity, inclusive of the aspects of writing beyond inscription. She quotes Ellsworth (2004) who argued:

> Learning never takes place in the absence of bodies, emotions, place, time, sound, image, self-experience, history. It always detours through memory, forgetting, desire, fear, pleasure, surprise, rewriting. And because learning takes place in relation, its detours take us up to and sometimes across the boundaries of habit, recognition, and the socially constructed identities within our selves. (p. 55)

In a study of writing development, being answerable to learning insists on a flexible, inclusive, and widening lens. If the major thrust of a study focuses on a person's written products across time, for instance, a researcher is want to trace the written product across time, space, and meaning for the writer. Patel (2016) also encourages researchers to be answerable to the contexts within and across which learning is studied. Compton-Lilly (2017), for instance, discusses the unique perspective on children's writing development that she gained through negotiating such answerability while researching with children and their families in her 10-year longitudinal literacy development research. By maintaining relationships with children and their families for several years she could trace not just the children's individuated writing activities, but how parents' experiences and expectations across longer timelines became indexed in their children's writing and learning pathways.

This came with a particular intensity as Compton-Lilly worked to maintain "coming-into-being-with" (Patel, 2016, p. 73) relations with her participants. For one young child, for instance, she was privy to know the parents who, during the course of the study, passed away while the child was too young to recall details about the parent. Researching with and being answerable to that child and their family meant staying in relationship with the family and passing along impressions, memories, and stories about the child's parent. Instead of distancing from research participants, as is often advocated, orienting toward researching with instead of about suggests maintaining proximity through responsive flexibility in the modes of research (Smith, West et al., 2019). Endeavoring to engage in lifespan work, writing researchers will be studying with individuals whose "bodies, emotions, place, time, sound, image, self-experience, history . . . memory, forgetting, desire, fear, pleasure, surprise . . . " (Ellsworth, 2004, p. 55) through time and across contexts become laid bare—a perspective on their learning pathways that no other individual has. This positions lifespan writing researchers not only with special insights, but more so with special ethical responsibility to tend and care for the relationship with participants (see Adsanatham, 2019).

CONCLUSION

The complexities and mobilities of writing practices across time and spaces challenge writing researchers to consider how we are ontologically oriented in researching lifespan writing development. In this chapter, I have suggested theoretical and methodological orientations that could assist in considering how writing development occurs through and across space-times, modalities, genres, communities, generations, etc. as we research with writers. These orientations embrace the complexity of lifespan writing by attuning researchers to aspects such as scale, mobilities, and answerability as we work toward coherence across, through, and with writers and writing.

The examples in this chapter are predominantly from an ethnographic and interpretive set of methodologies with research designs already focused on development *across*, *through*, and *with* but these orientations can be taken up with other methods and in methods combinations. Across this volume, the range of such approaches can be seen. For instance, Bowen (this volume) suggests a mixed method approach to lifespan writing research that features an observational "literacy tour" which emphasizes the spaces and materials across which writers write. A challenge offered to lifespan writing studies scholars then is to consider and perhaps reconsider how these orientations are applicable and would influence chosen approaches. Take, for example, longitudinal statistical approaches: How might a through orientation—that embraces the widely variable experiences of writers through time—inform the statistical modeling and interpretation of the inevitably uneven statistical distribution? Both Zajic & Poch (this volume) and Costa et al. (this volume) take up statistical modeling for writing research in ways that contribute to this conversation. Writing researchers might also consider how these orientations might change as we think across the various disciplines, methods, and participant ages, generations, and populations that can sometimes be overlooked (see Bowen, this volume; Poch et al., this volume; Lee, this volume) and which lifespan writing research represents.

REFERENCES

Adsanatham, C. (2019). REDRES[ing] rhetorica: A methodological proposal for queering cross-cultural rhetorical studies. In W. P. Banks, M. B. Cox, C. Dadas & C. Takayoshi (Eds), *Re/orienting writing studies: Queer methods, queer projects*. Utah State University Press. https://www.muse.jhu.edu/book/64315.

Andrews, R. & Smith, A. (2011). *Developing writers: Teaching and learning in the digital age*. Open University Press.

Bazerman, C., Applebee, A. N., Berninger, V. W., Brandt, D., Graham, S., Matsuda, P. K., Murphy, S., Rowe, D. W. & Schleppegrell, M. (2017). Taking the long view on writing development. *Research in the Teaching of English, 51*(3), 351–360.

Britton, J., Burgess, T., Martin, N., McLeod, A. & Rosen, H. (1975). *The development of writing abilities*. Macmillan.

Calkins, L. (1983). *Lesson from a child: On the teaching and learning of writing*. Heinemann.

Compton-Lilly, C. (2017). *Reading students' lives: Literacy learning across time*. Routledge.

Dippre, R. (2016, August 10–12). *"I'm not the same person": Tracing laminated literate practices through times, places, and selves* [Paper presentation]. 50th Anniversary Dartmouth Institute and Conference, Hanover, NH, United States.

Ellsworth, E. (2004). *Places of learning: Media, architecture, pedagogy*. Routledge.

Flower, L. & Hayes, J. R. (1981). A cognitive process theory of writing. *College Composition and Communication, 32*(4), 365–387.

Gee, J. P. (2014). *An introduction to discourse analysis: Theory and method* (4th ed.). Routledge.

Hawkins, M. (2018). Transmodalities and transnational encounters: Fostering critical cosmopolitan relations. *Applied Linguistics, 39*(1), 55–77.

Kell, C. (2009). Literacy practices, text/s and meaning making across time and space. In M. Baynham & M. Prinsloo (Eds.), *The future of literacy studies* (pp. 75–99). Palgrave Macmillan.

Lemke, J. (2000). Across the scales of time: Artifacts, activities, and meanings in ecosocial systems. *Mind, Culture and Activity, 7*(4), 273–290.

Nordquist, B. (2017). *Literacy and mobility: Complexity, uncertainty, and agency at the nexus of high school and college.* Routledge.

Paris, D. & Winn, M. (Eds.). (2014). *Humanizing research: Decolonizing qualitative inquiry with youth and communities.* Sage.

Patel, L. (2016). *Decolonizing educational research: From ownership to answerability.* Taylor & Francis.

Prior, P. (1998). *Writing/disciplinarity: A sociohistoric account of literate activity in the academy.* Lawrence Erlbaum Associates.

Prior, P. & Smith, A. (2020). Writing across: Tracing transliteracies as becoming over time, space, and settings. *Learning, Culture, and Social Interaction, 24.* https://doi.org/10.1016/j.lcsi.2018.07.002.

Roozen, K. (2020). Coming to act with tables: Tracing the laminated trajectories of an engineer-in-the-making. *Learning, Culture, and Social Interaction, 24.* https://doi.org/10.1016/j.lcsi.2019.02.009 .

Saldaña, J. (2003). *Longitudinal qualitative research: Analyzing change through time.* Altamira Press.

Shipka, J. (2011). *Toward a composition made whole.* University of Pittsburgh Press.

Smith, A. (2015). The serious work of writing. *English Journal, 105*(1), 81–84.

Smith, A. (2018). Waves of theory building in writing and its development, and their implications for instruction, assessment, and curriculum. In D. Alvermann, N. Unrau & M. Sailors, (Eds.), *Theoretical models and processes of literacy* (pp. 63–83). Routledge.

Smith, A., Hall, M. & Sousanis, N. (2015). Envisioning possibilities: Visualizing as inquiry in literacy studies. *Literacy, 48*(1), 3–11.

Smith, A. & Prior, P. (2020). A flat CHAT perspective on transliteracies development. *Learning, Culture, and Social Interaction, 24.* https://doi.org/10.1016/j.lcsi.2019.01.001.

Smith, A., West, A., McCarthey, S. (2020). Literacies across sponsorscapes: Mobilizing notions of literacy sponsorship. *Literacy, 54*(2), 22–30. https://doi.org/10.1111/lit.12199.

Stornaiuolo, A., Smith, A. & Phillips, N. (2017). Developing a transliteracies framework for a connected world. *Journal of Literacy Research, 49*(1), 68–91.

Tsing, A. L. (2012). On nonscalability: The living world is not amenable to precision-nested scales. *Common Knowledge, 18*(3), 505–524. https://www.muse.jhu.edu/article/485828.

Vandenberg, P., Hum, S. & Clary-Lemon, J. (2006). *Relations, locations, positions: Composition theory for writing teachers.* National Council of Teachers of English.

Wilkinson, A. (1986) *The quality of writing.* Open University.

Wynhoff Olsen, A. & VanDerHeide, J. (2020). Representations of students becoming as writers. *Language, Culture and Social Interaction, 24.* https://doi.org/10.1016/j.lcsi.2019.02.010.

CHAPTER 2.

ALWAYS ALREADY RELOCALIZED: THE PROTEAN NATURE OF CONTEXT IN LIFESPAN WRITING RESEARCH

Ryan J. Dippre
University of Maine

Anna Smith
Illinois State University

Writing is never without a context. Despite its prevalence, however, context is often backgrounded in the study of writing, rendered inert and uncomplicated by methodological choices. In this chapter, we wish to turn the spotlight on context, consider its role in the production of writing, and writing's reciprocal role in producing context. In our interests in writing across the lifespan, we argue, the relationship between context and writing becomes paramount: A defining feature of the "span" of life is the differing contexts across which and with which a writer moves. The Lifespan Writing Development Group (LWDG) center "context" in their attempt to "address the need for a vision of writing development that incorporates its complexities and many dimensions, and that accounts for the individuality of trajectories that can lead to distinctive voices and expressions" (Bazerman et al., 2018, p. 21). As its first of eight principles to inform such a vision, they foreground: "Writing can develop across the lifespan as part of changing contexts" (2018, p. 22). The LWDG note that "the growing body of texts that becomes part of each social grouping's resources and understandings forms the context of each new piece of writing, whether these are sacred texts and commentaries within religious communities, the research literature in an academic discipline, the regulations of a government agency, or the records of a school (Bazerman, 1999; 2013)" (2018, p. 24). In both the declaration of the principle and the elaboration that follows, the LWDG frames *context* as a site of ongoing change as people move across their lives, and the role that writing plays in establishing and moving forward those contexts, even as those contexts establish and move forward writers along particular developmental trajectories.

DOI: https://doi.org/10.37514/PER-B.2020.1053.2.02

This framing of *context* by the LWDG resonates with many of its uses in studies of rhetoric (Bitzer, 1968; Burke, 1945), semiotics (Volosinov, 1978), materiality (Pigg, 2014; Prior & Shipka, 2003), and literacy (Dyson, 2008). Context, in much of contemporary writing research, is treated as a setting of and respondent to unfolding social activity. In this chapter, we put argue that context is a more active agent than even many context-attentive writing researchers have articulated, and that a full appreciation of the agentive power of context can reveal productive insights for the ongoing study of writing through the lifespan. Drawing on New Literacy Studies and ethnomethodology, we develop an understanding of the protean nature of context in order to inform future lifespan-oriented writing researchers.

We take up the word *protean* to describe our vision of context because it highlights the highly variable character of context—the responsive flexibility that the so-called "background" of our social actions has to those actions. The term *protean* is derived from the Greek god Proteus, who was the warden of sea animals. He had the ability to shapeshift seamlessly, taking up forms as he moved. We see protean as a useful word located in interesting corners of literacy and writing research to articulate the complex social worlds within which writers and readers of texts live, work, and build. Bazerman (1989) draws on *protean* to expand upon the "ramshackle and ad hoc" process of reading student writing (p. 140). "In reading student papers," he argues, "we watch people coming and going, hiding and faking, being and becoming, and sometimes those people are ourselves" (1989, p. 139). The concept of reading as protean is a useful one for Bazerman, as it allows him to ask how the many "forms of life" that "leak through" (1989, p. 140) into the process of reading student texts should be shaping the reading of those texts, and the responsibilities that the teacher has to them. Delgado-Gaitan (1996) also draws on the word *protean* to articulate the transformative opportunities available to a complex, historically-layered, and dynamically-changing community. Likewise, Heath (2001) draws on the term to argue for seeing "literacy events" as never solely written or oral, but a dynamic confluence of literate forms that are always changing in relation to social situation and purpose. In each of these instances, *protean* serves to highlight the fluid, interactive nature of social action as well as the potential for transformation. Likewise, we hope that thinking of context as protean can launch the transformative possibilities of context to the fore of our thoughts when working to imagine writing through the lifespan.

A RADICAL RECONCEPTUALIZATION OF CONTEXT IN WRITING

Our reconceptualization of context begins with a conceptualization of social action that locates social structure in the moment-to-moment work of individuated actors. This framing draws on the ethnomethodological research program of Garfinkel (1967, 2002, 2006), Lynch (1993), and Cicourel (1964), among others. The ethnomethodological tradition argues that social facts—that is, the shared understandings of the world that make up society—are located in a place entirely different than the research sites of the then-reigning sociological program, structural-functionalism. Structural-functional theorists, they argued, saw individuals as "cultural dopes," producing "the stable features of the society by acting in compliance with pre-established and legitimate alternatives of action that the common culture provides" (Garfinkel, 1967, p. 68). Ethnomethodologists, on the other hand, came to see social order as emerging from ongoing, local, joint work of people interacting with one another and the world around them—it is, in other words, always an accomplishment, rather than a free-standing structure. Society, for Garfinkel and the ethnomethodologists who followed him, is not something "out there" to be taken for granted, but rather the product of regular, ongoing work of participants from one moment to the next. When an ethnomethodologist looks for a social fact, then, they look to the moment of its shared construction amongst members of a group.

By treating the social world as an ongoing accomplishment, the ethnomethodologists open the door to seeing contexts as also an accomplishment, something that is recognized, taken up, and understood by actors as they work together to produce social order. Central to the work of these creating and accomplishing contexts is through the work of *practices*—socially-recognized activity through which we make ourselves understandable to others and ourselves (and, by extension, through which we come to understand what others are doing). It is important, however, that we see practices as multiple (Scollon, 2001) and constantly in-flux, as always unfolding and responding to the actions of others as we co-construct situations of social (and, by extension, literate) action. In other words, as I (Ryan, in this case) work to *keep writing going* (Brandt, 1990) in the production of this section, I am undertaking my usual practices of literate action, but unsure of how they will unfold in a number of ways. Will I effectively realize this sentence that I start to write, or will I have to delete and start again? Will I be interrupted from my task by a phone call, a need to eat, my child's demands that I play with him? A practice's end is inherently unstable, in other words, until it is reached. And, by extension, so is the context that is created by and co-constructs that practice.

Pennycook (2010) offers useful language about practices and their role in perpetuating social action. Pennycook's work attends centrally to the locality of practices and, particularly, to language practices. A central concept for Pennycook is relocalization, which he uses to move toward "a notion of locality that includes theories of space and movement as part of a new way of thinking about how we relate to place" (2010, p. 35). The phenomenon of relocalization draws attention to the work of similarity, difference, and repetition: by seeing difference and not similarity or repetition as the constant in the flow of social action, Pennycook suggests difference is the given and that similarity and repetition must make themselves understood against a background of dynamic difference. The sameness that emerges in a sea of difference locates a given speech act within time and place, within a history that members of a given group can use to continue the work of producing sameness out of difference "for another first time" (Garfinkel, 1967, p. 9). In the work of making the different similar again, in other words, a locality is (re)constructed—a context is built.

RELOCALIZATION AS PROTEAN: LITERATE ACTION FOR ANOTHER FIRST TIME

Pennycook's framing of the local as being co-constructed anew in each instance of a given practice highlights the complex work of the production of social order that Garfinkel (1967, 2002) attempts to uncover with his "tutorials" and "experiments." Bringing students to see the actor-oriented perspective of clapping in time with a metronome, or encouraging students to experiment by acting as a boarder in one's own home, bring into sharp relief the complex, interconnected work of organizing and maintaining social order and, through it, the context that such social order emerges from. Seeing context as part and product of the ongoing work of social order is not entirely new to writing research, whether it be in the rhetoric and composition tradition or the tradition of New Literacy Studies (Street, 2003), but past research has not yet highlighted the truly protean object that context is for all social actors, particularly for those engaged in the work of writing. Writing coordinates social action at a distance (Bazerman, 2004), and so gives those involved in literate societies a sense of a broader structure through which they operate. When we complete a tax form, for instance, we can imagine a typified picture of the social actions of others that make that tax form do the things we intend it to do. For researchers following the work of Schutz (i.e., Miller, 1984), the underlying assumption of our understanding of this social action is that it emerges from our "stock of knowledge at hand" (Schutz, 1954, p. 8)—that is, the understandings of the world that we carry with us from one moment to the next. Other researchers drawing on more of a structural-functionalist paradigm (i.e., Devitt, 1991) may see our completion of a tax form as the result of our ongoing work to coordinate the many roles that we serve in as part of our broader participation in the structuration of society. In both of these models, we have something seemingly stable (a stock of knowledge; an enduring social organization) that we turn to when producing writing.

The sense of stability enables us to understand the task at hand, to freeze the context into place as a rock upon which a text may be constructed.

Ethnomethodology challenges such stability, encouraging researchers to reject such notions in order to turn to a closer look at the moment-to-moment work of *lived* practices in particular groupings. For ethnomethodologists like Livingston (1987), these practices could best be observed in *perspicuous settings* (Garfinkel, 2002), or sites that afforded easy access to viewing practices in use, such as bookstore lines at the start of the semester. Other ethnomethodologists have turned to the world of music (Sudnow, 2003) or the scientific laboratory (Lynch, 1993) in order to highlight the complex work of any given moment of practice, and its irreducibility to a pattern of social order or an indexed stock of knowledge in the mind. These researchers and others demonstrate that the stability of either social structure or stocks of knowledge prove insufficient to explain the complexity of keeping social action going on a moment-to-moment basis, and, worse still, that those explanations occlude the actor's vision of what is seen as possible from one moment to the next.

Setting aside the stability of social structure and stocks of knowledge leaves context hanging in the wind—caught up in an unending sea of difference reminiscent of Pennycook's (2010) argument. Yet somehow, despite this ongoing difference, we encounter situations that are familiar to us. We sit down to eat dinner with family, we exchange polite greetings in passing on the street, we run the red light because the cop is never on this stretch of road at this hour, etc. Disconnecting from the stabilities indicated above highlights the ongoing different-ness of each moment, but fails to account for recurrence. In other words, it takes care of the "first time" aspect of "each next first time" without accounting for the "next" (Garfinkel, 2002).

It is precisely this missing accounting that makes such a position so useful to understanding the complex co-construction of context from one moment to another. Because the "next-ness" of a given moment is not accountable in a sea of difference, researchers need to turn their attention to the mechanisms through which that next-ness is produced. Turning attention to the moment-to-moment work of literate action treats social order as inherently local, historical, and proleptic, and cognition as a set of structures (Coulter, 1991) through which patterns of interaction are signaled and interpreted, opening the door for researchers to attend to *how* literate actors move in their work of producing writing from one moment to the next, and how they keep the work of context going in the process of that work. Smith and Prior (2020) call for such research arguing that the profound heterogeneity and thorough lamination of practices, people, artifacts, and environments in each moment of writing requires close tracing attuned to sociohistorical threads and potential futures. They charge writing researchers to remember that as research contexts are protean and co-constructed, their common labels such as a classroom, home, or workplace "need to be seen as cultural ways of classifying many unfolding emergent assemblages" (Smith & Prior, 2019, p. 1).

If actors co-construct context as they construct social order, we can begin to think about the ways in which context participates in that co-construction. How, for instance, do the resources that actors talk and act into meaning in a given moment emerge from the talking and acting that went on in the moment before? In the moment that follows? Furthermore, how do these resources shape the talking and acting that goes on within that moment? If context is tied to history through the work of relocalization, how might the protean nature of that context enable actors to untie and retie various historic threads in the production of the moment? The protean nature of context enables a multiplicity of alternatives in any given moment of social action that might be recognized by members of the scene in question as legitimate and meaningful. In the next section, we articulate the benefits and limitations of such a perspective, and offer some potential paths forward for taking up this work in lifespan writing research.

CONSEQUENCES OF CONTEXT-AS-PROTEAN FOR LIFESPAN WRITING RESEARCH

BENEFITS

Thinking through context as a protean phenomenon brings with it several benefits for lifespan writing researchers. Perhaps most consequential is the way in which a protean nature of context draws attention to the moment-to-moment work of literate action. If context emerges from difference, if the basis of recurrence is social interaction, then researcher attention is directed to the ways in which actors create context together, from one moment to the next, over time. By thinking through the nuanced work of ongoing context-construction, researchers can attend more carefully to the subtle developmental work that occurs for writers across spaces and times. Smith (this volume) refers to this as being oriented as a lifespan researcher to details *through* which writing development occurs.

Such attention to moment-to-moment context construction can also provide researchers with significant insight into development from an *actor-oriented perspective*. Dippre (2016, 2017) has suggested elsewhere that the lived reality of writing across the lifespan—the felt experience of keeping writing going from one moment to the next—is the one constant that researchers can rely on when looking across the lifespan. Whatever the age, the social situation, or the kind of writing, there remains at the heart of things an active agent engaged in literate action for another first time. Treating context as protean, as responsive to the needs of the moment, as transforming social action while simultaneously being transformed by that social action, helps researchers think through the eyes of the actor—what they are seeing, how they are seeing it, how the work to make order out of the next passing moment synergizes cognitive structures and social expectations. Treating context as protean, in other words, highlights the actor-oriented perspective on acts of reading and writing and, by extension, shows the ways in which seeming islands of stability come to be seen that way. At the same time, this treatment provides a way out of these stability-driven understandings, by turning the researcher to the production of the moment.

The protean nature of context also signals the agency that individuals have in any given moment. In this sense, treating context as protean calls attention to post-humanist (Accardi, 2015; Dippre, 2018) understandings of agency: that agency is circulated through situations as they are constructed and can land not only in individuals but in any of what Latour (2003) would refer to as an *actant*. As individuated actants co-construct a context and a social situation, they circulate agency in a range of ways, through a variety of objects. A protean context, responsive to the ways in which agency can circulate, can address the complexity of the agentive work of writers across a range of writing tasks over time.

Finally, a protean treatment of context renders each passing moment, each social situation, as deeply laminated (Prior, 1998), and with individuated actors orchestrating—that is, foregrounding and backgrounding—multiple lifeworlds in any given moment. Treating context as protean enables researchers to follow the actor-oriented perspective of the writer across these lifeworlds, to trace the ways in which literate practices move beyond social boundaries in order to make possible the production of texts for somewhat-recurrent and somewhat-new circumstances. Work by Prior (1998, 2018), Roozen and Erickson (2017), Smith and Prior (2020), and others has begun the tracing of practices over time, and continued attention to the laminated lifeworlds present in a given moment may prove particularly useful to researchers interested in tracing the development of practices over time.

Problems

Attending to the protean nature of context brings with it some issues as well. The biggest challenge, by far, is that of data containment. Attending to the complexity of social action in a given moment requires an enormous amount of information, and isolating events without disturbing the phenomenon of interest can be particularly problematic. This would be an issue in any given research involving a protean conception of context, but attending in such detail to writing *through the lifespan* exacerbates the problem: issues of data collection and data storage alone become nearly insurmountable in such instances.

Lemke's (2000) argument calls attention the necessary and highly consequential work of data reduction in any study. In a lifespan study that recognizes the mutable and emergent boundaries of context as protean, drawing time and space boundaries around data or the representation of data is highlighted as an interpretive move on the part of researcher. In his work on longitudinal designs, Saldaña (2003) argues that three concepts are effectual in understanding phenomena in a longitudinal study: duration, time, and change. Each of these, he explains, are contextual, produced moment-to-moment through practices. Boundary-making decisions about data collection—that is, the act of reducing data for analysis—will have to be made on-the-move, as researchers follow one unfolding activity after another (Stornaiuolo et al., 2017). But if such decisions need to be made on-the-move, if there are no clear *a priori* guidelines for those decisions, how might researchers effectively both *make* decisions and *account* for those decisions to other researchers? Principles for making such research decisions in a context-as-protean framework have yet to be articulated.

A further issue with treating context as a protean phenomenon is scalability. The problems of data reduction indicated above hold true for a single-case study, let alone the work of multiple writers over extended periods of time. How might researchers attend to context as protean on a wide scale? In what ways might the complexity of context construction become analyzable to wider studies? Due to the massive undertaking of just perceiving let alone analyzing data drawn from a moment-to-moment approach, Lemke (2000) argues that "distributed communities of researchers" are needed, suggesting, "'It takes a village' to study a village" (p. 288). No doubt the treatment of context as protean in future research will unveil some mechanisms through which this work may be scaled, but at the moment more questions remain than answers on how to appropriately scale this work.

Data reduction and scalability are perhaps the most pressing concerns of treating context as protean, but they are far from the only ones. In the next section, we identify some ways in which we might begin to conduct research that assumes context to be a protean phenomenon and shapes its frameworks, methods, and sites accordingly. From these proposed early steps, we hope that future research can take on the work of identifying and resolving further problems in order to allow lifespan writing researchers to fully access the benefits of seeing context as inherently and unavoidably protean.

PRACTICE ↔ CONTEXT: ONE WAY FORWARD

The beginning of our work to see context as protean lies in a rather blunt instrument for supporting data reduction: focusing on one practice at a time. This work of focusing on particular literate practices (see Roozen, 2008 for instance) has had wide analytical purchase for writing researchers in the past, and we suggest that a continued focus on single practices will be a useful mechanism to provide researchers with a focal point while following literate action over a long span of time. Work by Dippre (2018), Roozen (2010), Woodard (2015), Rounsaville (2017), and others highlights the massive amounts of data that come from a careful look at a single practice or set of practices. Working through that data may provide a useful way for researchers to study writing over time while focusing on context and simultaneously honing approaches to reduce data in future, broader studies.

Such a focus on a single practice at a time may also suggest ways to scale up projects beyond the study of single writers. Focusing on particular practices (and how those practices get taken up and transformed across a range of subjects over time) can serve as a scalable mechanism through which development can be traced and, through it, the production of context over time. Studies of slightly wider scale than a case study—for instance, several stratified groups of writers assigned to particular researchers on a team trained to follow a particular literate practice—may offer insights for future, more complex studies on an even wider scale that accounts for the ongoing, protean nature of context over time.

Tracing one practice at a time would not require new methods, although a subtle tweaking of existing work might be required in order to make certain that context is treated as protean rather than as a stable given or a backdrop to the focal practice. Consider, for instance, the sociohistoric methodology enacted by Roozen (2008, 2009a, 2009b, 2010, 2019; Roozen & Erickson, 2017). This work highlights particular practices as they are repurposed (productively or not) in order to meet new demands across a range of lifeworlds. Roozen (2020), for instance, traces the emergent laminated trajectories (Roozen et al., 2015) of an engineering student, Alexandra Griffith, across three years and through retrospective interviews and document analysis through to childhood, turning attention in particular to the practice of composing data tables. Composing data tables—from puzzles to schedules to science labs—is the mechanism through which Alexandra's development as an engineer is seen. As Roozen traced the development of the practice of data tables in engineering, he noted the boundaries of writing in an engineering context were mutable to a range of data table composing practices Alexandra brought to each new data table. In this work, Roozen focuses on the "histories of reuse across heterogeneous times, places, and representational media" to trace the ontogenesis of practices and persons. In other words, he conducts a sociohistoric tracing of *similarity* across the wide array of *difference* operating in Alexandra's life. Roozen argues that analysis of practice should primarily focus on people's mediated action in relation to particular sites and groupings, but not end there. Rather, the writing researcher must be attentive to the "extensive historical trajectories that flow into and emanate from such sites" (p. 4). Tuning this sociohistoric approach to one that embraces fully the protean nature of context might further involve indexing Alexandra's dynamic writing activity with other socially demarcated yet evolving time-space-mattering boundaries.

CONCLUSION

Beyond approaching context as a setting of and respondent to unfolding social activity, in this chapter we argue that context is a far more ephemeral and active agent in the co-construction of social action than we've seen typically taken up in writing research. Each site of writing, we argue, must be approached as dynamic, complex, mediated, and historically-layered, and a writer's developing writing should not be considered outside of its concurrently developing context. This approach, we suggest, is one that treats context as protean.

Thinking about context as protean, as always variable and as the result of the ongoing construction of social order, does no favors to anyone hoping to simplify lifespan writing research. However, a protean sense of context opens up interesting and productive problems for understanding writing, its production, and the development of writers over time—problems that can be answered with new methods, theoretical viewpoints, and conceptual frameworks. Later chapters of this collection indicate some movement toward envisioning context-as-protean. Bowen (this volume), for instance, turns to specific decisions that writers make when materially constructing contexts for writing, which calls attention to the complex assemblages through which literate action emerges. Lee (this volume) turns attention to the broader historical and social contexts of writing across generations, showing how material affordances, changing social configurations, and changes to broader social structures create literate opportunities that resonate across generations of literate lives. Such steps toward articulating the protean nature of context in a range of sites and methods offers initial but productive steps toward embracing the study of writing in its deeply social, material, and historical complexity.

REFERENCES

Accardi, S. (2015). Agency. In P. Heilker & P. Vandenberg (Eds.), *Keywords in writing studies* pp. 1–5). Utah State University Press.

Bazerman, C. (1989). Reading student texts: Proteus grabbing Proteus. In B. Lawson, S. Ryan & W. Winterowd (Eds.), *Encountering student texts: Interpretive issues in reading student writing* (pp. 139–146). National Council of Teachers of English.

Bazerman, C. (1999). *The languages of Edison's light*. MIT Press.

Bazerman, C. (2004). Speech acts, genres, and activity systems. In C. Bazerman & P. Prior (Eds.), *What writing does and how it does it* (pp. 309–339). Routledge.

Bazerman, C. (2013). *Literate action: A theory of literate action,* (Vol. 2). The WAC Clearinghouse; Parlor Press. https://wac.colostate.edu/books/perspectives/literateaction-v2/.

Bazerman, C., Brandt, D., Rowe, D., Berninger, V., Matsuda, P. K., Applebee, A., Wilcox, K., Jeffery, J., Schleppegrell, M., Graham, S. & Murphy, S. (2018). *The lifespan development of writing.* National Council of Teachers of English.

Bitzer, L. (1968). The rhetorical situation. *Philosophy and Rhetoric, 1,* 1–14.

Burke, K. (1945). *A grammar of motives.* University of California Press.

Cicourel, A. (1964). *Method and measurement in sociology.* The Free Press.

Coulter, J. (1991). Cognition: Cognition in an ethnomethodological mode. In G. Button (Ed.), *Ethnomethodology and the human sciences* (pp. 176–195). Cambridge University Press.

Delgado-Gaitan, C. (1996). *Protean literacy: Extending the discourse on empowerment.* Routledge.

Devitt, A. (1991). Intertextuality in tax accounting: Generic, referential, and functional. In C. Bazerman & J. Paradis (Eds.), *Textual dynamics of the professions: Historical and contemporary studies of writing in professional communities* (pp. 336–357). University of Wisconsin Press. https://wac.colostate.edu/books/landmarks/textual-dynamics/.

Dippre, R. (2016, August 10–12). *"I'm not the same person": Tracing laminated literate practices through times, places, and selves* [Paper presentation]. 50th Anniversary Dartmouth Institute and Conference, Hanover, NH, United States.

Dippre, R. (2017, March 15–18). *Ongoing Renovation: Exploring the Development of Literate Action through an Ethnomethodological Lens* [Paper presentation]. Conference on College Composition and Communication, Portland, OR, United States.

Dippre, R. (2018). Faith, squirrels, and artwork: The expansive agency of textual coordination in the literate action of older writers. *Literacy in Composition Studies, 6*(2), 76–93.

Dyson, A. H. (2008). Staying in the (curricular) lines: Practice constraints and possibilities in childhood writing. *Written Communication 25*(1), 119–159.

Garfinkel, H. (1967). *Studies in ethnomethodology.* Prentice Hall.

Garfinkel, H. (2002). *Ethnomethodology's program: Working out Durkheim's aphorism.* Rowman & Littlefield.

Garfinkel, H. (2006). *Seeing sociologically: The routine grounds of social action.* Paradigm.

Latour, B. (2005). *Reassembling the social.* Oxford University Press.

Lemke, J. L. (2000). Across the scales of time: Artifacts, activities, and meanings in ecosocial systems. *Mind, Culture, and Activity 7*(4), 273–290.

Livingston, E. (1987). *Making sense of ethnomethodology.* Routledge.

Lynch, M. (1993). *Scientific practice and ordinary action.* Cambridge University Press.

Miller, C. (1984). Genre as social action. *Quarterly Journal of Speech, 70,* 151–167.

Pennycook, A. (2010). *Literacy as a local practice.* Routledge.

Pigg, S. L. (2014). Coordinating constant invention: Social media's role in distributed work. *Technical Communication Quarterly, 23*(2), 69–87.

Prior, P. (1998). *Writing/disciplinarity.* Lawrence Erlbaum Associates.

Prior, P. (2018). How do moments add up to lives: Trajectories of semiotic becoming vs. tales of school learning in four modes. In R. Wysocki & M. P. Sheridan (Eds.),

Making future matters. Computers & Composition Digital Press. https://ccdigital press.org/book/makingfuturematters/prior-intro.html#content-top.
Prior, P. & Shipka, J. (2003). Chronotopic lamination. In C. Bazerman & D. Russell (Eds.), *Writing selves/writing societies* (pp. 180–238). The WAC Clearinghouse; Mind, Culture & Activity. https://wac.colostate.edu/books/perspectives/selves-societies/.
Roozen, K. (2008). Journalism, poetry, stand-up comedy, and academic literacy: Mapping the interplay of curricular and extracurricular literate activities. *Journal of Basic Writing, 27*(1), 5–34.
Roozen, K. (2009a). "Fan fic-ing" English studies: A case study exploring the interplay of vernacular literacies and disciplinary engagement. *Research in the Teaching of English, 44*(2), 136–169.
Roozen, K. (2009b). From journals to journalism: Tracing trajectories of literate development. *College Composition and Communication, 60*(3), 541–572.
Roozen, K. (2010). Tracing trajectories of practice: Repurposing in one student's developing disciplinary writing processes. *Written Communication, 27*(3), 318–354.
Roozen, K. (2020). Coming to act with tables: Tracing the laminated trajectories of an engineer-in-the-making. *Learning, Culture, and Social Interaction, 24*. https://doi.org/10.1016/j.lcsi.2019.02.009.
Roozen, K. & Erickson, J. (2017). *Expanding literate landscapes: Persons, practices, and sociohistoric perspectives of disciplinary development*. Utah State University Press.
Roozen, K., Prior, P., Woodard, R., Kline, S. (2015). The transformative potential of laminating trajectories: Three teachers' developing pedagogical practices and identities. In T. Lillis, K. Harrington, M. R. Lea & S. Mitchell (Eds.), *Working with academic literacies: Case studies toward transformative practice* (pp. 205–216). The WAC Clearinghouse; Parlor Press. https://wac.colostate.edu/books/perspectives/lillis/.
Rounsaville, A. (2017). Worlding genres through lifeworld analysis: New directions for genre pedagogy and uptake awareness. *Composition Forum, 37*. https://compositionforum.com/issue/37/worlding.php.
Saldaña, J. (2009). *The coding manual for qualitative researchers*. Sage.
Schutz, A. (1954). Common-sense and scientific interpretation of human action. In *Collected Papers* (Vol. 1). Martinus Nijhoff.
Scollon, R. (2001). *Mediated discourse: The nexus of practice*. Routledge.
Smith, A. & Prior, P. (2020). A flat CHAT perspective on transliteracies development. *Learning, Culture, and Social Interaction, 24*. https://doi.org/10.1016/j.lcsi.2019.01.001.
Stornaiuolo, A., Smith, A. & Phillips, N. (2017). Developing a transliteracies framework for a connected world. *Journal of Literacy Research, 49*(1), 68–91.
Street, B. (2003) What's "new" in new literacy studies? Critical approaches to literacy in theory and practice. *Current Issues in Comparative Education, 5*(2), 77–91.
Sudnow, D. (2001). *Ways of the hand: A rewritten account*. MIT Press.
Volosinov, V. (1978). *Marxism and the philosophy of language*. Harvard University Press.
Woodard, R. (2015). The dialogic interplay of writing and teaching writing: Teacher writers' talk and textual practices across contexts. *Research in the Teaching of English, 50*(1), 35–59.

CHAPTER 3.

QUANTITATIVE PERSPECTIVES TO THE STUDY OF WRITING ACROSS THE LIFESPAN: A CONCEPTUAL OVERVIEW AND FOCUS ON STRUCTURAL EQUATION MODELING

Matthew C. Zajic
Teachers College, Columbia University

Apryl L. Poch
Duquesne University

As echoed throughout this edited collection, writing researchers are well aware of the complexities involved when adopting lifespan approaches to the study of written language. Writing researchers come from a wide array of fields (e.g., composition studies, rhetoric, psychology, education, and special education) that adopt different methodological approaches to answer a variety of research questions. A central issue to unpacking the complexities underlying the development of written language across the lifespan requires examining the available tools and methods offered by different research designs to pose and answer different types of research questions.

Typically, research approaches are categorized as quantitative or qualitative. Quantitative approaches generally focus on numbers (e.g., counting frequencies or measuring the associations between different skills) and reduce complex phenomena into measurable instances that can be analyzed using statistical analysis (Creswell & Creswell, 2018; Gelo et al., 2008). Qualitative approaches usually collect non-numerical data (e.g., texts, visuals, graphics, videos, or transcripts from interview and focus groups) that can be analyzed using inductive, interpretative analytical approaches (Creswell & Creswell, 2018; Gelo et al., 2008). These two approaches are often contrasted against each other as deductive vs. inductive, hypothesis-testing vs. hypothesis-generating, prediction vs. interpre-

DOI: https://doi.org/10.37514/PER-B.2020.1053.2.03

tation, generalization vs. contextualization, and explanation vs. comprehension (Creswell & Creswell, 2018; Gelo et al., 2008; Haig, 2013; Todd et al., 2004). Yet, juxtapositions aside, both approaches contribute to lifespan development research (Menard, 2008), suggesting that both approaches might inform ongoing lifespan writing research.

In this chapter, we offer a conceptual overview to quantitative research approaches with a focus on quantitative longitudinal research designs. While quantitative approaches will not answer all questions pertaining to lifespan writing development (see Bazerman, 2018), they are able to address many questions about how writing develops across the lifespan and, in some cases, consider research questions that qualitative approaches cannot. Furthermore, developmental methodologists have long applied quantitative approaches to issues concerning lifespan development (McArdle, 2010; Menard, 2008). We hope this chapter provides lifespan writing researchers with a starting point for mobilizing such methods to meet their research needs and a greater understanding of what such methods bring to lifespan writing research. Throughout the chapter, we emphasize conceptual understanding over technical jargon, especially as encouraging conceptual understanding fosters long-term statistical literacy (Harlow, 2013).

The first section broadly overviews quantitative longitudinal research approaches by drawing from recent longitudinal design frameworks (e.g., Bauer & Curran, 2019). In the next section, we introduce the concepts underlying structural equation modeling (SEM), a statistical, theory-driven framework commonly used to address both cross-sectional and longitudinal research questions. We discuss foundational SEM issues and provide examples based in writing research. The final section discusses longitudinal SEM through specific application of two different types of statistical models—autoregressive models and latent growth curve models (LGCMs).

LONGITUDINAL QUANTITATIVE RESEARCH DESIGNS

Longitudinal quantitative research designs and their analytical choices are guided by collecting numerical data and fitting statistical models. These statistical models are informed by theory, the research questions asked, and the types of data collected to make inferences about populations based on representative sample data. Scientific fields also use statistical models for theory building and for exploring the relationships between different variables using predictive, explanatory, and descriptive approaches (Shmueli, 2010). Singer and Willet (2003) offer a non-technical description of what statistical models aim to represent:

> Statistical models are mathematical representations of population behavior; they describe salient features of the hypoth-

esized process of interest among individuals in the target population. When you use a particular statistical model to analyze a particular set of data, you implicitly declare that this population model gave rise to these sample data. Statistical models are not statements about sample behavior; they are statements about the population process that generated the data. (Singer & Willet, 2003, p. 46)

Though statistical models underlie many quantitative approaches, the appropriate analytical approach differs based on the specific research questions asked and the sets of data collected. A robust set of available designs, methods, and tools fit under the umbrella of quantitative methods, and the following provides a categorized overview of different longitudinal research designs and some associated methodological approaches. Guided by the categorical approach taken by Bauer and Curran (2019), the remainder of this section introduces longitudinal quantitative approaches by focusing on two types of longitudinal data: time-to-event data and repeated measures data. These approaches can be useful to writing researchers to address research questions that may focus on whether or not an event occurred (e.g., a memorable writing experience during a particular time period of life); when it occurred (e.g., when do memorable writing experiences occur in postsecondary education?); and when changes occur in specific behaviors, attitudes, or feelings over time (e.g., does writing anxiety or apprehension change across time and context?).

Time-to-Event Data

Research questions based on time-to-event data focus on evaluating whether a particular event happens or when that event might take place. One way of addressing these questions is survival analysis (also named event history analysis, failure time analysis, hazard analysis, transition analysis, and duration analysis), a collection of flexible statistical methods specifically for describing, explaining, and predicting the timing and occurrence of events (Allison, 2010, 2019). For example, researchers might be interested in understanding more about when an event occurs, such as when students begin formal cursive or typing instruction in schools or when individuals first start writing via social media or instant messaging.

The event of interest falls at the center and focal point of survival analysis and is generally a qualitative change that occurs at some specific, observed point in time (Allison, 2010). This event may be simply observed and require little additional formal operationalization (e.g., the purchase and subsequent use of a cellular phone or other device for text or instant messaging), it may require considering multiple criteria to determine the exact timing (e.g., development of emergent literacy skills based on multiple accounts of different reading and writing behaviors), or it may require considering underlying quantitative variables to better specify the event occurrence (e.g., high social media writing activity may be contextualized by looking at the amount of writing being done across different social media platforms). Additionally, if events can happen multiple times, further consideration can be made regarding which occurrence to focus on (i.e., the first occurrence or a later occurrence) and to what degree events can be considered similar (i.e., can two events be qualitatively similar but differ in degree of their impact on some additional factor?) (Allison, 2010). Furthermore, survival analysis requires specifying a given interval of time for an event to have occurred, and these intervals may be specified given the research questions but also may vary given the underlying interests of the questions (Allison, 2010, 2019). For example, if researchers were interested in modeling the event of the first meaningful writing experience undergraduate students have during their postsecondary education, they might specify the origin point as the start date of students' first quarter or semester at college. However, if researchers were interested in understanding to what degree a meaningful writing experience preceded college entry or if their postsecondary experience was related to an event prior to college entry, then an earlier origin point may need to be considered. Further consideration should be made if concerns about censoring—that is, when an event fails to occur or demonstrates an unknown event time—are warranted and if the presence of censoring might influence the data collection or analysis.

Methods for survival analysis differ depending upon how much a researcher knows about the timing of an event. If the exact timing of an event is known, then continuous-time methods are appropriate (i.e., time is treated as continuous when the occurrence of events is known with a very high rate of precision). These methods may be appropriate for examining questions pertaining to occurrences of events during specific writing activities or the tracking of daily writing habits. However, if the timing of an event is only coarsely known (i.e., in months or years rather than seconds or days), then discrete-time methods are more appropriate (i.e., time is not continuous, and the events are known with lower rates of precision). These methods may be more appropriate for answering questions about an event that takes place over longer periods of time, such as the likelihood of first enrolling in a writing in the disciplines course in postsecondary education. Though the difference between the two methods appears to be a matter of conceptual semantics (as days may sound coarse for one event but precise for another), the selection of continuous versus discrete time methods has methodological implications for treating, analyzing, and interpreting the data (Singer &

Willet, 2003). One approach to distinguishing between the two sets of analyses entails looking to the number of ties within the data (i.e., an occurrence of two individuals experiencing an event at the same recorded time; see Allison, 2010). Discrete-time methods are better designed for handling high rates of ties, as the presence of ties has an extremely low occurrence rate under continuous-time methods (Singer & Willet, 2003). Consequently, survival analysis is a useful approach for when your research questions pass the "whether and when test": If your research questions include either word—whether or when—you probably need to use survival methods (Singer & Willet, 2003).

Repeated Measures Data

While research questions involving time-to-event data approaches focus on whether or when a particular event takes place, research questions involving repeated measures data focus instead on evaluating how abilities change over specific time periods. Like time-to-event data approaches, numerous methods and frameworks exist from which to study questions related to change in abilities over time. Bauer and Curran (2019) group approaches using repeated measures data into categories that depend upon the intensity of data collection (i.e., the number of times data are collected) and the number of units (i.e., abilities and items) being collected, resulting in three overarching research design categories: 1) time series analysis (intensive data collection involving few units); 2) intensive longitudinal data (intensive data collection involving many units); and 3) panel data (non-intensive data collection involving many units).

Both intensive data collection designs entail assessing one or more units on a high number of occurrences over a specified duration. The number of units included in these data collection points differentiates the focal point of these two approaches. Time series focuses on prediction or forecasting of a particular outcome and makes use of prior observations to predict expected change in the outcome at future time points. Intensive longitudinal data maintains a similar level of intensity but includes more units of data beyond a single outcome of interest to collect data on a higher number of individuals. Intensive longitudinal studies can include recording study units over many time points, often into the tens, hundreds, or thousands (see Walls & Schafer, 2006; Walls, 2013). Examples of such approaches include daily rating scales that might include self-reported ratings about different types of writing behaviors, like types of writing activities (e.g., text messaging or journal writing) or feelings about writing (e.g., instances of writing apprehension or motivation).

However, when only a handful of time points are included in a research design, a non-intensive panel data approach is most commonly used. This panel data approach is often what researchers imagine when thinking more generally about longitudinal data collection (Bauer & Curran, 2019) and formed the basis for initial longitudinal research rationales (Baltes & Nesselroade, 1979). Panel data are often collected across a small number of time points on a relatively large number of units with the ultimate goal of describing change over time. As with previous models, the topic of change is another nuanced concept, as different frameworks exist for considering mean-level change versus individual-level change, both of which are briefly discussed next.

Mean-level Change

Examining mean-level change puts the focus on group-level average change for a specific outcome over multiple time points. For example, researchers might be interested in the extent to which handwriting abilities change from preschool through secondary school. As such, these approaches draw on marginal models (Heagerty & Zeger, 2000) that estimate linear mean-level change (i.e., repeated measures analysis of variance, repeated measures multivariate analysis of variance, and analysis of covariance) and non-linear mean-level change (i.e., generalized estimating equations).

Individual-level Change

Researchers are often interested in examining not only how change may happen across specific groups but also to what extent individuals demonstrate variability in their change over time. Individual-level change is often first understood as a simple model that includes three or more time points to estimate a unique starting point (the intercept) and the trend of change over the remaining time points (the slope). But examining differences in individual-level change over time requires another choice about what the underlying question is regarding the nature of change in individuals for a given outcome: Are the differences in change due to differences of degree (i.e., quantitative variation) or differences in kind (i.e., qualitative differences between different change trajectories) (Bauer & Curran, 2019)? Differences by degree to investigate quantitative individual-level differences include approaches like multilevel models, mixed effects models, and LGCMs. Differences in kind to investigate qualitative individual differences include approaches like growth mixture modeling. Furthermore, additional models like general growth mixture models allow for exploration of differences by degree simultaneously with differences in kind when researchers are interested in examining research questions related to both degree and kind of differences. See Bauer and Curran (2019); Hoyle (2012); Little et al. (2000); and Muthén and Shedden (1999) for more thorough overviews.

Applications of Longitudinal Modeling Approaches for Lifespan Writing Researchers

Writing researchers interested in lifespan writing development may develop a variety of research questions requiring the use of time-to-event data or repeated-measures data approaches. Bazerman et al. (2018) offer a range of potential conceptual ideas to apply such methodological approaches, particularly as the complexity of the underlying factors involved with writing development are dynamic and not expected to develop in a rapid, linear fashion. Specifically, they emphasized that "writing needs time to mature, in fact decades, though at various moments motivated writers may make rapid progress on some dimensions. When and where those moments occur, however, may be hard to predict" (2018, p. 378). Survival analysis may be one useful approach to take to understand when these moments occur and how difficult they might be to predict among different writers. As survival analysis can take into consideration additional predictors of these moments (not discussed at length here; see Allison, 2010, 2019 and Singer & Willet, 2003), researchers can explore what factors may predict these experiences across distinct lifespan segments.

On the other hand, researchers might also use these moments to predict different types of writing outcomes. Graham's (2018) writer(s)-within-community model offers a range of potentially impactful factors that underlie writing development across different writing contexts. Though the theoretical basis for these factors is established, further empirical work is needed to examine how different underlying profiles based off these factors affect writing development differently over time and to what extent individual change in writing abilities may be measured using operationalized approaches to both the sociocultural and cognitive components of writing. Such an emphasis on connecting theory with data is at the heart of SEM, which we discuss next.

SEM: A FLEXIBLE STATISTICAL FRAMEWORK

SEM is a flexible statistical modeling approach that allows for rigorous examination of specified hypotheses connected to research questions about both cross-sectional and longitudinal research designs, and it is applicable across a wide array of disciplines (Hoyle, 2012; McArdle & Nesselroade, 2014). SEM is not a single statistical technique or model. It is an analytical process that covers several related procedures that posit multiple structural equations (i.e., mathematical statements that represent the strength and nature of specified, hypothetical relationships among sets of variables) to depict relationships and effects between observed and unobserved (or latent) variables (Hoyle, 2012;

Kline, 2016; Mueller & Hancock, 2019; Newsom, 2015). In other words, SEM provides a framework for answering theory-based, researcher-specified questions about relationships between abilities measured at a single time point or across multiple time points. As a model-based approach, it confers unique advantages to researchers of various fields that are unavailable in more traditional statistical techniques. Furthermore, though its capabilities have become more advanced in recent years, SEM can still serve as a framework for conducting other well-known univariate analyses (e.g., t-test, analysis of variance, regression, and multiple regression) and several multivariate analyses (e.g., path analysis and confirmatory factor analysis) (Grimm et al., 2017).

Some Necessary Terminology: Model Parameters, Covariances, and Latent Variables

Though our focus falls on the conceptual understanding of SEM, in order to clarify how SEM estimates relationships and effects between different variables, we briefly cover three statistical terms: model parameters, covariances, and latent variables. While SEM includes many other technical terms, these terms specifically cover some of the core terminology used across different SEM approaches.

First, a model parameter is a component of a statistical model that is generally not known to the researcher (i.e., a component that can be estimated) that can represent information about the relationships or effects between variables in that model (Raykov & Marcoulides, 2006). Parameters are not specific to SEM research, as parameters often generally reflect unknown aspects of statistical models that represent the phenomena under investigation. The goal of SEM is to estimate these parameters to answer underlying questions and hypotheses about the constructs under investigation (Raykov & Marcoulides, 2006). For example, in order to examine the relationship between two variables, a researcher would need to estimate their association given available data about those two variables.

Second, a covariance is a measure of the joint variance (the amount of shared variability present) between two (or more) variables that represents the strength of the linear association between variables and their variabilities (Kline, 2016). SEM primarily analyzes the variance-covariance matrix for a given dataset (i.e., a matrix that contains all of the variances and covariances of included variables). The importance of the variance-covariance matrix can be further seen by how SEM is often referred to as covariance structure analysis, covariance structure modeling, or analysis of covariance structures (Hoyle, 2012; Kline, 2016). However, non-covariance-based SEM approaches do exist, including latent class analysis (i.e., analysis of mixture models that contain exclusively observed categorical variables for a latent variable).

Third, a latent variable is an underlying characteristic that cannot be observed or measured directly, and instead requires at least one observed variable to estimate it (Bollen & Hoyle, 2012). Other terms for latent variables in the literature include unmeasured variables, latent factors, unobserved variables, or constructs, all generally meaning that they represent variables that are not immediately identifiable within a given dataset or that cannot be directly observed (or measured) from a sample of a specific population (Bollen, 2002; Raykov & Marcoulides, 2006). Latent variables can be both *a priori* and *a posteriori* and can be considered continuous, categorical, or hybrid depending on whether it is the presence of the latent trait that is the focus of the theory or if the latent trait has multiple gradations (Bollen, 2002). SEM has the capacity to measure relationships between multiple variables, regardless of whether they are observed or latent, while accounting for measurement error that is not accounted for when only investigating observed abilities (Raykov & Marcoulides, 2006). SEM accomplishes this by quantifying and removing the measurement error from the measurement of the latent variable, while simultaneously investigating relationships between distinct observed and unobserved abilities (Lei & Wu, 2007). Some examples of latent abilities include personality, attitudes, motives, emotions, and reading, as each are often measured using multiple observable measures to represent an underlying hypothetical construct (Bollen & Hoyle, 2012). Writing ability can similarly be thought of as a latent variable, as writing assessments are often tools that researchers use to make inferences about unobservable writing abilities. Multiple data points or assessments of specific writing abilities may provide a better estimate of an individual's unobservable writing ability, as assessments may capture different, smaller components of the larger unobservable ability.

STEPS TO IMPLEMENTING SEM

Different research designs require researchers to collect and analyze data using often very different approaches (see Gelo et al., 2008). SEM follows the research traditions of quantitative methodology, but different SEM approaches are used to answer different types of research questions, which requires different types of statistical models (see McArdle & Kadlec, 2013; Mueller & Hancock, 2019). However, most SEM approaches follow a similar overarching implementation framework, as described by Hoyle (2012). This brief-but-thorough overview of the implementation framework follows data acquisition and data preparation to include four required steps (specification, estimation, fit evaluation, and interpretation and reporting of findings) and an often required fifth step (respecification). We review these next in order to provide context to the types of questions researchers face when implementing SEM.

First, *specification* begins with a model (the formal statement positing the relationships to be explored within the given data) designed using theory-driven hypotheses. Model selection requires considering the different types of models available that would best fit the data collected (and how these data are related to the intended research hypotheses). Within the model, the researcher designates what variables will be included (both observed and latent variables) along with the relationships between the variables (i.e., unidirectional, allowed to covary, or unrelated) and their parameters (either fixed to a specific value or free to be estimated by information provided within the model). Specifying parameters requires attention to the need for model identification (i.e., all parameters must be identified by either being fixed or free, which is dependent on the number of observed variables included in the model).

Second, *estimates* are provided for parameters that are specified to be freely estimated as opposed to parameters that are fixed to specific values. The goal of estimation is to establish a model that minimizes the residual differences between the observed and the estimated covariance matrices given by the data and the model. Multiple estimation methods can be used depending on the characteristics of the data (e.g., the scales of the variables, distributional assumptions, and missing data), though most are iterative (i.e., they begin with one set of starting values for all free parameters and search for values that reduce the discrepancy between the model and the data).

Third, *fit evaluation* assesses how well the generated model represents the data by taking into consideration the discrepancy between the observed and implied covariance matrices. If fit appears poor (i.e., there is a large discrepancy in the covariance matrix) or is misspecified, then the model may be discarded or respecified (meaning that a new model may be generated to test a different underlying hypothesis; see fifth step). Different fit tests provide various fit statistics to make decisions regarding both absolute fit and comparative fit (i.e., how well one model fits in relation to other tested models) as well as corrections for parsimony.

Fourth and fifth are *interpretation and reporting of findings* and *respecification*, though the order in which researchers engage these steps depends on the results from fit evaluation. If a model does not demonstrate good fit, then respecification may be necessary to shift the focus to an exploratory approach to assess if alternative models may be better suited to the data. Choosing when to pursue respecification and what fit evaluation statistics to consider when deciding to move into either respecification or interpretation is a highly debated topic that cannot be thoroughly addressed in this brief overview. Nonetheless, readers need to be aware that the choice to consider respecification of a poorly fitting model requires a specific, theory-driven rationale.

If evaluation results in support for the originally specified model (or a respecified model), then interpreting and reporting the findings are done based on the stated hypotheses. Core components requiring interpretation include the basis for the model, the inclusion of and findings for specific parameters in the model, and how well the model accounts for uniqueness (i.e., variance) in the observed data. The way in which findings are interpreted depends upon the approaches taken during the implementation framework, as interpretation of a theory-driven model is more straightforward and meaningful than potentially uncertain rationales underlying exploratory models. Theoretical perspectives or previous empirical work should drive these interpretations, and researchers may need to consult further equivalent models (i.e., models that appear identical to the given model in terms of fit but include estimated parameters that contradict the chosen model).

This implementation framework outlines the overarching steps that researchers follow when using SEM to address specific research questions. Across these steps, researchers must make determinations (grounded in theory and empirical research) about their analyses beyond solely inputting numbers into a statistical program. Doing so allows researchers to understand better the relationships (or associations) between and among variables. However, while this framework briefly touched on some more technical aspects around planning and navigating the use of SEM, it did not adequately cover many of the technical decisions that researchers must make during the process (see Hoyle, 2012, and McArdle & Kadlec, 2013, for further technical discussions).

Examples of Writing Research using SEM Approaches

SEM is not a novel technique to writing research, yet only a few studies have addressed research questions using cross-sectional SEM research designs with different groups of individuals. Parkin et al. (2020) modeled the effects of an oral language latent factor on different level of language factors (including writing) and evaluated the effects of lower language levels on higher levels of language. In doing so, they found that a psychoeducational assessment demonstrated expected theoretically driven relationships that showed some variability in the relationships between language levels when comparing students in general and special education. De Smedt et al. (2018) investigated gender and achievement effects within the context of how cognitive and motivational challenges mediate and correlate with students' writing performance across different groups of students (boys and girls, and low, average, and high achievers). Their results highlight group-level differences in the relationships between these skills and suggest that research take into consideration different learner characteristics when considering how these skills relate to and predict writing skills.

Numerous other studies have adopted SEM approaches to examine writing skill development predominantly across the school-age years. Kim and colleagues examined if data from kindergarten and first grade students supported the theoretical relationships between writing, oral language, reading, and cognitive abilities (Kim et al., 2011; Kim, Al Otaiba, Puranik, Folsom & Greulich, 2014; Kim & Schatschneider, 2017). Limpo and colleagues examined relationships among transcription, higher-order writing processes, and writing performance in middle school students (Limpo et al., 2017) and compared relationships between transcription and self-regulation in late elementary and secondary students (Limpo & Alves, 2013). Berninger and colleagues investigated the relationships between writing with other language skills in typically developing writers (Abbott & Berninger, 1993; Berninger, Abbott et al., 2002; Graham et al., 1997) and writers with specific learning disabilities (Berninger, Nielsen et al., 2008; Nagy et al., 2003). Each of these studies generally sought to examine if theoretically driven questions about writing skills held for other skills among different groups when examined using highly specified modeling approaches. In all, they sought to examine if data supported the theoretically held beliefs about the relationships between writing skills and related linguistic, cognitive, and social cognitive skills. Though some studies included multiple samples from different age groups, these examples all discussed data collected from cross-sectional research designs.

SEM APPLICATIONS FOR LONGITUDINAL DATA ON LIFESPAN WRITING

Writing, like many skills, does not simply develop at one point in time. Writing skills are shaped across time and context. Understanding the ways in which individuals develop and apply these skills over time is a focal point of interest to lifespan writing researchers. In addition to its flexibility for analyzing cross-sectional data, SEM can be equally useful and appropriate for analyzing longitudinal data. As with cross-sectional SEM, one of the goals of longitudinal SEM is to identify models composed of a minimal number of estimated parameters that fit the data well, ideally with the intention of making predictions about future actions of individuals and groups of individuals or that identify sample characteristics associated with the development of a construct. SEM is a powerful tool for researchers interested in modeling the relationships between observed and latent skills over time (see Wu et al., 2013), and many different analytical tools are available to researchers interested in modeling longitudinal data (e.g., Grimm et al., 2017; Little, 2013; Little et al., 2000; McArdle & Nesselroade, 2014; Newsom, 2015). From the available modeling approaches, we selected two approaches we consider to be foundational to SEM that serve as illustrative introductions to the concepts underlying longitudinal SEM: autoregressive longitudinal models and LGCMs. Though presented separately, it is important to note that many SEM approaches for longitudinal data can incorporate features from both autoregressive models and LGCMs (Bollen & Curran, 2004; Curran & Bollen, 2001). However, for simplicity, we introduce and discuss them separately.

To assist with understanding how relationships between variables are modeled in the autoregressive model and LGCM examples, path diagrams are provided for each example (Figures 3.1–3.3). Though SEM is often represented using mathematical equations, path diagrams can also be used to visually depict these relationships (Ho et al., 2012; Little, 2013). Different path diagram components (i.e., parameter estimates and variables) are often labeled and named using Greek letters to convey their functions, though naming conventions can often differ. Little (2013) provides a cheat sheet for some of the commonly used Greek letters, and the conventions used for diagrams in this chapter draw from Little (2013) and Ho et al. (2012). The use of path diagrams was a deliberate choice for this chapter in order to visually depict the modeled relationships rather than rely on matrix algebra and mathematical equations, but path diagrams do not always provide as much detail as these mathematical representations. As cautioned by many methodologists (e.g., Kline, 2016; Little, 2013; McArdle, 2012; Mueller & Hancock, 2019), path diagrams are not a substitute for the equations they seek to represent, and researchers should be prepared to learn more about the mathematics underlying SEM after understanding the concepts (e.g., Harlow, 2013).

AUTOREGRESSIVE LONGITUDINAL MODELS

Are writing skills at one point in time predictive of writing skills at later points in time? Are specific writing skills predictive of other writing skills at different points in time? Questions specific to examining the degree that skills are predictive of themselves or other skills across time are well suited for autoregressive longitudinal models, a modeling approach used across disciplines for decades to investigate the relationships among specific variables over multiple time points (Biesanz, 2012; Little, 2013).

Autoregressive models conceptualize that performance at a specified time point is a function of earlier assessments of that variable plus new unique error that occurs with each time point (McArdle & Bell, 2000). Put differently, autoregressive models investigate the extent to which a future value for some variable is predicted from previous estimates of that variable. (Furthermore, *regressive* refers to the direct linear pathways between variables across time points, and *auto* refers to the pathways between the same variables across timepoints.)

Even with only one observed variable across multiple time points, this variable can be modeled as either only an observed variable or as a latent variable based on its observed variable, with the benefit of treating the variable of interest as latent to account for measurement error in the overall model (Biesanz, 2012). Autoregressive models can be useful to examine not only the predictive relationships within a single variable but also the cross-lagged relationships between multiple variables (i.e., the degree to which different variables can covary with or predict each other across multiple time points; Biesanz, 2012). Such cross-lagged approaches allow for temporal precedence in data collection to help assess for causal relations rather than correlational relations, as the cross-lagged specification sets up the framework for identifying causal relationships between abilities measured across multiple time points (Biesanz, 2012).

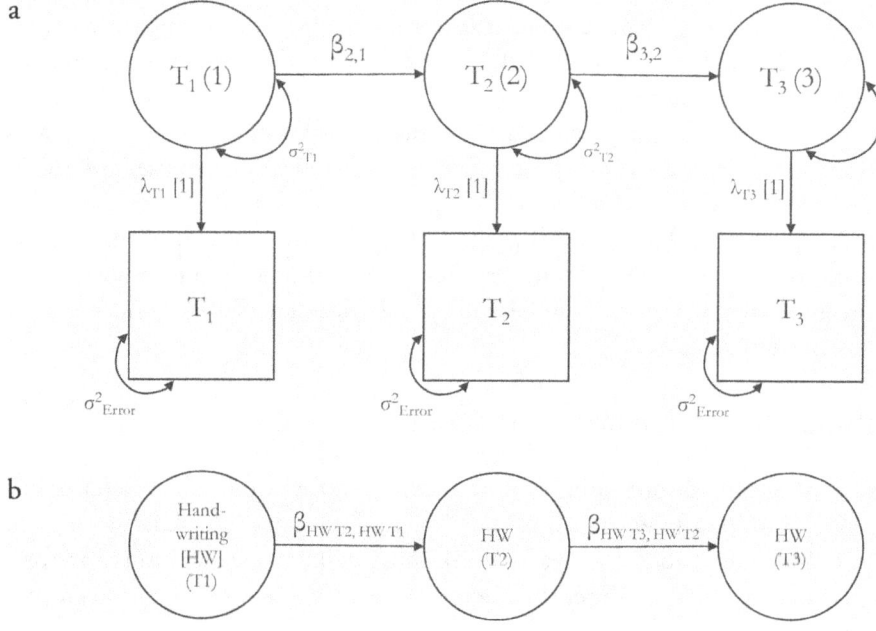

Figure 3.1. a) Path diagram example of an autoregressive model of one ability measured over three time points (T_1–T_3). Squares (□) represent the observed variables while circles (○) represent the unobserved latent variables. Curved, double-headed lines (↔) represent variances. Straight, single-headed lines (→) are directed, regressive relationships between observed or unobserved variables. See text for further information about specific parameter labels. b) Path diagram of handwriting skills assessed over three time points (showing only latent variable and autoregressive parameters).

Path diagrams shown in Figures 3.1 and 3.2 represent a first-order, single measure autoregressive longitudinal model and a cross-lagged, dual measure autoregressive longitudinal model, respectively. In Figure 3.1.a, an ability is depicted as having been assessed across three separate time points (T_1–T_3). Each latent variable represents the time-point-specific ability of interest, which is accounted for by the observed variable and the unaccounted-for error (or variance). In this example, the time-point-specific latent variables are based off a single observed variable (and the relationship between these is set to 1, as the observed variable is functioning as an indicator for the latent variable that is not freely estimated). The focal point of Figure 3.1.a falls on the regressive parameters between time points (i.e., $\beta_{2,1}$ and $\beta_{3,2}$), as these represent the stability of individual differences across the two adjacent time points. For any given time point, the performance of a variable of interest is the product of this regressive parameter, its value at the earlier time point (T_{1-3}), and its unexplained variance (σ^2_{1-3}) and unaccounted-for error (σ^2_{Error}). Figure 3.1.b shows what this path model would look like if applied to the measurement of handwriting skills measured over three time points. For simplicity in this example, we have included visual representations of the latent variables and regressive parameters only.

In Figure 3.2.a, there are now two different abilities assessed at each time point ($T_{1,A}$-$T_{3,A}$ and $T_{1,B}$-$T_{3,B}$), and the focus falls on both the predictive association within variables (autoregressive parameters) and the predictive associations across variables between timepoints (cross-lagged parameters). The regressive parameters depicting the relationships between the same variable at different time points (i.e., $\beta_{B2,B1}$, $\beta_{B3,B2}$, $\beta_{A2,A1}$, and $\beta_{A3,A2}$) can be interpreted as was done with the regressive parameters shown in Figure 3.1 (i.e., they represent the stability of individual differences across the two adjacent time points for that variable). However, the cross-lagged regressive parameters focus on the relationships between the two different abilities across time points, as these parameters (i.e., $\beta_{B2,A1}$, $\beta_{B3,A2}$, $\beta_{A2,B1}$, and $\beta_{A3,B2}$) represent the predictive relationship of one variable assessed at an earlier time point on the second variable assessed at a later time point (while controlling for the first variable). Additionally, the covariances between the unexplained variance (i.e., $\sigma_{\sigma^2_{T1B,T1A}}$, $\sigma_{\sigma^2_{T2B,T2A}}$, $\sigma_{\sigma^2_{T3B,T3A}}$) capture the extent to which changes in one variable are associated with changes in the other variable for that given time point. Figure 3.2.b shows what this path model would look like if applied to the measurement of handwriting and spelling skills. Again, for simplicity, we have included only visual representations of the latent variables, regressive parameters (both autoregressive and cross-lagged), and the covariance parameter between T_1 skills.

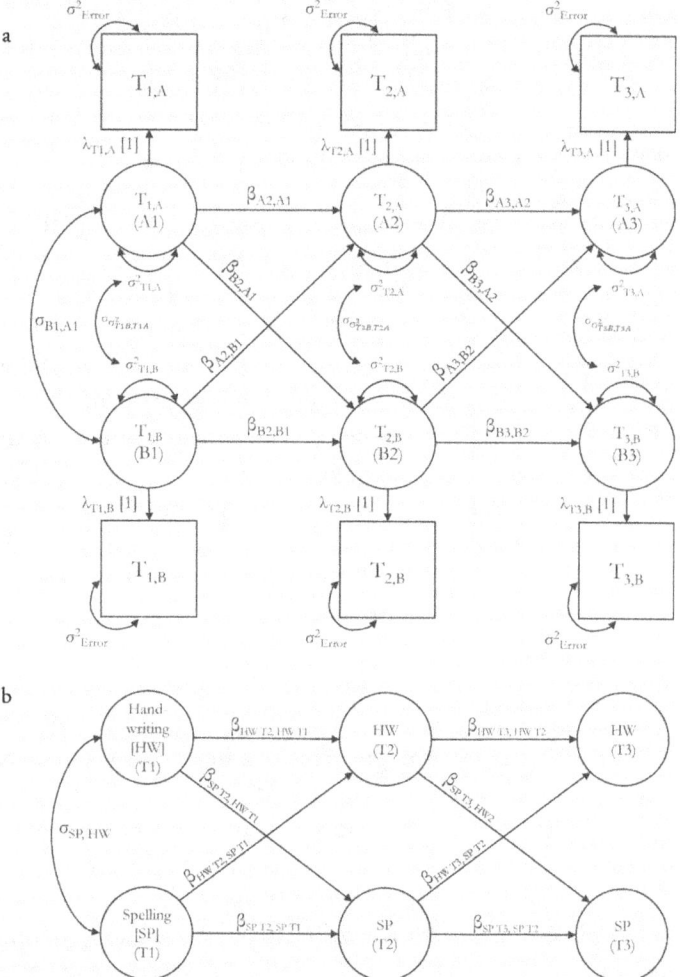

Figure 3.2. a) Path diagram example of a cross-lagged, autoregressive model of two abilities (A and B) measured over three time points (T_1–T_3). Squares (□) represent the observed variables while circles (○) represent the unobserved latent variables. Curved, double-headed lines (↔) can represent either variances (if they start and end within the same square or circle) or covariances (if they start and end on different squares or circles). Straight, single-headed lines (→) are directed, regressive relationships between observed or unobserved variables. See text for further information about specific parameter labels. b) Path diagram of a cross-lagged, autoregressive model of handwriting and spelling skills assessed simultaneously across three time points. Only the latent variables, the autoregressive and cross-lagged parameters, and the covariance parameter between T_1 skills are shown.

Using Autoregressive Models for Writing Research

Not many studies have used autoregressive models to analyze longitudinal writing development. One example by Abbott et al. (2010) adopted the multiple levels of language theory to examine the relationships within writing (autoregressive) and between writing and reading (cross-lagged) using an overlapping cohort design that included students in first grade through seventh grade.

The authors examined the longitudinal development of five measures (handwriting, spelling, word reading, text composition, and reading comprehension) in two cohorts of students using three different models. Model 1 analyzed three measures—handwriting, spelling, and text composition—with both specified autoregressive and cross-lagged parameters. Model 2 analyzed three measures—handwriting, spelling, and word reading—with both specified autoregressive and cross-lagged parameters between time points. Model 3 analyzed four measures—word reading, spelling, text composition, and reading comprehension—with both specified autoregressive and cross-lagged parameters between time points. As such, each model included three distinct types of paths: a) between-measure correlations for each grade level, b) within-measure autoregressive longitudinal paths between adjacent grades, and c) longitudinal cross-lagged paths between each measure for each set of measures at adjacent time points. Additionally, the authors used observed rather than latent variables due to minimal measurement error and a high degree of measure reliability (Abbott et al., 2010, p. 286).

The authors reported results for both standalone autoregressive models and autoregressive models with additional cross-lagged components. For the autoregressive models, the authors reported that individual differences across measures appeared consistently associated longitudinally between adjacent years from grades 1 to 7. Additionally, they found that the magnitude (i.e., the strength) of the associations differed upon the level of language, in descending order from word-level (spelling and word reading), text-level (reading comprehension and text composition), and subword-level measures (handwriting).

The models that included specifications for both the cross-lagged and autoregressive parameters demonstrated better model fit (i.e., better represented the data) than models with only the autoregressive parameters specified. Model 1 estimates highlighted some stability in measure-specific individual differences across grade levels with some unreliable longitudinal relationships between certain skills (e.g., handwriting with spelling and text composition) and unexpected reliable relationships between other skills (e.g., spelling and composition). Model 2 estimates highlighted consistent measure-specific individual differences across grade levels for handwriting, spelling, and word reading; a significant association (though small) between spelling and word reading; and no relationship between word reading and handwriting. Model 3 estimates highlighted consistent measure-specific individual differences and associations between different measures (e.g., spelling and word reading) across grade levels similar to those observed in Model 2 as well as new findings for consistent measure-specific individual differences (e.g., text composition and reading comprehension), associations between different measures (e.g., spelling and word reading; word reading and text comprehension), and no relationships between other measures (e.g., reading comprehension and spelling; text composition and word reading).

Abbott et al. (2010) provides one example as to how autoregressive models can be beneficial to longitudinal writing research. Their study focused explicitly on modeling the relationships within and between specific writing and reading skills across time to consider if data supported the multiple levels of language theory. Their findings offered a comprehensive examination of the relationships between multiple skills associated within writing and across reading and writing. These relationships highlighted not only the importance of multiple subskills within writing but also the extent to which different levels of language appear related across writing and reading domains at adjacent time points across the elementary and secondary school years (Abbott et al., 2010). However, this application of longitudinal SEM is but one of numerous approaches available to researchers.

Latent Growth Curve Models (LGCMs)

Autoregressive models highlight relations between multiple variables over time but do not emphasize information about individual- or group-level performance. What if, instead, our research questions focused on the trajectories of change in writing skills over time? What if we wanted to model overall change between scores and ask questions about whether this change is related to an individual's initial skill level or to their growth in writing skills over time? LGCMs represent a different class of models that focus on the extent to which individuals demonstrate change in specific abilities over time rather than solely performance-related bidirectional effects. The LGCM framework allows for evaluating hypotheses specific to between-person differences in within-person change and goes by many different names (e.g., multilevel models of change, latent trajectory analysis, latent curve modeling, and mixed effects or random effects models of change) (Shiyko et al., 2012).

LGCMs treat multiple observed time points of the same variable as indicators of (usually) two latent constructs that represent how individuals change over time. These latent factors include an intercept (i.e., the ability level at a single time point of interest and often the first time data were collected) and a slope (i.e., the change in an individual's ability over time). LGCMs use multiple time-point trajectories produced by individuals across different time points to provide a parsimonious representation of these trajectories via description of the average change trajectories and the degree to which inter-individual differences (i.e., between-person differences) in change occur. LGCMs allow for exploring a variety of different types of research questions related to the growth individuals demonstrate in a given ability measured over multiple time points and can range from simple to more complex models. LGCMs offer the flexibility of SEM with the advantage of modeling a variety of different random effects (e.g., means, variances, and covariances of individual differences for both the intercept and the slope) (Preacher, 2019).

Figure 3.3 depicts a path diagram of a simple LGCM representing the assessment of one ability across four time points. While the path diagram may share some visual similarities to the autoregressive models shown in Figures 3.1 and 3.2, the LGCM path diagram contains important distinctions. Working from the bottom of the diagram, the observed variables and associated errors are no different from those depicted in Figures 3.1 and 3.2 (i.e., a skill is measured four times). However, the two latent variables (labeled Intercept and Slope) are conceptually different from the latent variables depicted in Figures 3.1 and 3.2. Both latent variables contain unidirectional paths to each of the observed variables. Each path is labeled with a lower-case Lambda (λ) with subscripts to differentiate between different paths (e.g., $\lambda_{4,1}$ represents the path for the fourth observed variable for the intercept, while $\lambda_{4,2}$ represents the path for the fourth observed variable for the slope). The fixed values in brackets for this illustration represent what these path parameters would be set to when estimating a simple LGCM. While the fixing of each intercept path parameter to 1 follows the same rationale as used with the autoregressive models (in that each observed variable is acting as an indicator for the latent variable that is not freely estimated), the rationale behind fixing the slope paths is slightly different. In this example, each slope path parameter is fixed to a value between zero and three based on the time parameter (i.e., the fixed value represents the order of the time points beginning with zero as the first time point). These values may be fixed in this manner or left free to be estimated from the data (e.g., to assess for nonlinear growth, then these values would be freely estimated or partially fixed to allow for nonlinear estimation of time point slopes). The triangle represents that the initial intercept and slope values are assumed to be latent variables with fixed means ($\mu_{Intercept}$ and μ_{Slope}) but random variances ($\sigma^2_{Intercept}$ and σ^2_{Slope}) and covariances ($\sigma_{Slope, Intercept}$).

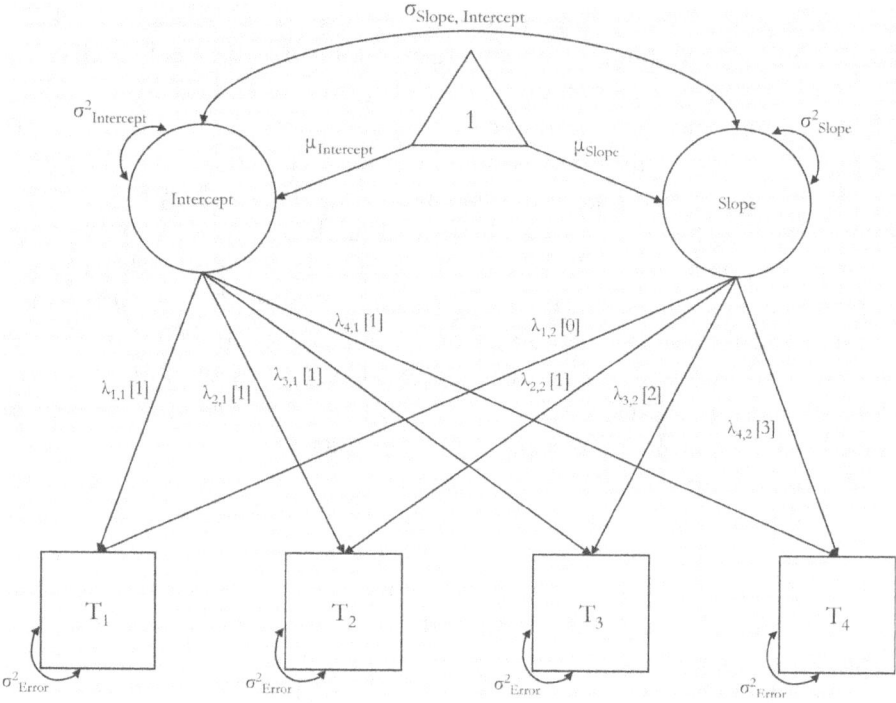

Figure 3.3. Path diagram example of a simple LCGM of one ability measured over four time points (T_1–T_4). Squares (□) represent the observed variables while circles (○) represent the unobserved latent variables. A triangle (△) represents a constant value. Curved, double-headed lines (↔) can represent either variances (if they start and end within the same square or circle) or covariances (if they start and end on different squares or circles). Straight, single-headed lines (→) are directed, regressive relationships between observed or unobserved variables. See text for further information about specific parameter labels.

Bollen and Curran (2006) offer three guiding questions to assist with thinking about research questions involving trajectories of change for a given sample of individuals for a given skill. First, *what is the trajectory of the entire group?* This initial question seeks to characterize the entirety of the dataset and does not consider potential subgroups or other distinctions within the data. This approach is needed to help understand what potential underlying trajectories exist for the entire dataset before more specific questions are asked. Second, *are distinct trajectories needed for each case?* This question requires considering how subgroups may demonstrate trajectories different from the overall average trajectory. By accounting for subgrouping factors, potential distinctions between different individuals are considered alongside the differences observed within individuals across time. Third, *are there additional variables that can be used to predict individual trajectories?* After establishing both an average trajectory and the presence of meaningful variation in this overall average trajectory (particularly in terms of both the intercept and slope), what other information could be useful for predicting these observed distinctions? This approach takes into consideration additional information that may be meaningful to predicting and understanding why distinct trajectory patterns exist within a given dataset for a construct measured multiple times.

LGCMs further offer the capability of examining research questions related to a wide range of different types of longitudinally oriented research questions (Grimm et al., 2017). LGCMs deal with investigating individuals in the same abilities over a number of distinct time points, allowing for investigations into intra-individual differences (i.e., how do individuals change across time points with respect to this ability?). LGCMs allow for testing different modeling approaches that assume different patterns of change for observed abilities and provide a structured approach to investigating such inter-individual differences within the context of earlier mentioned intra-individual changes (Grimm et al., 2017). As changes in multiple constructs can occur both simultaneously and sequentially, approaching questions about these inter-relationships requires simultaneous analysis of multiple variables alongside evaluations of how variables may precede, covary, and/or follow changes observed in another variable (Grimm et al., 2017). Furthermore, the flexibility of the SEM framework allows for considering different predictors for both intra-individual change and inter-individual differences in intra-individual change, such as allowing for the inclusion of multiple groups or the specification of time-invariant covariates (i.e., variables that occur at specific points in time that are included at only specific time points rather than reassessed at multiple time points).

Using LGCMs in Writing Research

Similar to autoregressive models, LGCMs have not yet been widely adopted for analyzing longitudinal writing development. However, Costa et al. (this volume) provide an investigation into the growth trajectories of written language and executive functions in 205 elementary-age children across first through fourth grade using LGCMs. Interested readers are directed to Chapter 10 for the full study, but what is of interest to this chapter is their consideration regarding key issues of model fit and estimation. Though their findings suggested interesting results relevant to the relationships between individual variability in written language (i.e., spelling, alphabet knowledge, and writing fluency) and executive functions (i.e., attentional control and planning) over time, they highlight particular concerns about model convergence and model fit, both of which showcase the complexity of issues that can occur when interpreting results from SEM. Even with their stated limitations, Costa et al. (this volume) present a worthwhile approach to using LGCMs for analyzing longitudinal writing data.

CONCLUSION

As highlighted by the Lifespan Writing Development Group (Bazerman et al., 2018), writing develops in a complicated, multifaceted process that should not be expected to happen rapidly or linearly. To address research questions related to the development of writing and writing-related abilities across the lifespan, researchers need to be diverse in their questions and their methodologies. This chapter offered a review of longitudinal quantitative approaches that writing researchers may draw on to investigate writing development across the lifespan. In doing so, we highlighted the application of SEM as a comprehensive framework whose structure provides researchers with the means to answer quantitatively oriented research questions via deductive, theory-driven, hypothesis-testing, and predictive approaches.

SEM and longitudinal quantitative research approaches more generally provide lifespan writing researchers with valuable tools to test and answer research questions about how writing develops and changes from early development through late adulthood across cognitive and social contexts. Quantitative methods have a longstanding history and continue to guide much of the methodological foundations across a wide array of fields within the social sciences (see Haig, 2013). The consideration for the broader role of quantitative methods—as well as the specific role of advanced approaches like SEM—provides frameworks to researchers interested in analyzing data collected over many different types of research designs. Broader longitudinal quantitative approaches aligned with time-to-event data and repeated measures data allow researchers to postulate and analyze an array of questions ranging from the importance of carefully defined events on later development to ways in which skills predict performance in similar or associated skills over any set period of time. SEM further provides researchers with a robust framework to specify carefully articulated research questions about data based on theoretical beliefs (and provides researchers with the capabilities of considering nuances in the data that are only covered briefly here) (see Kline, 2016 and Wu et al., 2013).

We hope this chapter has sparked an interest in readers from different disciplines with different methodological backgrounds in the multitude of roles that longitudinal quantitative approaches may have to help answer questions about the development of writing across the lifespan. However, quantitative methods do have their limitations and may not always be the best approach to take. Though SEM can be used for causal hypotheses, not all SEM approaches are causal in design, which can lead to overconfidence in data interpretation (see Hoyle, 2012; Jöreskog, 1993; or Kline, 2016). Additionally, the use of SEM does not magically transform correlational data into causal conclusions. Findings must be replicated across multiple datasets to avoid the capitalization of chance factors that might have been due to specific features of a dataset rather than the constructs under investigation (Raykov & Marcoulides, 2006). Furthermore, numerous researchers have called for additional considerations into the role of mixed methods in ongoing interdisciplinary research. These researchers argue that fewer distinctions may exist between quantitative and qualitative methods than many believe (see Haig, 2013) or that research designs may be strengthened by taking novel approaches that consider a wide array of methodologies (see Gelo et al., 2008 and Todd et al., 2004). Lifespan writing researchers should consider novel techniques across different approaches that may best answer their research questions and should build from findings across different lines of inquiry in the general pursuit of better understanding the ongoing development of writing abilities across the lifespan.

ACKNOWLEDGMENTS

Matthew C. Zajic received support during the drafting of this chapter from a Postdoctoral Research Fellow Training Program Grant in Education and Autism Spectrum Disorders from the National Center for Special Education Research at the Institute of Education Sciences (R324B180034) awarded to the University of Virginia.

REFERENCES

Abbott, R. D. & Berninger, V. W. (1993). Structural equation modeling of relationships among developmental skills and writing skills in primary-and intermediate-grade writers. *Journal of Educational Psychology*, *85*(3), 478–508. https://doi.org/10.1037/0022-0663.85.3.478.

Abbott, R. D., Berninger, V. W. & Fayol, M. (2010). Longitudinal relationships of levels of language in writing and between writing and reading in grades 1 to 7. *Journal of Educational Psychology*, *102*(2), 281–298. https://doi.org/10.1037/a0019318.

Allison, P. D. (2010). Survival analysis. In G. R. Hancock & R. O. Mueller (Eds.), *The reviewer's guide to quantitative methods in the social sciences* (pp. 413–424). Taylor & Francis.

Allison, P. D. (2019). Event history and survival analysis. In G. R. Hancock, L. M. Stapleton & R. O. Mueller (Eds.), *The reviewer's guide to quantitative methods in the social sciences* (2nd ed.) (pp. 86–97). Taylor & Francis.

Baltes, P. B. & Nesselroade, J. R. (1979). History and rationale of longitudinal research. In J. R. Nesselroade & P. B. Baltes (Eds.), *Longitudinal research in the study of behavior and development* (pp. 1–39). Academic Press.

Bauer, D. J. & Curran, P. J. (2019). *Conducting longitudinal data analysis: Knowing what to do and learning how to do it* [PowerPoint slides]. https://curranbauer.org/how-do-you-choose-the-best-longitudinal-data-analytic-method-for-testing-your-research-questions/ .

Bazerman, C. (2018). Lifespan longitudinal studies of writing development: A heuristic for an impossible dream. In C. Bazerman, A. N. Applebee, V. W. Berninger, D. Brandt, S. Graham, J. V. Jeffery, P. K. Matsuda, S. Murphy, D. W. Rowe, M. Schleppegrell & K. C. Wilcox (Eds.), *The lifespan development of writing* (pp. 326–368). National Council of Teachers of English.

Bazerman, C., Applebee, A. N., Berninger, V. W., Brandt, D., Graham, S., Jeffery, J. V., Matsuda, P. K., Murphy, S., Rowe, D. W., Schleppegrell, M. & Wilcox, K. C. (2018). *The lifespan development of writing*. National Council of Teachers of English.

Berninger, V. W., Abbott, R. D., Abbott, S. P., Graham, S. & Richards, T. (2002). Writing and reading: Connections between language by hand and language by eye. *Journal of Learning Disabilities, 35*(1), 39–56. https://doi.org/10.1177/002221940203500104.

Berninger, V. W., Nielsen, K. H., Abbott, R. D., Wijsman, E. & Raskind, W. (2008). Writing problems in developmental dyslexia: Under-recognized and under-treated. *Journal of School Psychology, 46*(1), 1–21. https://doi.org/10.1016/j.jsp.2006.11.008.

Biesanz, J. C. (2012). Autoregressive longitudinal models. In R. Hoyle (Ed.), *Handbook of structural equation modeling* (pp. 459–471). The Guilford Press.

Bollen, K. A. (2002). Latent variables in psychology and the social sciences. *Annual Review of Psychology, 53*(1), 605–634. https://doi.org/10.1146/annurev.psych.53.100901.135239.

Bollen, K. A. & Curran, P. J. (2004). Autoregressive latent trajectory (ALT) models a synthesis of two traditions. *Sociological Methods & Research, 32*(2), 336–383. https://doi.org/10.1177/0049124103260222.

Bollen, K. A. & Curran, P. J. (2006). *Latent curve models: A structural equation perspective*. John Wiley & Sons.

Bollen, K. A. & Hoyle, R. (2012). Latent variables in structural equation modeling. In R. Hoyle (Ed.), *Handbook of structural equation modeling* (pp. 56–67). Guilford.

Creswell, J. W. & Creswell, D. (2018). *Research design: Qualitative, quantitative, and mixed methods approaches*. Sage.

Curran, P. J. & Bollen, K. A. (2001). The best of both worlds: Combining autoregressive and latent curve models. In L. M. Collins & A. G. Sayer (Eds.), *New methods for the analysis of change* (pp. 107–135). American Psychological Association.

De Smedt, F., Merchie, E., Barendse, M., Rosseel, Y., De Naeghel, J. & Van Keer, H. (2018). Cognitive and motivational challenges in writing: Studying the relation with writing performance across students' gender and achievement level. *Reading Research Quarterly, 53*(2), 249–272. https://doi.org/10.1002/rrq.193.

Gelo, O., Braakmann, D. & Benetka, G. (2008). Quantitative and qualitative research: Beyond the debate. *Integrative Psychological & Behavioral Science, 42*(3), 266–290. https://doi.org/10.1007/s12124-008-9078-3.

Graham S. (2018). A writer(s)-within-community model of writing. In C. Bazerman, A. N. Applebee, V. W. Berninger, D. Brandt, S. Graham, J. V. Jeffery, P. K. Matsuda, S. Murphy, D. W. Rowe, M. Schleppegrell & K. C. Wilcox (Eds.), *The lifespan development of writing* (pp. 272–325). National Council of Teachers of English.

Graham, S., Berninger, V. W., Abbott, R. D., Abbott, S. P. & Whitaker, D. (1997). Role of mechanics in composing of elementary school students: A new methodological approach. *Journal of Educational Psychology, 89*(1), 170–182. https://doi.org/10.1037/0022-0663.89.1.170.

Grimm, K., Ram, N. & Estabrook, R. (2017). *Growth modeling: Structural equation and multilevel modeling approaches*. The Guilford Press.

Haig, B. D. (2013). The philosophy of quantitative methods. In T. D. Little (Ed.), *The Oxford handbook of quantitative methods* (Vol. 1, pp. 7–31). Oxford University Press.

Harlow, L. L. (2013). Teaching quantitative psychology. In T. D. Little (Ed.), *The Oxford handbook of quantitative methods* (Vol. 1, pp. 105–117). Oxford University Press.

Heagerty, P. J. & Zeger, S. L. (2000). Marginalized multilevel models and likelihood inference. *Statistical Science, 15*(1), 1–26. https://doi.org/10.1214/ss/1009212671.

Ho, M. R., Stark, S. & Chernyshenko, O. (2012). Graphical representation of structural equation models using path diagrams. In R. H. Hoyle (Ed.), *Handbook of structural equation modeling* (pp. 43–55). The Guilford Press.

Hoyle, R. (2012). *Handbook of structural equation modeling*. The Guilford Press.

Jöreskog, K. G. (1993). Testing structural equation models. In K. A. Bollen & J. S. Lang (Eds.), *Testing structural equation models* (pp. 294–316). Sage.

Kim, Y. S., Al Otaiba, S., Puranik, C., Folsom, J. S. & Greulich, L. (2014). The contributions of vocabulary and letter writing automaticity to word reading and spelling for kindergartners. *Reading and Writing, 27*(2), 237–253. https:/doi.org/10.1007/s11145-013-9440-9.

Kim, Y. S., Al Otaiba, S., Puranik, C., Folsom, J. S., Greulich, L. & Wagner, R. K. (2011). Componential skills of beginning writing: An exploratory study. *Learning and Individual Differences, 21*(5), 517–525. https://doi.org/10.1016/j.lindif.2011.06.004.

Kim, Y. S. & Schatschneider, C. (2017). Expanding the developmental models of writing: A direct and indirect effects model of developmental writing (DIEW). *Journal of Educational Psychology, 109*(1), 35–50. https://doi.org/10.1037/edu0000129.

Kline, R. B. (2016). *Principles and practice of structural equation modeling (4th ed.)*. The Guilford Press.

Lei, P. W. & Wu, Q. (2007). Introduction to structural equation modeling: Issues and practical considerations. *Educational Measurement: Issues and Practice, 26*(3), 33–43. https://doi.org/10.1111/j.1745-3992.2007.00099.x.

Limpo, T. & Alves, R. A. (2013). Modeling writing development: Contribution of transcription and self-regulation to Portuguese students' text generation quality. *Journal of Educational Psychology, 105*(2), 401–413. https://doi.org/10.1037/a0031391.

Limpo, T., Alves, R. A. & Connelly, V. (2017). Examining the transcription-writing link: Effects of handwriting fluency and spelling accuracy on writing performance via planning and translating in middle grades. *Learning and Individual Differences, 53*, 26–36. https://doi.org/10.1016/j.lindif.2016.11.004.

Little, T. D. (2013). *Longitudinal structural equation modeling*. The Guilford Press.

Little, T. D., Schnabel, K. & Baumert, J. (2000). Modeling longitudinal and multilevel data: Practical issues, applied approaches, and specific examples. Lawrence Erlbaum Associates.

McArdle, J. J. (2010). What life-span data do we really need?. In R. L. Lerner & W. F. Overton (Eds.), *The handbook of life-span development* (Vol. 1, pp. 55–88). John Wiley & Sons.

McArdle, J. J. (2012). Latent curve modeling of longitudinal growth data. In R. H. Hoyle (Ed.), *Handbook of structural equation modeling* (pp. 547–570). The Guilford Press.

McArdle, J. J. & Bell, R. Q. (2000). An introduction to latent growth models for developmental data analysis. In T. D. Little, K. U. Schnabel & J. Baumert (Eds.), *Modeling longitudinal and multilevel data: Practical issues, applied approaches, and specific examples* (pp. 69–107, 269–281). Lawrence Erlbaum Associates.

McArdle, J. J. & Kadlec, K. M. (2013). Structural equation models. In T. D. Little (Ed.), *The Oxford handbook of quantitative methods* (Vol. 2, pp. 295–337). Oxford University Press.

McArdle, J. J. & Nesselroade, J. (2014). *Longitudinal data analysis using structural equation models*. American Psychological Association.

Menard, S. (2008). *Handbook of longitudinal research design and analysis*. Elsevier.

Mueller, R. O. & Hancock, G. R. (2019). Structural equation modeling. In G. R. Hancock, L, M. Stapleton & R. O. Mueller (Eds.), *The reviewer's guide to quantitative methods in the social sciences* (2nd ed., pp. 455–456). Taylor & Francis.

Muthén, B. & Shedden, K. (1999). Finite mixture modeling with mixture outcomes using the EM algorithm. *Biometrics, 55*(2), 463–469. https://doi.org/10.1111/j.0006-341X.1999.00463.x.

Nagy, W., Berninger, V., Abbott, R., Vaughan, K. & Vermeulen, K. (2003). Relationship of morphology and other language skills to literacy skills in at-risk second-grade readers and at-risk fourth-grade writers. *Journal of Educational Psychology, 95*(4), 730–742. https://doi.org/10.1037/0022-0663.95.4.730.

Newsom, J. (2015). *Longitudinal structural equation modeling: A comprehensive introduction*. Taylor & Francis.

Parkin, J. R., Frisby, C. L. & Wang, Z. (2020). Operationalizing the simple view of writing with the Wechsler Individual Achievement Test (3rd ed.). *Contemporary School Psychology, 24*, 68–79. https://doi.org/10.1007/s40688-019-00246-z.

Preacher, K. J. (2019). Latent growth curve models. In G. R. Hancock, L. M. Stapleton & R. O. Mueller (Eds.), *The reviewer's guide to quantitative methods in the social sciences* (2nd ed., pp. 178–192). Taylor & Francis.

Raykov, T. & Marcoulides, G. A. (2006). *A first course in structural equation modeling* (2nd ed.). Lawrence Erlbaum Associates.

Shiyko, M. P., Ram, N. & Grimm, K. J. (2012). An overview of growth mixture modeling: A simple nonlinear application in OpenMx. In R. H. Hoyle (Ed.), *Handbook of structural equation modeling* (pp. 532–546). The Guilford Press.

Shmueli, G. (2010). To explain or to predict? *Statistical Science, 25*(3), 289–310. https://doi.org/10.1214/10-STS330.

Singer, J. & Willett, J. (2003). Applied longitudinal data analysis: Modeling change and event occurrence. Oxford University Press.

Todd, Z., Nerlich, B. & McKeown, S. (2004). Introduction. In Z. Todd, B. Nerlich, S. McKeown & D. Clarke (Eds.), *Mixing methods in psychology: The integration of qualitative and quantitative methods in theory and practice*. Psychology Press.

Walls, T. A. (2013). Intensive longitudinal data. In T. D. Little (Ed.), *The Oxford handbook of quantitative methods* (Vol. 2, pp. 432–440). Oxford University Press.

Walls, T. A. & Schafer, J. L. (2006). *Models for intensive longitudinal data.* Oxford University Press.

Wu, W., Selig, J. P. & Little, T. D. (2013). Longitudinal data analysis. In T. D. Little (Ed.), *The Oxford handbook of quantitative methods* (Vol. 2, pp. 387–410). Oxford University Press.

CHAPTER 4.

MAKING SENSE OF A PERSON'S LITERATE LIFE: LITERACY NARRATIVES IN A 100-YEAR-STUDY ON LITERACY DEVELOPMENT

Magdalena Knappik
University of Wuppertal, Germany

A longitudinal study sets out to collect data continuously as time passes; it assembles a whole picture by collecting a large amount of data at different points in time (Bazerman, 2018). Being retrospective in nature, literacy narratives may initially seem counterintuitive to the purposes of a longitudinal study. However, they offer invaluable insights into the processes of people making sense of their literate lives, and of the *meaning* they attribute to literacy as they tell and interpret their lives. If collected at different points in time and carefully connected to longitudinal data, literacy narratives may serve an important function in a longitudinal study on literacy development. In this chapter, I will demonstrate why we should try to make this connection, and how it can be achieved in data collection and analysis.

Literacy narratives are personal narratives or life stories with a specific focus on literacy development. Definitions of literacy narratives range from fictional to non-fictional texts; from written to oral texts; from texts elicited in a classroom setting, closely informed by a pedagogical agenda, to texts elicited in a research setting; and from texts that follow a biographical arc, such as in Brandt (1994, 1995, 1998), to texts that will zoom in on a few pivotal life events. For instance, Eldred and Mortensen (1992) define literacy narratives as fictional texts—"stories that foreground issues of language acquisition and literacy" (p. 513). Alexander (2011) and Carlo (2016) view the literacy narrative as a genre, while Lawrence (2015, p. 304) considers literacy narratives to be "personal accounts of literacy-related experiences." In this chapter, I will refer to non-fictional texts only. This does not mean I treat literacy narratives as factual, but that I consider them to be meant by their creators to be understood as non-fictional.

People's recollections of their past—or, in our case, of their literacy development—are necessarily shaped by a number of factors, for example their memories, or the overall meanings they attribute to their lives. And yet, literacy narratives offer insights into the *meaning* literacy takes on for writing individuals across different contexts and life events. However, to make use of literacy narratives, we need to be careful not to stop at the content level when we analyze them (Lawrence, 2015). To avoid dismissing literacy narratives on the grounds of their constructedness, we need to focus on exactly this quality—their constructedness—to deepen our analysis of the content.

I will make my argument for literacy narratives in four steps. First, I will argue why we should use literacy narratives in a longitudinal study. It is important, though, to consider that they cannot be treated as just facts about a person's literate life, as I will show in the following section. I will then highlight some key decisions that need to be considered when planning for the collection of literacy narratives and their connection with longitudinal data. Finally, I will suggest ways to deepen the analysis by including methodologies that focus on the constructedness of the narrative, using the neighboring field of life history research as a source for useful approaches to analysis. Life history research shares many of the interests of literacy narrative research: an interest in people's perspectives on their (writing) lives, on their meaning-making, and on their interpretations of their lives and writing development trajectories.

WHY WE SHOULD USE LITERACY NARRATIVES IN LIFESPAN WRITING RESEARCH

I want to point out four ways in which literacy narratives can be important for longitudinal lifespan writing research: First, they give us insight into a person's sense-making of their literacy development. Second, they tell us about social value systems towards literacy and thus provide important context for other data in the longitudinal study. Third, literacy narratives might themselves serve as sponsors of literacy development (Lawrence, 2015). Finally, a longitudinal, multi-site study on lifespan writing allows us to compare literacy narratives from very different social and institutional contexts and thus gain a deeper understanding of the genre itself.

The first contribution that literacy narratives offer to lifespan writing research is that they tell us about a person's sense-making of their literacy development. Autobiographical narratives tell us about the present of the narrator rather than their past (Bruner, 1991; Freeman, 2007; Schütze, 2007). In creating a coherent story, segmenting and ordering their past, research subjects are making sense of their present. If we follow this train of thought, we can use literacy narratives to gain profound insights into the present of a writer at one point in time and to find out about the meaning that person attributes to literacy—an important dimension of literacy development (Bazerman et al., 2018, p. 371). The literacy narrative's potential then would be the in-depth and structured analysis of a person's evaluation and sense-making of their literacy development at a given point in time.

In addition, literacy narratives may themselves be sponsors of literacy, as Lawrence (2015) points out. She argues that the genre of literacy narrative may be viewed as a scene for literacy development, in the sense that the "productive rhetoric" of the narrating event may actually sponsor literacy development: She points out that is important to view

> [t]he rhetorical practices of literacy narratives (autobiographical or otherwise) *as sponsors of literacy*—as material conditions that enable and constrain what and how literacy is thought, felt and lived by researchers and teachers, as well as by recounters of literacy narratives. (Lawrence, 2015, p. 306)

In a similar vein, Rosenthal (1995) talks about the "healing effect of biographical narrating" (p. 167; translation by MK). The process of creating and owning their life story, to experience the validation of their version of their life through an avid listener, and maybe just this very process of creating coherence and presenting their life story as the "history of a proper person" (Linde, 1993, p. 17) might have a healing or sponsoring effect on the narrator.

Furthermore, literacy narratives provide important insights into cultural and social value systems towards literacies and literacy development. Both master and little narratives (Alexander, 2011; Carlo, 2016; Daniell, 1999) can serve as key analytical tools for this. We can look out for both master and little narratives in a longitudinal study in order to learn more about cultural and social expectations about literacy at specific points in time. This might provide important context for analyzing other types of lifespan writing research data.

We might also compare literacy narratives across diverse populations to find out more about the culturally different and the universal structuring principles of the genre of literacy narratives. It might be interesting to research shared and changing systems of coherence, such as the "success story." It would also be possible to compare literacy narratives from education systems where this is not a well-known genre (and almost never a school-based assignment), to literacy narratives that were created in education systems where literacy narratives are a very common assignment.

Literacy narratives provide a rich source of data for lifespan writing research. However, we have to be careful not to treat literacy narratives as documents about a person's past. The next section will show the factors that shape a literacy narrative and that need to be taken into account when analyzing them.

LITERACY NARRATIVES AREN'T FACTS ABOUT A PERSON'S PAST: THE CONSTRUCTEDNESS OF LITERACY NARRATIVES

Literacy narratives cannot be taken as documents that provide facts on a person's (literate) life. Both life histories and literacy narratives are genres that entail strong cultural expectations as to the content and the shape of the stories that can be told. At its heart, a literacy narrative—and a life history—is expected to be a story of positive development, of learning, and of mastering a skill (literacy), or a life. There are two consequences of this: first, some things cannot be told in a literacy narrative; and second, some things will only be told because of the generativity of the genre. Webb-Sunderhaus (2016) uses the term *tellability* to draw attention to stories that are culturally favored, and to the stories that tend to be omitted or suppressed: "Tellability is a lens for evaluating which narratives are worth telling and for further assessing who can tell which narratives in what context" (p. 12). She critiques the portrayal of combined poverty and illiteracy in studies on marginalized persons that leave no room for their actual involvement with literacy, which might happen "in ways that are untellable in public discourse" (2016, p. 13). Likewise, Bowen (this volume) highlights how ageist ideologies frame age with intellectual and bodily decline and shows how this might shape our perception of writing in old age negatively. Also, writing development research tends to frame the gains of literacy development in a rather unchallengedly positive way, as Viruru (2003) critiques. As a consequence, any losses in that process, such as a loss of oracy, are not tellable and will not be told.

Some things might also not be remembered. The ability to recall memories at all could be enabled and limited by existing social frameworks, as Halbwachs' (1992) notion of *collective memory* conveys. He posits that the availability of frameworks within which memories can be placed is a precondition for people having those memories at all: "Many stories and histories simply cannot be told when the social frameworks are not there" (cited in Plummer, 2007, p. 402). For example, being homosexual only became a part of told life histories when the social frameworks to talk about being homosexual had been built and claimed by the LGBT community.

The genre itself provides a strong framework for the ways in which a literacy narrative will be told. This becomes most apparent when analysis is approached with a narratological lens. Both literacy narratives and life histories can be viewed and analyzed as "stories," as narrative texts with a plot, subscribing to the linearity of time as a structuring principle, with "nuclear episodes," "thematic lines," and "characters" (McAdams, cited in Plummer, 2007, p. 399–400). Nuclear episodes are "specific autobiographical events which have been reinterpreted over time to assume a privileged status in the story" while thematic lines are "recurrent content clusters in stories" and characters are "recognizable stereotypes" (Plummer, 2007, pp. 399–400). Norman Denzin (1999) points out that life histories usually are centered around a crisis-like event, something that Denzin names "epiphany." These genre-typical frameworks are productive or generative; thus a particular literacy narrative might be shaped in the way it is because genre conventions ask for it.

The generativity of the genre also shapes the interaction between listener and narrator, which influences the way a story is told and the self that is created in the process. Linde (1993) shows how life histories (she prefers the term "life stories") are shaped by the social demand of coherence: A story needs to be told in a coherent way in order to be comprehensible and narrators need to present a life story as a coherent course of events "in order for the participants to appear as competent members of their culture" (Linde, 1993, p. 16). There is also an internal demand for coherence, that is, "our own individual desire to understand our life as coherent, as making sense, as the history of a proper person" (Linde, 1993, p. 17). Narrators refer to systems of coherence or "popular versions of expert theories and systems" (Linde, 1993, p. 18), that they think they might share with their audience. And, with different audiences, narrators refer to different systems of coherence. Similarly, Angrosino (1989) highlights the role of the audience in the creation of the story. In his view, the story is a "document of interaction," the interaction is a "drama" between narrator and listener—"the process that creates the narrative" (1989, p. 4). Correspondingly, the narrated self that is created in this process is seen as fluid and changing, "not a timeless, finished product but . . . rather a fragment of an evolving process" (Angrosino, 1989, p. 105).

As a consequence of both the limitations and the generativity of the genre, there will be one prevailing form of the literacy narrative if it is given as an assignment: the success story. Daniell (1999), Alexander (2011), and Carlo (2016) make use of Lyotard's term "master narratives" to explain the potency of these cultural narratives. The most common master narrative in the field of literacy narratives seems to be the "success story," wherein literacy development is seen as a key to social and financial upward mobility and success and students tend to position themselves favorably within this frame. But Daniell (1999), Alexander (2011), and Carlo (2016) also encounter "little narratives," or stories that may counter and resist master narratives within their research.

All of these factors shape the form of literacy narratives yet this does not make them unsuitable for lifespan writing research. If we take this very quality—their specific constructedness—into account and make it part of the analysis, then we can gain valuable insights into the meaning of literacies for people and their lives.

COLLECTING LITERACY NARRATIVES: KEY DECISIONS

Before we start collecting literacy narratives as data in a lifespan study, we need to carefully consider several aspects that each allow for different research strategies. I want to highlight five of them: the different possibilities for collecting literacy narratives within a longitudinal study, the different forms they might take (written, oral, and visual), the prompts we might use to elicit a biographical arc, the impact of different listeners, and the institutional contexts for literacy narratives across sites.

Collecting Literacy Narratives within a Longitudinal Study

To make the most use of literacy narratives as part of a 100-year longitudinal study, I advocate for two types of data collection: a) the planned collection of literacy narratives across different contexts with different populations and at several points in a person's life; and b) the analysis of literacy narratives that occur as a by-product in an ethnography. Plummer (2007) distinguishes three types of data collection: everyday naturalistic, researched, and reflexive-recursive. "Everyday naturalistic" are life histories that occur as part of everyday interactions with subjects in an ethnography (Plummer, 2007, p. 396). "Researched" means that a researcher elicits a life history, usually with a prompt, while "reflexive-recursive" is a term to signify life histories that are more self-aware of their process of construction (Plummer, 2007, p. 396). They are often done by a researcher, for example as part of an autoethnography (e.g., Zebroski, this volume). We should both collect "researched" literacy narratives and "everyday naturalistic" stories on literacy development as part of ethnographies. Ethnographies will provide rich context data for the analysis of the literacy narratives that occur within them and literacy narratives will also allow insights into social and cultural values towards literacies that will then provide interesting context for analyzing other ethnographic data. It might also be interesting to compare researched and everyday naturalistic forms of literacy narratives.

Written, Oral, Visual and Material Forms

Literacy narratives are multimodal and may consist of written, oral, visual, or material forms and any combination thereof. Literacy narratives might be oral, in particular if they are everyday naturalistic types of data. Orally presented literacy narratives might create a more accessible space to persons who developed oracies rather than literacies in their lives, or to persons who developed both. To collect oral forms of literacy narratives could also serve to value oracy. This could be particularly important in light of Webb-Sunderhaus's and Viruru's critiques of literacy development research as being prone to overlook and/or devalue oracies or less socially valued forms of literacies. We could also try to elicit oracy narratives, i.e., stories about the development of a person's oracy and compare them to literacy narratives. Whilst this might be a worthwhile research objective in itself, this might also shed light on both productive and suppressing interrelations between oracy and literacy development. We also might combine the collection of visual and material data with written or spoken narratives. Bowen's suggestion (this volume) to do *literacy tours* with the research participants when listening to their narrative enables the narrators to include material objects into their story that serve a function for their writing activities, such as writing desks, clocks, and much more. It is important to be open to the multimodality of literacy narratives when deciding which type of data to collect so that participants are able to express the complexity of their experiences.

Prompts

It is important to ensure that the narratives we collect have a biographical arc. If the narrative only focuses on a few select episodes in life, it might become difficult to extract developmental trajectories. To achieve this, we need to construct our prompts carefully. In my study with 58 literacy narratives written by students who did not know literacy narratives as a genre or assignment (Knappik, 2018), this was accomplished by using a prompt with cues like "over the course of your life" or "in your life" ("Write your writing biography. Which kinds of writing have you encountered over the course of your life?" were the first two sentences of the prompt). The narratives took on the form of written life histories with a focus on literacy development. If we successfully elicit literacy narratives with a biographical arc (or "literacy life stories") we can make better use of existing methodologies for analyzing a person's sense-making of literacies in their life, (e.g., Linde, 1993 or Rosenthal, 1995) as I will discuss below.

Multiple Audiences

To account for the social expectations on literacy that different listeners/researchers might represent, we could ask participants to tell their literacy narratives to multiple listeners, including some that might share their economic, cultural or local backgrounds and some that might represent other backgrounds. We could also ask participants to interview other participants about their literacy development. As this might be tiring for research participants, this research strategy might only be feasible if some time has passed between the points of data collection.

CONTEXT: BEING AWARE OF ASSIGNMENTS

As the literacy narrative is such a well-known and ubiquitously practiced genre within US higher education, we should actively collect literacy narratives in institutions in different contexts where literacy narratives are scarcely known as a genre and contrast them with literacy narratives collected in the US. We should also consider collection sites outside of institutions since we might encounter different varieties of narratives if the genre is not a well-known writing assignment. For instance, success stories were not the master narrative in my study, even though it was conducted in an institution of higher education. Instead, narratives of resentment towards the types of literacies that the narrators developed were quite common. There were also stories that mourned the loss of other, more joyful types of writing as part of their portrayal of development (Knappik, 2018). It will be interesting to compare literacy narratives across contexts where they are well-known genres and where they are not.

ANALYZING LITERACY NARRATIVES: MOVING BEYOND THE CONTENT LEVEL

Literacy narratives are clearly shaped by genre and by broader institutional and cultural factors. Those factors both limit and enable individuals to use literacy narratives for making sense of their literacy development and the meaning of literacies in their lives. To unlock the potentials this holds for lifespan writing research, we need to equip our analysis with tools that are able to recognize meaning beyond a content level. Methodologies within life history research provide excellent tools for this. In this section, I will present two of them: (1) a story-focused approach that will foreground narratological devices in the narrative to highlight which parts of a (literacy) narrative might be subject to social frameworks rather than individual experience (Linde, 1993); and (2) a methodology that combines a story-focused and a content-focused approach in order to find out which guiding principle a narrator uses to make sense of their (literate) life (Rosenthal, 1995). I present both of them to show that there exists a range of approaches to analysis that move beyond the content level. Linde's is more narratological while Rosenthal decidedly advocates for an inclusion of the content level into the analysis, albeit in a very sophisticated and form-conscious way. Both Linde and Rosenthal argue that the sequentiality of a life story[1] is the most important guiding principle of the analysis of life stories, as they view the way

---

1   I choose to use the term "life story" in this section because Linde uses the term "life story" and Rosenthal uses "Lebensgeschichte" in German, which translates directly to "life story."

a life story is structured as a most important tool to understand the processes of meaning-making expressed in this structuring.

LINDE: THE CREATION OF COHERENCE

Linde's (1993) approach is very useful to gain a deeper understanding of socially established principles that speakers (and listeners) presuppose when they create and make sense of a life story. In her investigation of principles of construction and coherence in life stories, Linde presents a wide array of useful linguistic vocabulary to describe and analyze the discourse units of a narrative. Drawing on Labov & Waletzky's (1967) definition, the following are typical parts of narratives: "the optional abstract, the orientation, the narrative clauses, and the optional coda" (p. 69). These parts are usually sequential. Narratives often also include evaluations—why the story was worth telling—which may occur at different locations throughout the narrative. In a narrative, the evaluation "is socially the most important part" because it conveys "how [its addressees] are to understand the meaning of the narrated sequence of events and what kind of response the speaker desires" (Labov & Waletzky, 1967, p. 72). It will be very productive to look out for evaluations in literacy narratives since they will tell us about the expectations of the narrator and what we as researchers represent to them in regard to literacies. Research on literacy narratives suggests that the "success story" might be one of the main systems of coherence that narrators draw on when telling a literacy narrative. This is important in particular for all research interested in developmental aspects. A success story will usually describe at its core some kind of development. This means that we need to reconstruct the narrator's expectations of what constitutes development in between the narrator and the listener.

ROSENTHAL: CONTRASTING THE LIVED AND THE TOLD LIFE

As Rosenthal (1995, p. 14–15) incorporates both "the lived life" and "the told life" into her analysis, her approach lends itself most usefully to the analysis of retrospective data within a longitudinal study. In Rosenthal's terms, the narrated story is the "told life." The "lived life" needs to be reconstructed from context information about the narrator's biography and their historical and social contexts. If a literacy narrative is part of a longitudinal study, for instance an ethnography, it will easily be possible to gather these facts. The longitudinal study might even provide considerable detailed facts about a whole lived literacy/life.

Rosenthal aims to contrast the "lived life" with the "told life" in order to find out about possible life courses that did not happen and to look for things that the narrator might have been silent about. Those omissions transpire when we contrast the lived against the told life. This is a way to account for the tellability of literacy narratives and the non-tellability of unvalorized forms of literacy: We can find out what was not told.

Rosenthal's goal is to reconstruct the overall "gestalt" of the life story. This, again, is a contrasting technique. There is the idea in gestalt theory that we can interpret a part only in relation to its whole and that the whole is more than the sum of its parts. The parts/segments that we analyze will be continuously contrasted against the whole. The whole—the gestalt—is the guiding principle that a person chooses to organize their life story—the "red thread," as it were. For her, this individual guiding principle is something that a person has actively formed, rather than a given framework within which someone might operate. To find this guiding principle is, for Rosenthal, the key to understand a person's process of sense-making.

As we do not know this guiding principle at the start of our analyses, we will generate multiple hypotheses about it as we move from segment to segment. For any line of data interpreted, Rosenthal asks us to imagine consequences of this interpretation—fantasies about how a life will unfold if the initial interpretation proves true. When continuing our analysis sequentially, the data will show that some of those interpretations are rendered implausible while others may be affirmed. We will dismiss the implausible readings and continue with the plausible ones, generating multiple new ones as we go along. This is important in order to break up routine assumptions made by the researcher and to avoid jumping to conclusions based on the specific ideas of normalcy any researcher might hold.

Rosenthal's approach allows us to make use of both literacy narratives and any data that we have gathered across a person's lifespan. In a longitudinal study, we are well positioned to collect both types of data, contrasting told lives against lived lives to find out what people decided to include or omit in their literacy narratives. Rosenthal's abductive process of analysis helps to avoid, or at least reflect, our preconceptions about literacy development. It seems very promising to reconstruct different guiding principles that people created to make sense of their (literate) lives and to contrast and compare them across different contexts and sites.

CONCLUSION

In this chapter, I aimed to show how literacy narratives can make an important contribution to longitudinal writing research. While they are not suitable as a source of facts about a person's life because they are shaped by a number of factors, they offer a number of other possibilities to researchers. The generativity of the genre "literacy narrative" with its requirements for a story arc (Denzin, 1999; Plummer, 2007) and the creation of coherence (Linde, 1993) influence the narrative as well as the social expectations that the researcher represents. Collective memory (Halbwachs, 1992) and social expectations for the literacy or illiteracy of research participants (Viruru, 2003; Webb-Sunderhaus, 2016) form frameworks that enable "tellable" stories and dismiss others. Literacy narratives are necessarily highly constructed forms of data on literacy development.

Literacy narratives reflect social frameworks, interactional demands, and the narrator's choices to select and order the events that, in their perspective, form their literacy development. And this is exactly why they are valuable for lifespan writing research: They allow us to analyze how people are making sense of their literate lives. Smith (this volume) warns that we might overlook analyzing change in itself if we just compare data from different points in a person's literate life. She invites researchers to look at "the in-betweens . . . to draw focus to the means and mechanisms *through* which writing development is realized." Research participants' ways of ordering their pasts—of attributing meaning to literacy and life events while omitting others—is a way to analyze these means and mechanisms from the writers' own perspectives. What counts as change to a person? What counts as development to a person? What is valued or devalued by a person and their environments? How do their definitions of "change," "development," and "values" function in their processes of making sense of their lives?

Literacy narratives also make an important contribution to understand different and, with Dippre and Smith (this volume), ever-changing, protean contexts. Their narratives reflect the expectations of their listeners as well as social valorizations and devalorizations of literacies at specific points in time and space. Linde's (1993) methodology of analyzing the construction of coherence in a narrative allows us to deepen our understanding of the interactional and social relationships between narrator and listener and how they translate to the shape of the narrative. The social frameworks that we can reconstruct in this analysis serve as important context for longitudinal studies.

The act of sense-making that a narrator undertakes in a literacy narrative might also in itself be a sponsor of literacy development (Lawrence, 2015). This idea is highly valuable for lifespan writing research. If we are able to collect literacy narratives of the same person at different points in the lifespan, we may analyze how this narration might have changed their views on themselves or their literacy practices, and how this might have stimulated changes in their literacy practices.

As the members of the Writing Through the Lifespan collaboration consider how to launch a 100-year study on writing development, I suggest that literacy narratives have an important role to play, especially when combined with longitudinal approaches such as ethnography and when researchers have the opportunity to collect more than one literacy narrative per research participant across the lifespan. By combining retrospective and longitudinal data, we are able to contrast both types of data. This is, admittedly, very ambitious, but also highly promising. Rosenthal's (1995) methodology is built around the careful comparison between the "told" and the "lived" life. If we have longitudinal data on the "lived" life, we have a source of data that is unprecedented in its richness. To contrast this data with the narrative that a person constructs out of the same thing—the lived life—must be an incredibly interesting analysis. It will allow us to analyze very thoroughly which life and literacy events have been omitted, which have been highlighted, and what overall guiding principle a person uses to convey their story. This guiding principle might shed light on what it is about literacy that matters most to persons.

To use literacy narratives as part of a longitudinal study opens a pathway to an important dimension of lifespan writing research, the dimension of the *meaning* of literacy in a person's life (Bazerman et al., 2018). We can analyze what (changing) meaning a person attributes to their literacies and their literacy development, we can investigate the functions that literacy narratives have for making sense of a person's life, and we can research the ways in which the act of narrating one's literate life is a sponsor of literacy development in itself. A longitudinal approach to lifespan writing research provides an excellent site to make the most use of literacy narratives as complementary and contrasting data, and as data of its own merit.

REFERENCES

Alexander, K. P. (2011). Successes, victims, and prodigies: "Master" and "little" cultural narratives in the literacy narrative genre. *College Composition and Communication*, 62(4), 608–633.

Angrosino, M. V. (1989). *Documents of interaction: Biography, autobiography, and life history in social science perspective.* University of Florida Press.

Bazerman, C. (2018). Lifespan longitudinal studies of writing development: A heuristic for an impossible dream. In C. Bazerman, A. Applebee, V. Berninger, D. Brandt, S. Graham, J. Jeffery, P. Matsuda, S. Murphy, D. Wells Rowe, M. Schleppegrell & K. Campbell Wilcox (Eds.), *The lifespan development of writing* (pp. 326–365). National Council of Teachers of English.

Bazerman, C., Applebee, A., Berninger, V., Brandt, D., Graham, S., Jeffery, J., Matsuda, P. K., Murphy, S., Wells Rowe, D., Schleppegrell, M. & Campbell Wilcox, K. (2018). The challenges of understanding developmental trajectories and of designing developmentally appropriate policy, curricula, instruction, and assessments. In C. Bazerman, A. Applebee, V. Berninger, D. Brandt, S. Graham, J. Jeffery, P. K.

Matsuda, S. Murphy, D. Wells Rowe, M. Schleppegrell & K. Campbell Wilcox (Eds.), *The lifespan development of writing* (pp. 369–381). National Council of Teachers of English.

Brandt, D. (1994). Remembering writing, remembering reading. *College Composition and Communication*, *45*(4), 459–479. https://doi.org/10.2307/358760.

Brandt, D. (1995). Accumulating literacy: Writing and learning to write in the twentieth century. *College English*, *57*(6), 649–668. https://doi.org/10.2307/378570.

Brandt, D. (1998). Sponsors of literacy. *College Composition and Communication*, *49*(2), 165–185.

Bruner, J. (1991). Self-making and world-making. *Journal of Aesthetic Education*, *25*(1), 67–78. https://doi.org/10.2307/3333092.

Carlo, R. (2016). Countering institutional success stories: Outlaw emotions in the literacy narrative. *Composition Forum*, *34*. http://compositionforum.com/issue/34/countering.php.

Daniell, B. (1999). Narratives of literacy: Connecting composition to culture. *College Composition and Communication*, *50*(3), 393–410.

Denzin, N. (1989). *Interpretive Ethnography*. Sage.

Eldred, J. C. & Mortensen, P. (1992). Reading literacy narratives. *College English*, *54*(5), 512–539. https://doi.org/10.2307/378153.

Freeman, M. (2007). Autobiographical understanding and narrative inquiry. In D. Clandinin (Ed.), *Handbook of narrative inquiry: Mapping a methodology* (pp. 120–145). Sage.

Halbwachs, M. (1992). *On collective memory*. University of Chicago Press (L. A. Coser, Trans.). (Original work published 1952 as *Les cadres sociaux de la mémoire*, and 1941 as *La topographie légéndaire des évangiles en terre sainte: Etude de mémoire collective*).

Knappik, M. (2018). *Schreibend werden. Subjektivierungsprozesse in der migrationsgesellschaft*. wbv.

Labov, W. & Waletzky, J. (1967). Narrative analysis: Oral versions of personal experience. In J. Helm (Ed.), *Essays on the verbal and visual arts* (pp. 12–44). University of Washington Press.

Lawrence, A. M. (2015). Literacy narratives as sponsors of literacy: Past contributions and new directions for literacy-sponsorship research. *Curriculum Inquiry*, *45*(3), 304–329. https://doi.org/10.1080/03626784.2015.1031058.

Labov, W. & Waletzky, J. (1967). Narrative analysis: Oral versions of personal experience. In J. Helm (Ed.), *Essays on the verbal and visual arts* (pp. 12–44). University of Washington Press.

Linde, C. (1993). *Life stories: The creation of coherence*. Oxford University Press.

Plummer, K. (2007). The call of life stories in ethnographic research. In P. Atkinson, A. Coffey, S. Delamont, J. Lofland & L. Lofland (Eds.), *Handbook of ethnography* (pp. 395–406). Sage.

Rosenthal, G. (1995). *Erlebte und erzählte lebensgeschichte: Gestalt und struktur biographischer selbstbeschreibungen*. Campus.

Schütze, F. (2007): *Biography analysis on the empirical base of autobiographical narratives: How to analyse autobiographical narrative interviews—Part 1*. INVITE –

Biographical Counselling in Rehabilitative Vocational Training. Further Educational Curriculum. EU Leonardo da Vinci Programme. https://doi.org/10.2307/J.CTVDF09CN.7.

Viruru, R. (2003). Postcolonial perspectives on childhood and literacy. In N. Hall, J. Larson & J. Marsh (Eds.), *Handbook of early childhood literacy* (pp. 13–21). Sage.

Webb-Sunderhaus, S. (2016). "Keep the Appalachian, drop the Redneck": Tellable student narratives of Appalachian identity. *College English*, *79*(1), 11–33.

CHAPTER 5.

A DEFINITION OF EVERYDAY WRITING: METHODS FOR A WRITER-INFORMED APPROACH TO LIFESPAN WRITING

Jeff Naftzinger
Sacred Heart University

On the opening page of Bazerman et al.'s (2018) *The Lifespan Development of Writing*, the authors point out that "[w]e may readily grant that learning and development are life long, yet we stay focused—as we must—on the immediacies of our academic locations" (p. 3). If we do not expand our scope beyond these locations, they argue, "we [will] know too little about how writing develops before, during, and after schooling; too little about how a person's writing experiences relate to each other developmentally across the lifespan" (Bazerman et al., 2018, p. 4). Similarly, in this chapter I argue that if we stay focused on the immediacies of our scholarly assumptions of what writing is and how it should be defined, then we will be unable to more fully understand the ways that writing is defined by everyday writers and how these definitions are shaped across the lifespan.

One way that we can begin to expand and enrich our understanding of everyday writers, and the ways they use writing, is to use a writer-informed approach. This kind of approach, which has been taken up by researchers like Bowen (this volume), Rosenberg (this volume), and Prior and Shipka (2003), gives the writers we study a role in collecting and selecting the data we analyze, in shaping our interviews, and, ultimately, in guiding the trajectory of our research and results. Importantly, this kind of approach can aid in the discovery of not just how and why people are writing through their lifespans and how they define writing, but it can also—and perhaps more importantly—aid in the discovery of where our scholarly assumptions and understandings diverge from those engaged in writing in their everyday lives. In other words, a writer-informed approach provides an opportunity for us to supplement our own assumptions and understandings with those of the everyday writers, and vice versa. Working with writers to shape these findings also has the potential to help the writers we work with more fully understand, and see the importance of, their writing practices.

DOI: https://doi.org/10.37514/PER-B.2020.1053.2.05

My own writer-informed approach to studying everyday writing asked five writers (most of whom did not even consider themselves to be writers) to define writing as they use it in their daily lives. The writers participated in the selection and collection of data about their writing habits, and they made the decisions about what counts as everyday writing and what does not. This kind of approach attempts to, borrowing from the previous Lifespan Writing Development Group, "more wholly democratize a complex, slow-growing" *definition* of a "human capacity that no longer belongs in the hands of the few" (Bazerman et al., 2018, p. 4) and put it into the many hands of the non-academic and non-professional writers who engage in it.

In this chapter, I will discuss previous research that has shown the value of a writer-informed approach to studying writing. I will then outline the methods used in my own writer-informed approach to define everyday writing. Finally, I close with two examples that illustrate the benefits of a writer-informed approach: first, it can help us strengthen our understandings of writing through the lifespan by pointing out where our scholarly definitions and understandings of writing diverge from those of the practitioners we study; and, second, it can help positively change the way our participants think about their own writing.

WRITER-INFORMED APPROACHES TO UNDERSTANDING WRITING

Though the term *writer-informed approach* might be new, the benefits of letting participants guide investigations into writing practices—especially those that span the length or width of our lives—have been illustrated by some scholars in writing studies like Bowen (this volume), Prior and Shipka, (2003), and Roozen (2008; 2012). Looking more specifically at Bowen's "literacy tours" (this volume), Prior and Shipka's maps and document curation, and Roozen's interviews can demonstrate a research tradition similar to what I call a writer-informed approach.

In her chapter in this collection, Bowen discusses "Literacy Tours" as a method for better understanding the material influences on elder participants' writing practices. Though she does not use the term, these literacy tours are part of a writer-informed approach, since the writer "*leads* the researcher on a narrated walk-through of the physical and sometimes virtual spaces in which they engage in literate activity" (this volume, emphasis added). As Bowen explains, this writer-informed method "interrupts . . . the assumptions that might otherwise be embedded within the interview" and "elicits details about a life story that might not otherwise appear in [them]." Bowen argues that giving the writers the opportunity to lead us to findings, to shape our investigations, and to participate in the selection and curation of data as much as possible is the major benefit of a writer-informed approach. Scholars like Prior and Shipka (2003) and Roozen (2008, 2012), whose work often looks at the sociohistorical aspects of writing, have also utilized methods that allow the writers to take the lead in helping us better understand the ways that writing practices are materially, socially, and personally situated.

In "Chronotopic Lamination: Tracing the Contours of Literate Activity," Prior and Shipka (2003) trace the ways that "literate activity" consists of "dispersed and fluid chains of places, times, people, and artifacts that come to be tied together in trajectories of literate action" (p. 181). As outside observers, it would be difficult to envision these laminations themselves, so they asked academic writers (students and professors) to take the lead: to draw maps of both their writing processes and the spaces that those processes take place in, to curate a collection of supplemental "material[s] they used in their writing" (Prior & Shipka, 2003, p. 180), and to participate in a semi-structured interview about their maps, artifacts, and writings. Put another way, Prior and Shipka let the writers select what was most important or apparent to them.

This process gave the participants the opportunity to exert more control over the conversations about their writing and, ultimately, inform the results of the research. By letting the writers direct their focus, Prior and Shipka were able to look at a range of writing (from a multimodal assignment, to a dissertation, to a manuscript), spaces (from a dorm room, to a bar, to a house), influential artifacts (from movies, to notebooks, to annotated books), and the interconnections between these factors. Their writers were able to point them towards activities and connections that might otherwise have been missed by more rigid, prescriptive scholar-driven selection criteria.

Similarly, Roozen (2012) has used a writer-informed approach to complicate "dominant perspectives of basic writers' self-sponsored literacies [that] tend to overlook the important roles such activities can play in literate development" (p. 99). Over five years, Roozen collected texts, conducted semi-structured interviews, and observed writing activities to illustrate how one writer, who was classified as a basic writer in the university, engages in a diverse range of writing tasks outside the university. In composition courses, Roozen's writer struggled with issues like grammar and sentence structure. Outside of his courses, however, he successfully wrote for the school newspaper, wrote jokes as a standup comedian, and published his poetry. Because he worked so closely with this writer and let the writer's interests and activities guide the investigation, Roozen (2008) was able to engage in a "complicated, messy, and yet fascinating exploration of the role that non-school literate practices played in [the student's] development as an 'academic writer'" (p. 8).

As with Prior and Shipka (2003), Roozen (2008) let his participant inform the research by engaging in "open-ended interviews" that were primarily guided by the artifacts the student brought in (p. 9). When Roozen would request artifacts of writing from his student, the student often "volunteered to provide [Roozen] with additional texts that he thought might be useful . . . " (2008, p. 9). As before, the writer was able to exert more influence over their discussions and ultimately shape Roozen's findings. As a result, Roozen was able to come up with a more robust understanding of the ways that the overlapping academic and non-academic activities this student engages in complicates the rigid understandings of who counts as a basic writer. Without a more writer-informed approach to his investigation, Roozen's discussions of the permeability between academic and extracurricular writing would have been limited by his own understandings of this participant's life and experiences.

These three examples point to the benefits of a writer-informed approach to studying writing, and all three of these approaches also, in various degrees, look towards everyday writing—the writing that writers engage in in the course of our daily lives. These examples also illustrate what might be missed if we do not let writers inform our research: the contexts, the practices, the artifacts, the new understandings that would be overlooked without their input. That being said, none of these examples attempt to *define* writing or everyday writing, which means our definitions of writing, and our understandings of how those definitions are shaped by writer's lives and experiences, lack the nuance that writer-informed approaches add.

Rather than utilizing writer-informed approaches, studies that have attempted to define everyday writing (or a related term) tend to take one of three scholar-directed approaches: 1) deductively, with scholars creating a definition and illustrating it with tasks and/or artifacts (see Nystrand & Duffy, 2003); 2) inductively, constructing a definition after observing the tasks and/or artifacts of everyday writers (see Barton & Hamilton, 1998); or 3) synthetically, constructing a definition from other scholars studying this area (see Lillis, 2013). The writers are certainly integral to these various approaches, but the researchers make the determinations about what does and does not count as everyday on behalf of the practitioners.

Bowen (this volume), Prior and Shipka (2003), and Roozen (2008, 2012) have shown how writer-informed approaches can more fully illustrate the ways that writers' contexts shape their writing practices, and how they can lead us to new understandings. To that end, the remainder of this chapter demonstrates how a writer-informed approach can also be used to let writers lead us to definitions of everyday writing, and how this process can benefit both the researchers and the writers.

A WRITER-INFORMED APPROACH TO DEFINING EVERYDAY WRITING

To define everyday writing, my writer-informed approach relied on three sources of data collection: 1) time use diaries (TUDs) that catalog the writers' writing tasks over the course of a week; 2) artifacts of writing that illustrate some of those writing tasks; and 3) discussions with the writers about the TUDs and artifacts and their definitions of, and experiences with, writing. Together, these three data collection methods offer an overarching portrait (the TUDs), a portrait of specific practices (the artifacts), and a definition and its influences (the interviews).

These methods, in particular, have been influenced primarily by two earlier studies of everyday writing: the investigation into the overarching everyday writing habits of American adults by Cohen et al. (2011) in "A Time Use Diary Study of Adult Everyday Writing Behavior" and the investigation into the contextual influences on, and purposes of, adult writing habits in Barton and Hamilton's (1998) *Local Literacies*. The designs and methods of these two studies have been adapted to the goals of this particular approach; namely, using multiple streams of data to give the writers more opportunities to direct my attention towards and away from certain practices and influences on their writing, and more opportunities to insert their voices into the findings.

The TUDs utilized for my writer-informed approach asked the writers to log their writing tasks for seven days and fill out six data points for each entry. The six data points for each writing task are: 1) the date/time of the task; 2) what was written; 3) where it was written; 4) what materials were used to write it; 5) how much time was spent writing it; and 6) for what purpose it was written. The writers were able to decide the level of detail for their responses to these points, which I then asked about during the interview process.

In terms of what counts as writing and what should thus be cataloged in the TUD, the instructions for the writers asked them to

> Record any activity in which you have used a keyboard (e.g., connected to your computer, on your smartphone, etc.) or a writing implement (e.g., a pencil, a pen, a crayon, etc.) to compose something. This can include activities like sending a text, writing a journal entry, posting on Facebook, jotting a shopping list, or other related activity.

Although there were some examples of writing implements and activities that could be included, these vague instructions were intended to give the writers more agency in determining what they counted as writing and so, what did and did not get cataloged. For example, one of the writers (Bill) included his Facebook Likes as a writing task in his diary, which I would not have thought to include as a writing task. These instructions also sometimes encouraged the logging of tasks, like adding books to a reading list (Rose), that the writer indicated they might otherwise have excluded. The writers' decisions about what did and did not get put in their TUDs were discussed in the interviews, which gave them more of an opportunity to explain their definitions of writing and everyday writing.

Both the individual TUDs and the collated TUD data helped to illustrate the relationship between the writers' definitions and the writing they actually engage in, which we were then able to more concretely discuss in our interviews. In these discussions, the writers looked over their TUDs and looked for patterns in the data; they then used these insights to inform their definitions of everyday writing and offer illustrations of the kinds of tasks that fit, or did not fit, in their definitions. As will be discussed in more detail, the writers' definitions of everyday writing were mostly based on its functions, and this was corroborated by the data in the TUDs. For example, the writers emphasized communication as part of their definition of everyday writing, and their TUDs illustrated that most of their writing is for communicative purposes. Similarly, the writers who emphasized organization as part of their definition logged a large number of organizational tasks (e.g., lists and planning documents) in their TUDs and pointed to them in our discussions as illustrations of that function.

While the TUDs are intended to provide one picture—in broad strokes—of the writers' writing habits, the artifacts they selected were able to provide a more detailed illustration of that writing. The writers were asked to select ten artifacts of writing that had been recorded in their TUDs, and these instructions were also designed to let the writers curate their selections. These artifacts provide more information, and opportunities for questions, about the specific ways these writers were composing, what the compositions look like, and what factors—either immediate or distant—have influenced the artifacts they selected. These artifacts also aided in understanding the participants' definitions of writing and looking for connections/disconnections between definitions and practices.

Finally, after collecting the TUDs and artifacts, I conducted semi-structured interviews, or discussions, with each of the writers to talk about their writing practices (both generally and in the TUD/artifacts) and their definitions of both writing and everyday writing. The TUD can only attend to the range of writing tasks the writers are engaging in, and the artifact collection can only attend to the specific composition. The interview, on the other hand, can attend to the more contextual factors—like the social, historical, and/or personal factors—influencing the writers' practices and understandings; these can, in turn, illustrate the information from the TUDs and artifacts. The interviews also provided the opportunity for the writers to define both writing and everyday writing in their own words. While this aspect of data collection certainly had the most scholarly intervention, the questions were open-ended and provided many opportunities for the writers to guide the discussion.

These three sources of data were then read across holistically and inductively in an attempt to find similarities and differences among the writers' practices and definitions. The definition was the result of finding similarities and repeated references to definitions of writing in different parts of their interviews, and the TUDs and artifacts were used to illustrate those definitions in our discussions.

THIS WRITER-INFORMED APPROACH

As this study is a writer-informed approach, selecting a group of writers who would inform it was particularly important. This group consisted of five self-described "non-writers" each representing a decade between 20 and 60 years of age and who are each quite different from one another in terms of demographic and personal factors such as race, occupation, location, level of education, and individual interests. They are:

- **Rose**: a white woman in her mid-20s, who at the time of study was living in Tallahassee, Florida after having driven across the country camping in her van. She has some college experience, mostly in the field of nursing, but no degree. She has worked primarily in the service and hospitality industry and was in between jobs while participating in the study.
- **Alison:** a white woman in her early 30s living in Minneapolis, Minnesota. She has a BA in art history, which she finished in her late 20s. She spent many years working in retail, although she is currently self-employed and running an Etsy store selling vintage/antique home goods.
- **Danny:** a white man in his late 40s living in Clinton, New York. He has a BA in studio art, which he finished in his early 40s. Since graduating, he has overseen the day-to-day operations related to the studio art workshop at a small liberal arts college.
- **Laura:** a black woman in her early 50s living near Chicago, Illinois. She has a BS in psychology and pre-med, which she completed at age 22. She is a manager and compliance analyst at a large insurance corporation in Illinois, where she oversees casualty and loss reporting and training.
- **Bill:** a white man in his early 60s living near Akron, Ohio. He has a BS in engineering and started, but did not finish, an MBA. He

worked at a large aircraft manufacturing company as an engineer, manager, and internal educator for two decades and is now "semi-retired." He has recently patented a plane/boat/car hybrid, which he is designing and building himself.

This group of five was deliberately selected for this investigation based on two major factors: 1) their lack of professional/scholarly experience with writing and 2) the range of demographic factors the writers represent. The reasoning behind the first criterion was to ensure that the writers' contributions to this study would not be swayed by professional or scholarly expertise. The second criterion is connected to Dippre and Smith's chapter in this collection, which highlights the importance of context in the development of writing.

Selecting based on age groups yielded a group of writers who could speak to a range of different age-related experiences that happen through the lifespan, for instance, adapting to new writing technology, moving to new locations, and embarking on different careers (see Bazerman et al., 2018; Bowen, this volume; Dippre and Smith, this volume). The other demographic factors were also helpful in generating a portrait and definition of writing that speak to a range of experiences, interests, and contexts. Interestingly, despite the writers' age differences and the differences in their individual writing practices, their definitions of writing were quite similar.

The data collected from the five writers provided interesting insights into what writing looks like for, and how it is defined by, a diverse group of writers. With the constraints of space, however, I will focus on two findings that illustrate the usefulness of writer-informed approaches as we continue our research into writing through the lifespan. The first finding focuses on the disconnections between the writer-informed and the scholarly definitions of everyday writing as a way to highlight how scholarly concerns do not always align with those of the writers studied. The second finding focuses on how this kind of approach can also result in new understandings for the writers who inform our studies.

A Writer-Informed Definition

In their article, Cohen et al. (2011) define "everyday writing" as "any writing that is carried out in the daily lives of an individual," which "can range from writing a formal multipage academic paper to jotting down a phone number or making a list" (p. 4). This definition is especially capacious and includes *all* writing under the umbrella of everyday writing. While this term does direct our attention towards *not just* academic writing, it does not necessarily emphasize the more mundane tasks that writers engage in. In order to specifically highlight these mundane writing tasks, I, with colleagues, have defined everyday writing as "the ubiquitous self-sponsored writing typically operating outside the regulation and oversight of an institution or representative of an institution."[1] The explicit exclusion of writing that is sponsored (Brandt, 2001), which tends to happen in school and at work,[2] was a deliberate choice made to more fully orient discussions towards the unsponsored writing tasks that, in our view, make up the bulk of writing. While we appreciated the common goal of turning scholarly attention to non-scholarly writing, we thought that existing definitions of everyday writing and related terms (see Barton & Hamilton, 1998; Hauser & mcclellan, 2009; Nystrand & Duffy, 2003; White-Farnham, 2014) did not go far enough to separate the everyday from the academic and the professional, which are already more commonly studied. These concerns, however, are scholarly; a writer-informed approach to defining writing can help us discover what the actual practitioners believe everyday writing is and what possible benefits, if any, the term everyday writing can offer them.

Although there were small distinctions across the writers' definitions of everyday writing, there was one common thread that linked them: an emphasis on the functions of everyday writing, particularly communication and organization. While the definition informed by this group of writers was more closely aligned to Cohen et al.'s (2011) definition than it was to my own, it was also not as capacious as Cohen et al.'s. At the same time, the writers' focus on the functions of their writing, as opposed to genre or location, was also quite different from others who have defined terms akin to everyday writing (Hauser & mcclellan, 2009; Nystrand & Duffy, 2003; White-Farnham, 2014). The writer-informed definition was, perhaps, most similar to Barton and Hamilton's (1998) functions of vernacular literacies, though these scholars identified four more functions than this group of writers did. These differences illustrate the ways that a writer-informed definition can help to fill in the gaps of our own scholarly ones.

The emphasis on communication was evident in almost all the writers' definitions of everyday writing. Rose, for example, explained that she sees everyday writing as including basically any writing task that does not involve introspection or payment, but when she discussed the value of the practice, she said it provides the "opportunity to *connect* with people" (emphasis added). Danny's definition of everyday writing was simply "communication," and Laura similarly defined everyday writing as writing that is used "for communicating." Bill said that he sees everyday writing as writing that deals with "emotional stuff: relationships or

---

1   This definition was crafted with Kathleen Blake Yancey, Joe Cirio, and Erin Workman as part of an early draft of a manuscript arguing for Everyday Writing as a means of categorizing seemingly disparate scholarship in Composition research.

2   Where we are most often in the presence of "agents . . . who teach, model, support, recruit, extort, deny, or suppress literacy and gain advantage by it in some way" (Brandt, 2001, p. 19).

keeping people happy," which he explained later in the interview (and illustrated through his artifacts and TUD) is primarily enacted through communicating.

The data collected in the TUDs helped to illustrate this primary function of everyday writing: 76 percent of the tasks logged by the writers were for another person, and the remaining 24 percent were for the writer him/herself.[3] The artifacts, however, were much more evenly divided among these two categories, with 54 percent being written for others and 46 percent for the writer him/herself. This disparity slightly complicates their collective definition of everyday writing, which is primarily focused on its communicative function, though it also helps to highlight the second major function they identified.

Many of the self-directed artifacts and writing tasks in the diaries enacted the function of organizing the writers' lives. Alison's definition of everyday writing as "putting words on a page—be it meaningless or not" does not necessarily exclude everyday writing's communicative function, but her definition was the only one that does not specifically point to that communicative function. Instead, Alison's discussion of her own writing, and the illustration of that writing in her TUD and artifacts, focused on everyday writing's value for memorializing and organizing her life. Many of the artifacts that Rose selected also pointed to this function of everyday writing, though she did not emphasize it in the definitions she provided in her interview. The artifacts that Rose and Alison selected for this study were primarily organizational writing tasks like shopping lists, Bullet Journal plans and pages, a planning document for a trip, and so on. Danny and Laura also logged these organizational tasks in their TUDs, and their discussions of their writing practices included references to this type of writing task.

For Danny and Laura, these organizational tasks, and most of their writing, occurred at work, which also highlights the role of function in their definitions. As they expanded on their definitions of everyday writing, these two writers—the only two who have full-time jobs—specifically included their work-related tasks that were used for communicating with others and organizing their days, like sending emails and writing notes. Their TUDs and selected artifacts also indicated that this is the primary purpose of their writing: 67 percent of Danny's writing tasks were work related, as were 79 percent of Laura's. The other three writers—Rose, Alison, and Bill—did make a distinction between everyday writing and work writing, but they did so in different ways. Rose used the promise of payment as a factor to separate them. Alison used the relative length of workplace documents, in terms of word count and time devoted, to delineate them. Bill said that workplace writing is not everyday writing because

---

3   Although there were some writing tasks, like shopping lists, that were initially composed for personal reasons but might later be shared with another person.

it does not, or should not, have an emotional aspect (his evaluative criterion for everyday writing).

Taken together, the writers' definitions of everyday writing are primarily shaped by the writing they regularly engage in, which includes writing used for communicating and/or organizing. Although this group's definition of everyday writing is similar to Cohen et al.'s (2011), since it, too, focuses on the "everydayness"—or regularity—of the writing, this group's definition is much more restrictive. While Cohen et al. included everything, this group of writers excluded tasks such as writing for pay, writing for introspection, and writing for academic purposes. At the same time, though, the writers' definitions of everyday writing were much less restrictive than mine, and they did not use sponsorship to delineate writing and everyday writing. Since Rose, Alison, and Bill do not write for work, they excluded workplace writing in their definition; conversely, since Danny and Laura write primarily for work, they specifically included it in their definition (though they do not see themselves as writing for pay).

These findings, and the ways that the writer-informed definition does not wholly align with the scholar-informed definitions discussed here, highlight the relationships between writers' lives and their definitions of writing and thus the usefulness of a writer-informed approach: working closely with the writers allows them to map connections for us, and allows them to show us what is most influential. Though we may not fully agree with the writers' definitions, this approach points to how our understandings as scholars can become more nuanced by including the opinions of the writers themselves. Rather than including as much as Cohen et al. (2011) have, or excluding as much as I have, the writer-informed definition of everyday writing in this study is a kind of middle ground focusing on function, and a more limited set of functions, rather than just regularity or sponsorship as other scholars have posited.

A Writer-Informed Perspective Shift

Working with this group of writers to develop a definition of everyday writing resulted in a second finding about a writer-informed approach: it can help the writers we study see themselves as writers and help them see the value of their writing. As scholars of writing, especially those of us interested in lifespan writing, we tend to see a wide range of writing, if not all writing, as valuable. The writers who informed this study of everyday writing did not come to the study with the same belief, but their roles as co-researchers informing this study helped to shift that.

While their definitions of everyday writing, discussed above, were quite expansive, the writers' definitions of what they considered to be "real" writing was quite restrictive. These five writers view "real writing" as what they did in school or what "real" writers—like journalists, novelists, and poets—are paid to do. Even Danny and Laura, whose writing tasks were primarily connected to their occupations, did not see themselves as writers, nor did they see the tasks they logged in their diaries as writing. Because of these assumptions, all five of the writers were concerned that their participation wouldn't be useful to this study, since they believed that they did not write—or did not write enough.

As it turns out, their trepidations were closely connected to their definitions of "real" writing. This was especially evident in my discussion with Rose, who said that she didn't know if her participation was "going to be helpful to, because [she was] not even writing" during the week she logged in her TUD. Rose explained that "real" writing (or "*writing* writing," as she called it) "is intentional," it is "[p]utting . . . pen to paper. Like an introspective kind of a release . . . " that involves making an effort " . . . to sit down to really take the time [to write]." When I asked Rose whether or not she thought of herself a writer, she said, "I guess, no," because, she explained, she was not engaging in the intentional, introspective tasks she includes in her definition of "real" writing. Jokingly, Rose said that looking over her TUD "made [her] feel like a shallow bitch," because the week of tasks showed that all she "did was text people."[4] The rest of the writers, with the exception of Bill, reported similar feelings of perceived inadequacies: they logged writing tasks in their TUDs, but they weren't *"real"* writing tasks. (Bill's concern was that he did not log enough writing tasks).

Although it is true that some of the writers do not write very much, their TUDs illustrate that they do at least some writing during the course of a week. Their initial definitions of "real" writing, however, caused them to basically ignore the writing they actually engage in. This, in turn, caused the writers to overlook the importance of this writing in terms of the functions that they ultimately included in their definitions of everyday writing (communicating and organizing). After they looked over their TUDs and constructed their definitions of everyday writing, however, some of the writers' feelings about their writing tasks changed.

After looking over their TUDs and constructing a definition of everyday writing for themselves, three of the writers—Rose, Alison, and Danny—indicated that term helped them see that they *are* writers and they *do* write.[5] Similarly, this new term helped all five of the writers see that the mundane writing tasks they engage in are actually a valuable part of their lives. Rose, who was so dismissive of her own writing at the outset of our discussion, directly addressed

---

4 51 percent of the tasks Rose logged were texts.

5 Laura reported that she still didn't feel like she was much of a writer, and Bill said that, although he does not write much, he still believes he is a writer.

this, saying "in the very beginning [of the interview] I talked about how I was like disappointed in myself for my lack of valuable writing—or writing that I saw as valuable. Whereas . . . my perspective has changed now." After seeing the previously overlooked writing tasks that were logged in her TUD—like texting, posting on social media, and keeping lists—and discussing the *functions* of that writing, Rose now "think[s] that [everyday writing] is just as valuable" as *writing* writing, since it allows her to communicate with friends and keep track of her life. Alison also said that many of the tasks she logged in her TUD and selected as artifacts were tasks that she basically "did without even thinking" and did not think of as writing. After studying this writing and thinking about how it functions, however, she said she now thinks this kind of writing is "more valuable than people probably realize."

This change in perspective seems to suggest that a writer-informed approach can not only help us better understand writing through the lifespan, but it can also help writers better understand what writing is, what counts as writing, and who they are as writers. After their participation, this group of writers seems to have a more robust understanding of how writing functions as a part of their lives and a better understanding of its value—even the seemingly mundane "words on a page, be [they] meaningless or not" that would have previously been overlooked.

CONCLUSION

As we attempt to more fully understand writing through the lifespan, it seems important that we do more to include the writers in our research so that they too can benefit from their participation. Writer-informed approaches to understanding writing through the lifespan are one way to give those who engage in the practice(s) we study more of a role in shaping our research and findings. As these two examples from my own writer-informed approach to studying everyday writing indicate, these methods can help to augment, and add detail to, both our scholarly conceptions about writing phenomena and those of the writers we work with.

While I went into the study with my own definition of everyday writing that focused on sponsorship as the criterion for in/exclusion, this writer-informed approach has helped me see that this distinction is not important to actual everyday writers. For these writers, the *function* of their writing—for communication and organization—is much more important, and these definitional functions are directly tied to the writing they engage in—rather than to a more abstract understanding of the practice. Writer-informed definitions of other lifespan related writing phenomena may offer insights that complicate some of our commonly held assumptions.

At the same time, utilizing writer-informed approaches in studying writing across the lifespan can also help us share our results with the writers we study. Simply studying writers has the potential to increase the knowledge that benefits the field of writing studies, but working closely *with* writers as part of our studies has the potential to benefit the field, the researchers, and the writers. This study, for example, complicated my own understanding of what everyday writing is, but it also changed the ways that the writers who constructed the definition think about their own writing. Rather than seeing the mundane tasks logged in their diaries as meaningless, the writers, through collecting data and discussing their findings, now see that these tasks serve important functions in their lives. Adopting this approach to other areas of lifespan writing research may help other writers see the value of their writing and/or the value of studying that writing.

REFERENCES

Barton, D. & Hamilton, M. (1998). *Local literacies: Reading and writing in one community*. Routledge.

Bazerman, C., Applebee, A. N., Berninger, V. W., Brandt, D., Graham, S., Jeffery, J. V., Matsuda, P. K., Murphy, S., Rowe, D. W., Schleppegrell, M. & Wilcox, K. C. (Eds.). (2018). *The Lifespan development of writing*. National Council of Teachers of English.

Bazerman, C., Applebee, A. N., Berninger, V. W., Brandt, D., Graham, S., Jeffery, J. V., Matsuda, P. K., Murphy, S., Rowe, D. W., Schleppegrell, M. & Wilcox, K. C. (2018). Introduction. In C. Bazerman, A. N. Applebee, V. W. Berninger, D. Brandt, S. Graham, J. V. Jeffery & K. C. Wilcox (Eds.), *The lifespan development of writing* (pp. 3–19). National Council of Teachers of English.

Brandt, D. (2001). *Literacy in American lives*. Cambridge University Press

Cohen, D. J., White, S. & Cohen, S. B. (2011). A time use diary study of adult everyday writing behavior. *Written Communication, 28*(1), 3–33. https://doi.org/10.1177/0741088310381260 .

Hauser, G. A. & mcclellan, e. d. (2009). Vernacular rhetoric and social movements: Performances of resistance in the rhetoric of the everyday. In P. M. Malesh & S. M. Stevens (Eds.), *Rhetoric of movements* (pp. 23–46). State University of New York Press.

Lillis, T. (2013). *The sociolinguistics of writing*. Edinburgh University Press.

Nystrand, M. & Duffy, J. (Eds.). (2003). *Towards a rhetoric of everyday life: New directions in research on writing, text, and discourse*. University of Wisconsin Press.

Prior, P. & Shipka, J. (2003). Chronotopic lamination: Tracing the contours of literate activity. In C. Bazerman & D. R. Russell (Eds.), *Writing selves/writing societies* (pp. 180–238). The WAC Clearinghouse; Mind, Culture, and Activity. https://wac.colostate.edu/books/perspectives/selves-societies/.

Roozen, K. (2008). Journalism, poetry, stand-up comedy, and academic literacy: Mapping the interplay of curricular and extracurricular literate activities. *Journal of Basic Writing, 27*,1, 5–34.

Roozen, K. (2012). Comedy stages, poets projects, sports columns, and kinesiology 341: Illuminating the importance of basic writers' self-sponsored literacies. *Journal of Basic Writing, 31*,1, 99–132.

White-Farnham, J. (2014). "Revising the menu to fit the budget": Grocery lists and other rhetorical heirlooms. *College Composition and Communication, 56*(2), 208–226.

CHAPTER 6.

REVISITING PARTICIPANTS AFTER PUBLICATION: CONTINUING WRITING PARTNERSHIPS

Lauren Rosenberg

University of Texas at El Paso

Chief, an adult learner who has been negotiating changes in his literacy practices, reflects on his decision to switch from one learning center where he studied for many years to a different informal educational site. His remarks offer a snapshot of how an individual who is continuing to develop as a writer later in life maintains a commitment to studying while also facing the complexity of assimilating new knowledge. Chief's ongoing relationship to literacy education, and the ways that I learn about his process from my perspective as a writing researcher doing longitudinal work, are the center of this chapter in which I look at the potential of revisiting research participants as a methodology for lifespan studies. He reflects:

> Say you doing math. . . . You didn't get one thing that you're learning. . . . They push you on to something else. But, hey! I learned a lot. But I had to rush. . . . You know, uh, when you get home, you got to study. . . . You want to learn, you really got to study at home. . . . But the reason I went down to [a new learning center] was because of up there [previous learning center] you could be missing so many hours [referring to attendance]. And the [new learning center], you go down, you can get one-on-one; and you don't even have to worry about timing. . . . Till you get that subject down pat.

Chief's experiences as an older American who has become literate through informal education later in life offer lifespan researchers an opportunity to challenge presumptions about formal schooling. In the third principle for lifespan studies, established in "Towards an Understanding of Writing Development Across the Lifespan" (Bazerman et al., 2018), the authors assert, "Writing development is variable; there is no single path and no end point" (p. 28). Though they recognize diversity of educational experience, the authors nevertheless assume that schooling is central to—and shapes—writing experience. They admit:

DOI: https://doi.org/10.37514/PER-B.2020.1053.2.06

"Poverty and other marginalizing social factors, although they may be overcome by individuals, may limit resources and development opportunities as well as create stigmatizing social attributions that affect writing development" (2018, p. 30). I argue further that, for writers whose racial and economic experiences place them outside of the mainstream culture of schooling, there is no predictable pathway toward writing development. Traditional schooling with its benchmarks and grade levels determines, and thus limits, our idea of how learning is supposed to progress. By looking at the trajectories of people whose literate experiences are not typical and studying the choices they make, we can get a fuller sense of writing pathways as idiosyncratic.

Therefore, in this chapter, I introduce a methodology of revisiting that evolved from my experiences reconnecting with former participants. When I saw the people who had worked with me on a qualitative study of writing ten years after the original research and a few months after their words (spoken and written) had been published, the participants led our conversations in new directions that reopened the research and caused me to challenge my own assumptions about the researcher-researched relationship. Though much of the chapter focuses on constructing a methodology of revisiting, during the second half I reflect on an encounter with Chief that illustrates what he taught me about the value of revisiting and what it can look like as a research practice.

THE IDEA OF REVISITING EMERGES THROUGH PARTICIPANTS' NARRATIVES

In 2015, I published a monograph based on a study of four people (including Chief) who attended an informal adult education center in Springfield, Massachusetts where they were learning to read, write, do math, and use computers (Rosenberg, 2015). I learned from the participants that motivations for becoming literate were more complicated than amassing skills or meeting school and workplace demands. Particularly for people who had not acquired literacy through compulsory schooling, the decision to become more proficient readers and writers later in life was a blend of personal and social impulses. They wanted to disrupt the autobiographical scripts that had written them into the position of "illiterate" and redefine their roles for their own purposes.

After the book came out, I contacted the participants to give them each a copy. Although I had hoped for such reunions while I was writing the book, I hadn't imagined what those meetings could be like. This was partly because of my fear that the participants might have died (none of them was young, and some were in poor health), and partly my inability to imagine such scenes. Would the four people be as I remembered them? Would they want to speak with me? I deliberately visited without a recorder or prepared questions, without the premise of approaching them as research subjects. As a responsible, feminist qualitative researcher, it was part of my ethic to go back and share results.

The participants in the study that led to my book, adults who were acquiring new literacies, were not concerned with the ways they would be presented in a published report. The idea of working with an academic researcher was new for them, and nothing in their experience had prepared them to question how I might represent them. Their unawareness of the perils of representation at the time of research reinforced their vulnerability in the project; therefore, it was my responsibility to treat their testimonies and written texts with respect and to work towards presenting their narratives with a conscious effort to resist appropriation.

Other researchers who use ethnographic methods express similar concerns about appropriating participants' experiences. Problems of ethical representation are not limited to the write up of the researcher's findings but can involve additional aspects of the researcher-participant relationship, including its closure. The promise to return to the research site to continue interactions after the research period has ended can be disappointing and confusing for participants when researchers break that promise. Haitian anthropologist, Gina A. Ulysse (2008) grapples with the surprising response she received when she returned for follow up visits with her participants, Jamaican traders and organizers for the United Vendors Association. They were accustomed to the presence of academic researchers who would record them and publish their words and then never return to Kingston. Ulysse's participants knew that the researcher would gain career benefits from the published products, which would not benefit those who had been researched. In contrast, lifespan research seeks to challenge the fixity of research that Ulysse's participants identified by maintaining collaborations between researched and researcher, avoiding the re-subordination of participants. The researcher has a responsibility, as Ulysse puts it, "to write culture against the discipline's hegemony" (2008, p. 98).

I argue that revisiting participants and reflecting with them after publication can be viewed as an important part of the research process that has not been considered in writing studies and that can offer a valuable lens for lifespan research. Through revisiting, researchers and participants can work toward undercutting a one-way knowledge-making tradition that privileges the researcher's findings at the moment of publication as final, limiting possibilities for partnership. Participants' responses to the published text contain possibilities for expanding the way they continue to interpret their stories. We can challenge the conventions of research when we foreground the insights of participants as they continue to reflect on and analyze their experiences.

I propose that we extend the research tradition by paying greater attention to the ways we are informed by the people we study. Researchers can learn from participants about how they value the published text and how it might potentially circulate within their networks in ways unknown to academic researchers. We can deepen our research and our understanding of the nature of writing partnerships by following pathways that are determined by participants' interests and life course. Anna Smith suggests in this volume that we can "consider lifespan writing research as an activity not just *about* a developing writer, but research conducted *with* developing writers" (p. 17).

Thus, I advocate for, and this chapter will demonstrate, a kind of writing partnership rooted in ongoing interactions between writers and moments of collaboration that create possibilities for engagement. I am not literally speaking of composing together or of my writing inspiring research participants to produce on their own; rather, my view of partnership is relational and organic, following the events and patterns of our lives as they intersect with the research. As Smith (this volume) describes it, ": "Researching with a developing writer and with their families and communities makes [writing researchers] privy to critical in vivo insights and provides proximity to practice that cannot be otherwise articulated" (p. 22). It is not unusual for ethnographic researchers in writing studies to involve participants in their work; feminist qualitative researchers in composition have long claimed that "we must be prepared to make the case for new forms of research and writing in our discipline" and that "we need to continue experimenting with new ways of reporting research" (Kirsch & Ritchie, 1995, p. 24). In this chapter, however, I refer to a different situation. The participants in my research were all adults who developed new literacies later in life. None of them was a mainstream learner; only one person identified as a writer. It would not have been possible for them to participate in conventional collaboration because of their literacy histories and orientation to formal education. Further, it could be insulting to ask adults in the process of acquiring new literacies to read an academic text and offer feedback, as it might remind them of being gazed upon as "stupid" or unable to learn. Instead, I chose to connect with former participants by reading together and listening to their interpretation of the text. I didn't know that their commentary would lead us back into the material, nor could I have guessed that their reflections on their own literacy would prompt me to examine the research process as I do now.

EXTENDING THE RESEARCH PROCESS THROUGH ONGOING COLLABORATION

My motivation to meet with participants was personal; I was not collecting data. What I realized about the limitations of research came as a result of the revisits. Going in, I could not have known that the act of revisiting would be so powerful, or that it would teach me to examine the research process as I do now. The perfunctory statement of the original IRB approved study, in which I promised to follow up by sharing drafts and inviting feedback, led to the more serious commitment to reopen the research process, guided by participants.

My interest in revisiting began with the participants' narratives. Afterwards, I searched for scholarship on the subject. When I approached other researchers in writing studies, no one I spoke with knew where to turn. Our unawareness suggested that returning to participants after publication has not yet been valued as part of the process of creating scholarship. The revisits allowed me to understand that interacting with participants after a period of time has passed can take both researcher and researched to another level of collaboration in response to the document that already exists. Participants cycle back through their own narratives and add to them based on the literacy agency they have continued to develop. They restate, verbally revise, and reflect on their past comments in light of recent experiences.

Longitudinal researchers, in contrast with those conducting shorter span work, value extended, personal engagement with participants, emphasizing time as significant to writing development (Bazerman, 2018; Bazerman et al., 2017; Bazerman et al., 2018; Compton-Lilly, 2014; Herrington & Curtis, 2000; Smith, this volume; Sternglass, 1997). Linguistic anthropologist Shirley Brice Heath devotes an entire book to the research that resulted from the researcher returning. In *Words at Work and Play* (2012), Heath continues relationships with the children and grandchildren of two communities that she studied during the 1970s and 1980s. Although she never directly states what motivated her work with participants and their families over more than thirty years, Heath implies that there is tremendous value in maintaining the research connections that became central relationships in her life. For example, in the first chapter, she references the epilogue of *Ways with Words* (1983), quoting her own closing line: "what seem limits or losses can be beginnings as well as endings" (p. 376), suggesting that her inquiry into the lives of participants must continue. She concludes the Prologue to *Words at Work and Play* (2012) by concentrating on the importance of analyzing stories:

> Human beings hold primary interest in two things: reality and telling about it. . . . Any story differs with each passing moment, new purpose, and favored vantage point. Neither the whole story nor the true one ever exists, however much we may wish for it. If we could achieve wholeness and absolute truth in our stories, we would have no more stories to tell. And tell stories, we must. (p. 7)

It is through the personal that Heath extends her research process and creates new partnerships. Her data collection and analysis over three generations show that a longtime commitment to participants allows for the research process to travel along unpredictable pathways. She remarks:

> We all want to find out what happened to those who will forever be part of our lives. We want to understand how they develop new roles, economic alignments, and rearrange their ways of socializing the young in the ever-evolving frameworks of time and space. We want to learn from their processes of adapting, improvising, and creating. (2012, pp. 183–184)

Together with Heath, the children of Trackton and Roadville reflect on the progression of their lives. They listen to recordings of their past and make comparisons of then and now. Grandchildren of the original participants are folded into the data collection process when they are given "activity logs" and instructions by Heath on how to do anthropological research by documenting conversations and experiences. Through layered informal and formal interactions, the research partnerships extend, following the unpredictable direction of additional players and their experiences.

Time isn't the primary feature of my analysis, as it is for Heath and other scholars cited here. I wanted to reconnect with the people whose literacy experiences were the core of my research and get a sense of them in the present moment in relation to the literate lives I had explored years earlier. I was also curious about ways their writing might correlate with other ordinary life practices. As Brandt (2018) notes, "While often congruent with certain stages of life (i.e., youth, middle age, old age) the multiple and simultaneous roles most people play in families, communities, and workplaces condition developmental trajectories and possibilities even as they interact with one another" (p. 251). Shifting stages of life, responsibilities, health, roles in family and work situation, all contribute to an individual's ongoing sense of self as a writer.

Compton-Lilly's (2003) work on the reading practices of urban children makes a similar case for the "contradictions and complexities" (p. 110) that not only surround but significantly impact literacy practices, which studies across time can help researchers to identify more clearly. The first of Compton-Lilly's books, *Reading Families* (2003), lays the groundwork for an extensive study of "the ways parents and children in one urban community conceptualize reading" (p. 10) that Compton-Lilly then traces through her ongoing research. In a 2014 report on her decade-long study of one student's writing development, she concludes, "While longitudinal research can be targeted to explore particular questions, its longitudinal nature increases the propensity for research to take new directions and uncover unanticipated findings" (p. 30). The fluid, unpredictable quality of this kind of research makes it compelling. The researcher can't know what turns participants' lives and choices will take. Compton-Lilly's study reflects on her participant's school performance as well as his "long-term trajectory of becoming" (2014, p. 29). She found that, "becoming a writer was a longitudinal journey that entailed dispositions that extended across home, school, and peer community involving both writing practices and a broader set of tangential dispositions" (2014, p. 30).

Through the act of revisiting participants and contemplating their narratives with them after the results are published, we might become more open to changes in our research methods, so that participants figure more prominently in our future scholarship. If we are to maintain relationships across time, and if our work is to reflect the decisions participants make in regard to literacy shifts and life changes (both major and ordinary), we must follow their lead, watching the turns that mark new writing pathways. By extending our interactions, we might add a layer of collaboration that can increase both of our knowledge, a change that is important for the future life of the published project and for future research. Reflecting together on the finished document and the research process itself can lead to deeper thinking from a different angle. By consulting with participants after research, I have learned that knowledge-making is never static; rather, it keeps going, steered by their insights.

REVISITING CHIEF

At this point, I shift the focus of this chapter from theorizing a methodology of revisiting to offering an example of revisiting in practice. I tell a story of the visit with Chief to characterize the interaction with my longtime participant and show that it expanded our research trajectory. The visit also gave me the opportunity to get to know Chief's wife who has since become a participant in my research. This experiment with revisiting opened a new avenue of research that I have followed in my ongoing longitudinal work with Shirley and Chief. Through our interactions, I learned more about the possibilities and limitations of writing partnerships as they continue to develop.

As a seventy-seven-year-old African-American man who was raised on a sharecropper's farm in rural South Carolina during the 1950s, Chief had limited exposure to formal education, although he always craved opportunities to read and write. Despite his occasional access, and the segregated conditions of schooling when it was available, Chief was able to make a decent living because of his extensive early work experiences and the skills he developed as a laborer. During his long career, he worked as a welder and a forklift operator. He owned his first home at the age of seventeen and sent his children to college. Only after he retired following a motorcycle accident that injured his back, did he seek informal education at a number of adult learning centers. Since then, Chief has become an avid writer and reader. He was editor of the newsletter at the literacy center where I got to know him, and he was involved in a family literacy program there. He has been committed to circulating his writing among known and unknown audiences so that more people can learn about the importance of education based on his example. And, he is a singer-songwriter who has recorded and toured with nationally recognized men's gospel choirs.

We reconnect at his home so that I can deliver my book. After chatting about our lives over the last few years, our discussion turns to the text. I am sure Chief will read it on his own because of the way he holds the book gently in his hands and gazes at its covers. He tells me, "I'm going to give this to my teacher over there [at the literacy center he attends] on Monday, and she can read it. I told her about 'Chief and Rabbit,'" which is one of his favorite stories that he wrote while he was a student at the literacy center where we met. For consistency, I use the approach I have developed with the others of reading aloud and marking passages, but I get the impression when Chief gazes away that he would prefer to read alone. Still, I show him his interview extracts, his essays on Jim Crow and domestic violence, his editor's letters, and the story of "Chief and Rabbit." Every so often when I glance at him, Chief is holding the book in his hands and whispering, "I am so proud of this book." Our revisit gives me the chance to witness Chief's pride over a text he literally claims as his own—he refers to it as his book.

When Chief holds the book and murmurs about his pride, it takes on "the status" of a "social actor" (Brandt & Clinton, 2002, p. 348) imbued with the ability to act upon him. In re-spinning the literacy event to a "literacy-in-action" concept, Brandt and Clinton claim (referencing Bruno Latour), that the objects which surround our literate acts are a significant part of our literacy interactions: "[But] we also want to consider the additional question of how literacy acts as a social agent, as an independent mediator (i.e., literacy, itself, in action)" (2002, p. 349). When I observe Chief's connection with the text, I see what Brandt and Clinton consider an expression of the "ontological relationships between people and things" (2002, p. 353). Chief is a human agent with his own complex relationship to literacy; yet, his handling of the book reveals how the book acts upon him as well, mirroring his idea of literate achievement and affirming Brandt and Clinton's (2002) point that, "When we use literacy, we also get used. Things typically mediate this relationship" (p. 350). The pride Chief speaks of is in his own ever-developing relationship to literacy. The object represents literacy itself, something I understand after our visit that would have been impossible to know while writing *The Desire for Literacy* (Rosenberg, 2015). His comments demonstrate that ownership does not reside solely with the author. In claiming the text, he can use it for his own changing literacy purposes, purposes that exceed what either of us could have imagined while discussing interview transcripts or when I wrote alone. Chief's choices about the book, combined with his continued literacy education, open up new spaces for him to contemplate literacy, and for us to mutually contemplate (an idea I first proposed in *The Desire for Literacy* [2015] and develop further in "Listening to research as a feminist ethos of representation" [Rosenberg & Howes, 2018]). He directs the research as it is relevant to him. By following Chief's lead as someone who knows more about literacy education from his experiences than I ever can, it becomes possible for us to disrupt the usual path of research, to thread back into a project that was closed by publication, and to re-open it for further exploration. In this way, we push back against the confines of traditional research. We can define our writing partnership so that it reflects the situation that exists for us as researched and researcher relating to a published text and to one another. Our interactions with a common text show the intersections of our literacy communities and become the topic of future research.

Midway through the visit, Chief's wife arrives. This is the first time I have spoken with a participant's family member. She reclines on the sofa behind us, talking about the morning run at the food pantry where she volunteers, and then she joins the conversation about literacy. "I love to read," Shirley says. As I speak with them, I realize that Shirley has always had something Chief wants. I wonder whether Shirley's literacy practices were what drew Chief and her together. We discuss the tension that occurs among some couples when one partner is more literate than the other.

A few months after the visit, Chief invites me to the literacy center where he studies once a week so that his teachers can see his book. Initially, he went there for help studying for his 7D bus driver's license. His varying interests and needs have led him to select different learning environments at different periods of his life. When he comments, "I'll probably be going to school for the rest of my life because I have to learn so much," I am reminded that Chief will always seek informal education as a way to maintain agency and dignity. He steers our writing partnership, restorying it by asking me to experience literacy education on his terms. My knowledge of adult basic education changes when I join Chief at this small social service agency that offers one-on-one tutoring. He introduces me to an educational model that he believes better suits him as a learner. In this setting, his teacher prepares individual lessons for him and shifts her expectations in response to his learning. By taking me to this place, he is preparing me for our research to come. During the study that develops as a result of these interactions, Chief will contrast the educational styles at the different literacy centers where he has studied, as he demonstrates in the opening quote.

PARTICIPANTS EXTEND OUR WORK IN NEW DIRECTIONS

Revisiting came as a surprise. I was not expecting to find the kernel of a new methodology when I met with Chief and his peers, but our interactions revealed something substantial about the nature of research relationships and how they change focus and character based on the directions that participants take them—if we remain open to participants leading the research. When we meet, it is to contemplate literacy together. Another surprise was finding out how my future intentions for research, and the methods I will use, take shape because of these encounters.

For example, after the visits, I receive holiday cards from Shirley, then lengthy handwritten letters. And, once my partnership with Chief expands to include Shirley, I design a project that concentrates on Chief and Shirley's trajectory as a couple that is continuing to develop as writers (see Rosenberg, 2018). The project responds to an unexpected turn in my interpretation of Chief guided by him and Shirley as knowledge-makers. Their example demonstrates how revisiting opens new pathways for research not already predicated by the researcher's intentions. Rather, it is what I learn in the moment of the revisit when I listen to Chief and Shirley that causes me to fold back into my study of Chief's literacy development and envision it differently.

As I write this, I am thinking ahead to the next phase of this work, which will be with Shirley. Now that I am aware of my research changing methods, methodologies, and purposes based on participants' initiatives, I can take more of a spectator's role to observing where Shirley directs us. While my work with Shirley and Chief ultimately leads to new publications that will give me academic credit in my field, the process of creating texts also offers Shirley and Chief opportunities to participate in an ongoing writing partnership that they interpret and reflect on individually, as a couple, and with the researcher. The benefits for them may not be the same as those that I gain professionally, yet they matter. Our ongoing discussions of literacy are part of their lives and mine.

Revisiting participants challenges lifespan researchers to examine our compliance with disciplinary hegemony as we (perhaps unwillingly) perpetuate an academic tradition that locks the people we research into the role of subject. A goal of lifespan writing research is to push back against assumptions about what writing does and what writers can achieve throughout the course of their lives. By looking across time and the material and social conditions of our lives, research becomes more relational, responding to various situations rather than adhering to a single pathway. Led by participants, researchers learn to be flexible in our approaches and methods.

The four participants from my original study engaged willingly in the revisits. They were not doing it out of obligation; their obligation to my research had ended years earlier. I had the chance to witness them taking in the contents of a book about acquisition of literacy whose subject was their literacy. Revisiting gave us the opportunity to contemplate their spoken and written words at a time beyond the period of the study. Reflecting together, reading aloud, marking passages for future reference, and discussing their current life experiences provided a new lens for evaluating research. The book became a social actor (Brandt & Clinton, 2002) that was part of their ongoing pursuit of literacy. They could extend the conversations in contexts that matter to them now and that are shaped by their literacy agency. Participants' expressions of their ongoing relationship to their own literacy taught me to investigate the value of literacy in people's lives in ways that I could never know from my position as an academic researcher.

Interactions like the ones I describe here are significant for exploring what literacy means and how we understand collaboration. This curious, listening perspective is especially important for researchers in lifespan studies as we figure out new possibilities for collaboration and how we can better understand writers' experiences. Lifespan studies can benefit from the insights of people outside of academic settings who embody literacy differently from those of us who are informed primarily by our academic reality.

Chief's reactions to the book reveal that the production of knowledge does not end with publication. It continues as researcher and participants keep learning from one another in real, ongoing relationships. The participants' involvement in research interactions keeps the conversations open and fluid so that their positions do not remain fixed. This is how participants continue to become knowledge makers. Together we contemplate and create knowledge.

REFERENCES

Bazerman, C. (2018). Lifespan longitudinal studies of writing development: A heuristic for an impossible dream. In Bazerman et al., *The Lifespan development of writing*. (326–365). National Council of Teachers of English.

Bazerman, C., Applebee, A. N., Berninger, V. W., Brandt, D., Graham, S., Jeffrey, J. V., Matsuda, P. K., Murphy, S., Rowe, D. W., Schleppegrell, M. & Wilcox, K. C. (2017). Taking the long view on writing development. *Research in the Teaching of English*, 51(3), 351–360.

Bazerman, C., Applebee, A. N., Berninger, V. W., Brandt, D., Graham, S., Jeffrey, J. V., Matsuda, P. K., Murphy, S., Rowe, D. W., Schleppegrell, M. & Wilcox, K. C. (Eds.) (2018). *The Lifespan development of writing*. National Council of Teachers of English.

Brandt, D. (2018). Writing development and life-course development: The case of working adults." In Bazerman, C., A. N. Applebee, V. W. Berninger, D. Brandt, S. Graham, J. V. Jeffery, P. K. Matsuda, S. Murphy, D. W. Rowe, M. Schleppegrell

& K. C. Wilcox (Eds.), *The Lifespan development of writing* (pp. 244–271). National Council of Teachers of English.

Brandt, D. & Clinton, K. (2002). Limits of the local: Expanding perspectives on literacy as a social practice. *Journal of Literacy Research, 34*(3), 337–356.

Compton-Lilly, C. (2003). *Reading families: The literate lives of urban children.* Teachers College Press.

Compton-Lilly, C. (2014). The development of writing habitus: A ten-year case study of a young writer. *Written Communication, 31*(4), 1–33. https://doi.org/10.1177 /0741088314549539.

Heath, S. B. (1983). *Ways with words: Language, life, and work in communities and classrooms.* Cambridge University Press.

Heath, S. B. (2012). *Words at work and play: Three decades in family and community life.* Cambridge University Press.

Herrington, A. J. & Curtis, M. (2000). *Persons in process: Four stories of writing and personal development in college.* National Council of Teachers of English.

Kirsch, G. E. & Ritchie, J. S. (1995). Beyond the personal: Theorizing a politics of location in composition research. *College Composition and Communication, 46*(1), 7–29.

Rosenberg, L. (2015). *The desire for literacy: Writing in the lives of adult learners.* NCTE/Conference on College Composition and Communication.

Rosenberg, L. (2018). "Still learning": One couple's literacy development in older adulthood. *Literacy in Composition Studies, 6*(2), 18–35.

Rosenberg, L. & Howes, E. (2018). Listening to research as a feminist ethos of representation. In Blair, K. & Nickoson, L. (Eds.), *Composing feminist interventions: Activism, engagement, praxis* (pp. 75–91). The WAC Clearinghouse; University Press of Colorado. https://wac.colostate.edu/books/perspectives/feminist/.

Sternglass, M. S. (1997). *Time to know them: A longitudinal study of writing and learning at the college level.* Lawrence Erlbaum Associates.

Ulysse, G. A. (2008). *Downtown ladies: Informal commercial importers, a Haitian anthropologist and self-making in Jamaica.* University of Chicago Press.

PART 2.
LEVERAGING OUR TRADITIONS

We encouraged the authors of Part 1 to be bold—we wanted to see the new vistas that opened up by innovating well beyond the disciplinary boundaries that often constrain. In Part 2: Leveraging Our Traditions, we return to more familiar methodological and theoretical approaches and consider them through a lifespan lens. The authors of Part 2 thus work within the boundaries of a variety of established research traditions, sharing research projects that feature focused innovations to their methodologies to better equip them for lifespan writing research. In so doing, their research suggests new pathways that these traditions might (and perhaps need to) explore.

The first chapters in Part 2 do this while focusing on specific segments of the lifespan. These chapters give readers from Composition Studies a glimpse into writing at other stages of life, but they also operationalize lifespan writing research by demonstrating how to add a lifespan lens to ongoing studies. Lauren Bowen takes a sociohistoric approach with novel methodological choices by diving deeply into the complex literate actions of one senior writer in order to uncover the sometimes-unimaginable complexity of a literate life. Yvonne Lee then expands our attentions beyond a lifespan segment by considering the writing lives of not only one writer across a lifetime, but of several writers across multiple, overlapping, and related lifetimes. This exploration of new innovations within particular disciplinary traditions continues with an autoethnographic investigation of how one author—Zebroski—negotiates the complex writing tasks demanded of him during the challenging social and emotional work of retirement. Costa et al. then employ the Structural Equation Modeling that Zajic and Poch (Chapter 3) described in a study of the executive functioning of students in Grades 1 and 4, considering ways to orient such work through the lifespan.

The remaining chapters in Part 2 also work to expand our understanding of how we make meaning. Arya et al. engage not just the production of texts but also their reception as they examine acts of data representation and the emergent understandings that school-aged children have about them. Data representations, in this chapter, serve as a strategic site for uncovering the complex work that readers engage in to construct data in their reading of it. Next, Poch et al. highlight the complex cognitive landscapes that semiosis occurs with and through, bringing to light the work of producing texts and the challenges with textual production that individuals with learning disabilities and autism spectrum disorder may face. They also provide some paths forward for thinking about semiosis across the internal-external divide and using psychometric techniques to locate semiosis within contemporary psychological thought. Erin Workman, like Knappik earlier, asks us to think about how we make sense of our own literate development, but Workman achieves this by adapting cognitive researchers' mind maps for lifespan writing research. Kevin Roozen concludes Part 2 by tracing inscriptions via the interpretive work of Latour (1990) and Gries (2015), rendering more robust the complexity of semiotic acts that Poch et al. and Arya et al. build up in their work.

Just as Part 1 provided some starting points for writing researchers to reconceptualize their thinking about theoretical orientations and methods toward the lifespan, Part 2 allows writing researchers to imagine new approaches that are more tightly tied to existing disciplinary structures—new, creative methods of repurposing that take advantage of the insights and innovations of existing fields and traditions. If we are to conceive of lifespan writing research as a long-term endeavor requiring both immediate and extended pay-offs, then Part 2 provides the short-term return on innovation that the ideas in Part 1 do not easily support. Leveraging Our Traditions also paints a picture of the incredible variety of disciplines, methods, and theories interested in the phenomenon of writing through the lifespan.

CHAPTER 7.

LITERACY TOURS AND MATERIAL MATTERS: PRINCIPLES FOR STUDYING THE LITERATE LIVES OF OLDER ADULTS

Lauren Marshall Bowen
University of Massachusetts, Boston

This chapter proposes guiding principles for researching the literate activity and development of older adults. The Lifespan Writing Development Group (LWDG) was rightly deterred from "attempting a general, typified, age- or stage-based account" of writing development (Bazerman et al., 2018, p. 13). In alignment with this thinking, this chapter does not attempt to offer a standard characterization of "old age" as a discrete phase of writing and literacy development, but instead illustrates the need to examine old age as a part of the long view of the lifespan—without failing to account for the differences that old age can make.

Following an overview of proposed principles, this chapter illustrates the value of such principles through a mixed-methods approach featuring an observational method called the literacy tour, which, through its simultaneous emphasis on materiality and the narrative "long view" of lifelong literate development, illustrates the multifaceted role of aging in elder participants' writing and literacy development.

THE DIFFERENCE OLD AGE MAKES: AN OVERVIEW

Experiences in old age are individually, culturally, and historically situated, yet several commonly shared realities of aging have implications for the research of writing through the lifespan. Central to this framework is the caution against either ignoring or overdetermining the role of biological aging in late-life writing. However essential the physiological dimensions are to studies of aging, focusing exclusively on the biological aspects of old age presents an impoverished view of later life stages, and, by extension, of literacy over the lifespan. For this reason, these principles for studies of writing through the lifespan account for both the biological and the sociocultural elements of aging.

Principle 1: Old Age Involves Physiological Changes

As with any other life stage, old age involves physiological development. Although specific physical changes differ from individual to individual in both kind and effect, most age-related change impacts the capacity to engage in literate activity and learning. Decline in visual acuity, hearing loss, fatigue, arthritis, and other common physical factors in old age can have a significant impact on the ability to engage in literate activity and learning (Weinsten & LaCoss, 1999).

Because biological aging is an ongoing and individual process of change and adaptation, the felt effects of physical change on literate activity are specific to individual experience. In some instances, physical changes may prompt the adoption of new literate activity, such as taking up audiobooks when declining eyesight makes book-reading impossible (Rumsey, 2018). In other instances, a physical change makes it impossible to continue with a treasured literate activity, such as a post-stroke tremor rendering handwriting illegible (Rosenberg, 2018). Further, age-related physical changes—and the ways those changes are experienced as constraints on literacy and learning—are correlated with non-age factors. Individuals' socioeconomic status, prior experiences with disability, race/ethnicity, gender, and other identity factors can contribute both to the onset of physiological change and the individual's ability to adapt, both physically and psychologically, to that change.

Principle 2: Older People Have Long and Deep Histories with Literacy and Learning

Perhaps the most obvious consideration for researching writing through the lifespan is that older people have "more lifespan" to account for in analysis of any current literate activities. Older adults have had more time to develop durable dispositions toward literacy, including values, attitudes, and beliefs about literacy and its uses. For some, longer lives bring opportunities for inhabiting a broader range of social roles; as Brandt (2018) notes, "Development comes to people through the roles they play or are expected to play at different times of life; the historical events to which they are exposed; and the reconfigured meanings and potentials that accumulate around these experiences" (2018, p. 245). As longevity improves and as cultures of work and retirement continue to change—for example, through the elimination of mandatory retirement policies—the expectations for how older people should spend their time and contribute to their communities is diversifying. Alongside this change, the diversity of roles in which older adults learn, use, and sustain literate activities is increasing. An extended life history often includes greater opportunities for exposure to major social, cultural, and technological shifts. Given these realities, the perspective of old age may be particularly advantageous for researching writing through the lifespan.

Principle 3: Ideologies of aging shape perceptions of and expectations for older adults

Although not often recognized as such, aging is also a process of socialization: we learn how to be old (Cruikshank, 2009). This learning occurs, in part, through encounters with meanings of old age and aging that circulate within a curriculum of aging, the assemblage of historically and culturally situated discourses that define and promote values, attitudes, and beliefs about old age (Bowen, 2012). The language and literacy practices of older people quickly become entangled with the curriculum of aging, which not only shapes elders' literate lives, but also inflects the ways that elders' lives are seen (or not seen), represented, and interpreted—even in ways that we represent ourselves as aging individuals.

For instance, prominent in a contemporary U.S. curriculum of aging is a decline ideology, through which old age, and everything that comes with it, is necessarily framed in terms of loss (Gullette, 1997). The decline ideology of aging gained prominence in the mid-nineteenth century, as industrial capitalism increased value in labor that was fast, accurate, and consistent; workers whose bodies could not move fast enough—especially older and/or disabled workers—were devalued. As characterized by age historian Thomas R. Cole (1992), the nineteenth-century embrace of industrial values fostered a suspicion of old age:

> Westward migration, the growth of cities, the rise of manufacturing, and the creation of national transportation, communication, and financial networks testified to liberal capitalism's economic power. . . . Enormous material progress revealed its dark side—fear of decline, of degeneration, of being left behind. (p. 74)

This fear of decline was amplified by the professionalization of modern medicine, which granted institutional legitimacy to medicine's centuries-old habit of pathologizing old age. Within this sociocultural context, inevitable physiological changes associated with aging become conflated with decline in all aspects of human experience, and the decline ideology of aging propagates adverse beliefs about old people: that they are senile; that they are nonsexual beings; that they are culturally irrelevant; and, most germane to lifespan writing studies, that they are incapable of and/or disinterested in learning.

The decline ideology of aging is germane to studies of writing development through the lifespan in at least two ways. First, elder participants of lifespan research may have internalized cultural lessons about being old that impact their literate activity: for instance, they anticipate age-related limitations on new learning and development, and thus do not choose to engage in activities that would mark, for the purposes of lifespan research, new development or change. Alternatively, older participants may be highly sensitive to the decline ideology of aging, such that they make choices to avoid the perception of being in decline. Second, researchers, too, may be predisposed to the decline narrative, and either overdetermine the role of biological aging in literate activity and development, or else altogether ignore older adulthood as a part of the developmental trajectory. Therefore, while attending to and acknowledging the role of the aging body, which inevitably includes some reduction of physical and/or cognitive capacities, studies of writers in later life must also be conscious of the constraining effects of a decline ideology of old age.

In sum, I propose that studies of older adults' literate activity should:

1. Attend to the impact that age-related physiological change might have on the capacity for literate activity and learning, while also contextualizing the actual impact of physiological changes on literacy from the larger context of an individual life.
2. Contextualize late-life choices, behaviors, and orientations toward literacy within the larger context of the lifespan, including prominent social roles inhabited over a lifetime. This can best be accomplished by adopting capacious views of literacy, writing, and development in order to recognize specific late-life choices and behaviors (including decisions not to write) as a part of the lifelong trajectory of literacy development.
3. Interrogate the ideologies of aging that shape the values and perceptions of older adults' literate activity.

Given the above principles, studies of older adults' literacies require methodological orientations toward corporeal and material dimensions of literacy; toward the "long view" of literate history; and toward the ideological dimensions of literate activity and experience. In an effort to model ways of addressing the above principles through research design, I present an overview of a mixed methods approach that combines life story interviews with the spatially-oriented interview method I call literacy tours, followed by a brief overview of a case study to illustrate this method in use.

LIFE STORIES AND LITERACY TOURS: TOWARD A METHODOLOGY OF MATERIAL MEANDERING

Retrospective narrative accounts of an entire life—as used in what is sometimes called life story research (Atkinson, 1998; Cohler & Hostetler, 2003; Bertaux &

Kohli, 1984) and as illustrated in the influential grounded theory work of Deborah Brandt (2001)—lend themselves well to accounting for the sociocultural and ideological contexts of development. As Knappik (this volume) reminds us, cultural frameworks both limit and generate the stories we tell about our lives. Shaped by social and developmental contexts, life stories are not told the same way over an entire lifetime and can therefore provide important evidence of the ideological and social underpinnings of a particular moment on the developmental timeline.

Reflecting their ideological contexts in form and theme, life stories carry ideologies of aging and literacy, alike. Yet, life story narratives elicited during interviews are distinct in character from those stories told independently of the research scene. Interviews are not neutral data collection tools, but are themselves particular genres or communication events bearing conventions and norms that influence the kinds of questions researchers ask and the responses participants give (Briggs, 1986). Life stories are co-constructed narratives that can reproduce the ideological framework of both the participant and the researcher, and as such, the design and representation of narrative writing research follow and establish aesthetic patterns that, in part, "we have been acculturated to tell" (Journet, 2012, p. 16). Researchers are always at risk of allowing unrecognized assumptions about old age and aging—assumptions informed by a curriculum of aging, which propagates decline ideology—to guide a priori decisions about what merits our attention and analysis.

In response to this dilemma, I will describe and illustrate the use of a supplemental qualitative data collection method, the literacy tour, which I first developed as a means of attending to materiality and embodiment in a study of older adults and digital literacies (Bowen, 2011). Much like other interview techniques used by writing studies research, such as writing process drawings (Prior & Shipka, 2003), video recording (Rule, 2018), and visual-mapping (Workman, this volume), literacy tours are an alternative interview method for eliciting writers' tacit knowledge. The method itself is simple: a participant leads the researcher on a narrated walk-through of the physical and sometimes virtual spaces in which they engage in literate activity. Participants can be prompted (e.g., "Can you show me where you usually set up your laptop?"), but touring moments can also happen organically, perhaps even interrupting the flow of a traditional interview. During tours, the researcher may ask questions about particular objects that catch their attention, but for the most part, the researcher's role is similar to that of a tourist: to look, listen, take notes, snap pictures, and record video of what participants choose to show.

The literacy tour as a supplement to the life narrative interview provides at least two distinct advantages for researching writing through the lifespan. First, the introduction of the literacy tour as a data collection tool interrupts the interview scene—and the assumptions that might otherwise be embedded within the interview script itself—by introducing the genre of the guided tour. Prompted by the presence (or absence) of objects in a particular space, the literacy tour provides a means through which to divert the traditional interview exchange and elicit details about a life story that might not otherwise appear in the interchanges of an interview.

In the context of archival research, Kirsch & Rohan (2008) identify openness to serendipity as a necessary dimension of historical research. Recounting the serendipitous trail of research on physician and women's rights advocate Mary Bennett Ritter, whose papers are kept at the archives at the University of California Berkeley campus, Kirsch explains that, while serendipity cannot simply be arranged, "one can be open to the possibility" (Kirsch & Rohan, 2008, p. 20). Kirsch (Kirsch & Rohan, 2008) describes how her ability to attain a fuller, more contextualized understanding of Ritter's life came from "the simple fact of being there," as taking campus tours, exploring nearby trails, and walking local streets made it possible for Kirsch to more fully understand the local knowledge that was assumed by the documents she encountered. Likewise, literacy tours provide an expansive—and often serendipitous—framework through which to contextualize and further prompt life narrative data gathered through interviews. In this way, researchers may be better able to grasp how participants experience aging, both within and in tandem with the stories about the life course that they have been acculturated to tell.

The spatial orientation of the literacy tour offers a second advantage to lifespan writing research through opportunities for deeper analysis of the role of materiality in literacy development—which, in turn, opens up opportunities to further examine age identity and age ideology. Literacy tours are oriented toward what Brodkey (1987) calls *scenes of writing*, or what Cydney Alexis (2016) conceptualizes as a *writing habitat*. Recent writing studies research has already found writing habitats—and objects found within them—to be important to the study of writing processes. Rule (2018) proposes the study of "writing's rooms" as a means of "budg[ing] the clingy assumption that composing processes are ultimately only linear, goal-directed mental action" (p. 405), thereby adopting new materialism's expanded sense of agency, which extends to nonhuman artifacts and material environments. Literacy tours are, in other words, a way of capturing and examining environmental contexts as "active agents" in literate activity (Dippre & Smith, this volume).

As an environment in which someone typically writes, the writing habitat is "populated . . . with objects," shaped by preferences, and host to routinized behaviors (Alexis, 2016, p. 83). During literacy tours, participants show me predictably literacy-related objects, such as books, computers, writing instruments, and notebooks, as well as less obviously literacy-related artifacts: photographs, chairs, maps, model vehicles, clocks, and other objects. These material discoveries reflect the ways in which "[e]verything matters to writing; all matter is fair game" (Micciche, 2014, p. 491). Focusing on the objects that populate writing habitats has made it possible for writing studies researchers to identify how objects insert themselves into a writer's processes, tuning consciousness and managing affect in ways that facilitate or even disrupt textual production, as writers actively recruit objects to mediate a writing process: a timer on a microwave to regulate writing time (Prior & Shipka, 2003); a distraction-free digital writing environment to direct attention (Ching, 2018); dogs to provide calming companionship and a perhaps-welcome interruption (Blewett et al., 2016). For the purposes of researching writing development through the lifespan, attention to the minutiae of writing habitats is useful for considering the ideological context in which writers write: the objects and spaces of writing habitats reflect the beliefs, values, and attitudes of the humans who designed them (Alexis, 2016). Further still, literacy tours embrace the new materialist view of writing as "a curatorial, distributed act" and as a process of "curating materials to create narrative, identity, community, or other significant meanings" (Micciche, 2014, p. 494). The literacy tour is a direct methodological response to this understanding of writing as curation—not just curation of words, source materials, or writing technologies, but also as curation of environments, narratives, and selves.

Alongside the life narrative, literacy tours help researchers to account for material and ideological contexts of literate activity and narrative research. Touring has the potential to disrupt the literacy narratives that researchers and participants have been acculturated to tell, and the materialist orientation of touring brings the ecologies of writing development more sharply into focus. In the next section, I present the case study of a 78-year-old retired electrical engineer named Don. Although not originally designed as a study of writing development, the methods by which I came to understand Don's literate life illustrate a means of accounting for the decline ideology of old age in the literate lives of older people.

CASE STUDY: DON

Don shared his story with me when I met him in 2010, in his sunny house in an economically depressed manufacturing town in the northeastern United States. After his wife greeted me warmly at the door, Don led me to a finished basement, which had been designed by and for him, alone. Knowing that I was primarily interested in his digital literacy practices, Don seated himself at a workstation which boasted a desktop computer with dual monitors and shared his story.

Don's Life Story

Born in 1930, Don was raised by his grandparents in a New England island fishing village. Don's grandfather worked in the upper echelons of a steamship company that shuttled passengers to and from the island in the early 1900s, until a bridge was built to connect the island to the mainland, after which he worked as custodian of the village school. Don recalls, with deep admiration, his grandfather's pursuit of photography. After high school, Don followed his grandfather into a short-term career producing photographic postcards of local nautical icons.

In 1950, the Korean War prompted Don to join the Air Force, through which he attended "electronic school" and learned about radio technologies before being stationed in New Mexico to work on emergency communications. In 1954, Don took advantage of the GI Bill and enrolled in an electrical engineering program at a state university. In the summer months, Don would return to familiar territory and install and maintain airplane guidance systems throughout the eastern United States. After successfully completing his degree, Don worked for a major defense contractor, teaching air force technicians across the country how to use fire control systems electronics. While stationed in his home state during one teaching job, Don met and married his wife.

Spurred by the launch of Sputnik, Don's company transferred him to field service in order to lab test Syncom—a NASA-run satellite project that would yield the first orbiting geosynchronous communications satellite. Following the Communications Satellite Act of 1962, Don signed on as a satellite engineer for COMSAT, overseeing the construction of "earth stations" out of Washington, DC, and eventually became an assistant station manager at one of these sites until a new earth station opened in his home state, where he would serve as manager for the remainder of his career. When Don retired at age 60, he "went out, closed the door, so to speak, and never looked back."

Happily retired for nearly two decades, Don's electronics engineering life was hardly over. In his basement den, Don would use his computer to organize digital photos he took (mostly of the island where he grew up), to shop online, and to play single-player CD-ROM flight simulator and golf games. Occasionally, he would help his daughter fix her own computers to remove viruses and malware, and perform basic hardware upgrades or repairs to computers for himself or his friends.

Literacy Tours and Material Matters

Don's Literacy Tour

Guiding me on a tour of his PC, Don spent a good deal of time clicking through file folders on his desktop to show his carefully ordered filing system, and eventually set one folder of his own digital photos to play as an automatic slideshow while we talked. Frequently, Don interrupted our interview to point to one of the photos rotating through the slideshow. Most photos were landscapes he had recently taken of the island where he grew up, as well as photos of bridges. Don shared lessons about the architecture of each bridge as it appeared on screen.

After his PC tour was complete, Don pulled a palm-sized "flip phone" out of a messenger bag on the floor. Clamshell-style phones were still common, but the first Apple iPhone had already been released in 2007, and earlier mass market smartphones such as the BlackBerry were nearly at their peak and had already sparked complaints about smartphone addiction (Richtel, 2007). Don spent this brief "stop" on our tour by talking about his adult daughter:

> She gets wrapped up in this iPod iTunes stuff and downloads tunes and she has a little pod that will play the things into earphones and they'll have a little picture and so forth, and she tries to explain it to me. She uses a BlackBerry, and I don't care. My cell phone is just a little thing like this. Right now, it's not on. It's got that thing, takes pictures, you know? I don't care. All I want to do is to be able to call and be able to receive a call. And then I found that this thing opened up [flips open his phone], now if I want to do text and crap like that, I can, but I don't. I don't care about that stuff.

Shifting to a walking tour of the basement, Don showed me some predictable literacy objects, including nonfiction books on subjects closely related to his career interests and expertise, such as theoretical physics, astronomy, and operating system guides. In passing, Don turned to a set of models suspended from the ceiling on fishing line. The models included a lobster boat, an airplane, and the International Space Station. All were left as unfinished balsa wood skeletons. While presenting the models to me, Don explained, "I didn't want to put skin on them or fabric because it would hide the mechanical structure."

EXTENDING AND COMPLICATING NARRATIVE THROUGH THE LITERACY TOUR

Studies of older people—including those who, like Don, do not claim to do much writing of any sort—have a great deal to tell us about writing and literacy development over the lifespan. In order to recognize the value of such cases, we need expansive frameworks (Principle 2, above) that capture what Brandt (2018) describes as "powerful aspects of writing development that are easy to miss when developmental models are too simple, too narrow, too linear, or too disconnected from context" (p. 244). Life story data provides one avenue for gathering evidence of many such easy-to-miss aspects, including the role of ideologies of old age and aging. It is noteworthy that Don's life story is heavily populated with technologies and career milestones rather than human relationships. The narrative's heavy emphasis on career replicates the cultural scripts for elder men who, according to gerontologist Ruth Ray (2000), have been acculturated to focus their life stories on career milestones rather than people. This culturally appropriate narrative helpfully illuminates what Brandt calls the "role of role" in literacy over the life course (2018, p. 251). Don's account traces his inhabited social roles, made available to him as a straight, white, middle-class, cisgender man at particular sociocultural moments: the Korean War, the birth of satellite communications, the rise of home computing. As with other adults, Don's earlier social roles continue to hold meaning in later life, even when those roles are no longer institutionally recognized. Retired, Don continues inhabiting his role of technology expert, continually upgrading his home computer, snapping and displaying digital photos, and by fixing his friends' and family members' devices.

Adopting the success story arc reflective of his own values, Don's life story presents an uninterrupted chain of roles, each building on the previous one, carrying forward through retirement. With the literacy tour, however, Don's streamlined chronology of his lifespan must expand lifewide, as he accounts for the material environment that he has curated for himself. The space—located down a flight of stairs, absent of assistive devices—indicates that physiological changes have not yet required much adaptation of Don's literate activity (Principle 1, above); instead, Don's technology and literacy habitat in retirement, with its maps and photos of the island where he grew up, slideshow of bridge photos, and bare model vehicles, reveal what Barton and Hamilton (1998, p. 75) call "ruling passions": those near-obsessive motifs in human lives that become important to understanding dispositions and motivations for literate activity and learning. The place of honor Don creates for his digital photo collection and the choice to display skeletal balsa wood models become significant indices of Don's disposition toward technology. As a tour guide, Don curates a sense of himself not just as a successful engineer, but as someone who has, over his lifespan, composed more comfortably with hardware than with words, and who is more interested in curating technology than in using it to mediate social relationships. We see, in other words, evidence that the salient aspect of Don's literate activity is extending his habits of "geeking out" and "messing around" (Horst et al., 2013) with technology and composing with materials and images.

The literacy tour also yields evidence of the social and cultural role of old age and aging in Don's literate life. His demonstration of the cell phone provides a case in point. As a tour guide, Don did not tell me when he bought the phone, why he bought that particular phone, or whom he might want to communicate with it, nor did he present the phone with the same reverence as he did more beloved objects in his room. Speaking from the perspective of a historical moment when smartphones and text messaging were rapidly gaining popularity alongside social networking platforms like MySpace and Facebook, Don's tour became less about his own phone and more about his daughter's iPod and BlackBerry. Don described, but did not demonstrate, what his phone could do, and showed that he did not "care about that stuff."

In this moment of the tour, we begin to see how ideologies of aging might play a part in constructing and interpreting Don's literacy values (Principle 3, above). As a white middle-class man who has inhabited the role of father, engineer, teacher, and repairman, Don's role as expert has been secure throughout his adulthood. However, in presenting his cell phone, Don's tour needed to account for a technological development that positioned his daughter as expert and he as novice ("she tries to explain it to me"), thus reversing roles that normative age identity and familial roles (and, perhaps too, gender identity) otherwise prescribed for him. As Rumsey's (2018) research on the literacy practices of elders finds, old age amid bodily and technological change brings new kinds of developmental opportunities and the chance to make agentive choices: to adopt new practices, to adapt familiar ones, or to alienate oneself from new changes. Consciously aware of the different choices younger generations were making in 2010, Don opts for "alienation," dismissing those emergent literacies that, to him, have no significant value. By describing his daughter as "wrapped up" in her mobile technology, by referring to mobile tech as "stuff" and "crap," and by overtly stating that he could make another choice but did not care to, Don's tour presentation strives to cast his unwillingness to use a phone not as inability, but disinterest—and, too, as a marker of generational distinction that maintains a comfortable age identity, and keeps the decline narrative of aging out of his account of literate activity.

As Don's case reveals, the three principles proposed at the beginning of this chapter steer toward a flexible, multidimensional framework. By attending to writing habitats and individuals' accounting of them, we are able to access the material, corporeal elements of literacy in later life, without falling into the decline ideology trap that would conflate old age with bodily incapacity.

In turn, this methodological resistance to the decline ideology of aging supports capacious definitions of writing and development. The LWDG defined writing development by its association with "a reorganization or realignment of previous experience that registers through writing or in a changed relationship to writing"—in short, development correlates with achievement of, or pursuit of, change (Bazerman et al., 2018, p. 7). However, as studies of older adults have already begun to show, demonstrating change in behavior in later life may provide an incomplete picture of the agentive literate choices older adults—particularly elderly adults—often make. In this way, studies of older adults as representatives of a later stage in the literate lifespan can mark developmental change in terms other than decline and loss—where even moments of "not-writing" can become a valuable piece of the writing-through-the-lifespan picture.

CONCLUSION

Because age is both a biological phase of human life and a social category bearing normative expectations, studies of writing through the lifespan need methods that account for the material and ideological dimensions of literate activity. Narrative-based methods, such as the life story interview, in combination with materialist (but still narrative-driven) methods like literacy tours, provide a means of gathering evidence of age ideology and age identity with a "long view" lens. Taking the material environment of literate activity as its primary focus, the literacy tour captures the ideological dimensions of literacy as it is reflected in the design, selection, and arrangement of objects in the space. How those objects are used, cherished, hidden, or ignored all provide important evidence of a lifetime of forming particular attitudes, values, and beliefs relevant both to literacy and to aging.

This long view approach re-integrates old age into the development picture, after modern conceptions of old age as foremost a medical and social problem long ago marked it as the provenance of gerontology rather than writing, human development, or education. And still, the materialist bent of the literacy tour also presents a tangible means of addressing the unique conditions of old age. The literate habitats one curates are, in part, responsive to the changes brought on by advancing age. This might include the presence of adaptive or assistive tools to support age-related physical decline, but it also includes tools and habits that are pointedly absent or obscured, such as Don's cell phone. By orienting life story research to the curation of material environments, the literacy tour can begin to trace the agentive choices that elder adults make, either with or against the mainstream of mass literacy. The focus on curated environments (which may well extend to environments which one is not able to curate) elicits important evidence of the "tacit knowledge" of writing and literacy (Roozen, 2016), including the dispositional and affective dimensions of literacy that have been built up over a lifetime, from youth to the present. In Don's case, the interest in "messing around" and "geeking out" with technology (Horst et al., 2013), an orientation toward technology—introduced early by a tech-oriented grandfather and sustained in a government-sponsored career in electronic and satellite engineering—takes priority over using technology for the purposes of inscription.

Studies of older populations that strive to acknowledge old age as part of an entire lifespan, but which also acknowledge the biological and sociocultural dimensions that mark old age as a distinct phase of human life, reinforce a need for capacious definitions of writing and of development. Given what cases like Don's have to teach us, literate development must be marked not only in evidence of a changed relationship to writing (Bazerman et al., 2018), but in agentive choices about literate activity made in response to the course of a particular human life—including "changes that occur in relationships between people and their life worlds over time" (Brandt, 2018, p. 245). While the decline ideology of aging might otherwise mark later life as a period of stagnation and regression, research on writing development through the lifespan should mark not only moments when literate activity exhibits something new or different, but also moments when literate activity does not outwardly appear to change, as when Don makes an agentive choice not to write text messages.

In committing to a project that includes the study of writing at all ages, from birth to death, the Writing through the Lifespan Collaboration has taken an enormous—and historic—first step. But there is more yet that we might do. Consider Smith's call (this volume) to examine writing not just in, but across: How might the Lifespan Collaboration remain alert to the social and ideological dimensions of aging not only in a variety of age groups, but across them? Age—not just old age—always carries ideological weight, as all age groups, birth cohorts, and generations are imbued with cultural meaning. As the Lifespan Collaboration aims for actionable coherence, it is important that we continue to resist a normative stance by deepening our understanding of the impact of age ideology on literacy, both as a practice and as a subject of study.

REFERENCES

Alexis, C. (2016). The material culture of writing: Objects, habitats, and identities in practice. In S. Barnett & C. Boyle (Eds.), *Rhetoric, through everyday things* (pp. 83–95). University of Alabama Press.

Atkinson, R. (1998). *The life story interview*. Sage.

Barton, D. & Hamilton, M. (1998). *Local literacies: Reading and writing in one community.* Routledge.

Bazerman, C., Applebee, A. N., Berninger, V. W., Brandt, D., Graham, S., Jeffery, J. V., Matsuda, P. K., Murphy, S., Rowe, D. W., Schleppegrell, M. & Wilcox, K. C. (Eds.). (2018). *The Lifespan development of writing.* National Council of Teachers of English.

Bertaux, D. & Kohli, M. (1984). The life story approach: A continental view. *Annual Review of Sociology, 10,* 215–237.

Blewett, K., Morris, J. & Rule, H. J. (2016). Composing environments: The materiality of reading and writing. *CEA Critic, 78*(1), 24–44. https://doi.org/10.1353/cea.2016.0007.

Bowen, L. M. (2011). Resisting age bias in digital literacy research. *College Composition and Communication, 62*(4), 586–607.

Bowen, L. M. (2012). Beyond repair: Literacy, technology, and a curriculum of aging. *College English, 74*(5), 437–457.

Brandt, D. (2001). *Literacy in American Lives.* Cambridge University Press.

Brandt, D. (2018). Writing development and life-course development: The case of working adults. In C. Bazerman, A. N. Applebee, V. W. Berninger, D. Brandt, S. Graham, J. V. Jeffery, P. K. Matsuda, S. Murphy, D. W. Rowe, M. Schleppegrell & K. C. Wilcox (Eds.), *The Lifespan development of writing* (pp. 244–271). National Council of Teachers of English.

Briggs, C. L. (1986). *Learning how to ask: A sociolinguistic appraisal of the role of the interview in social science research.* Cambridge University Press.

Brodkey, L. (1987). Modernism and the scene(s) of writing. *College English, 49*(4), 396–418. https://doi.org/10.2307/377850.

Ching, K. L. (2018). Tools matter: Mediated writing activity in alternative digital environments. *Written Communication, 35*(3), 344–375. https://doi.org/10.1177/0741088318773741.

Cohler, B. J. & Hostetler, A. (2003). Linking life course and life story: Social change and the narrative study of lives over time. In J. T. Mortimer & M. J. Shanahan (Eds.), *Handbook of the life course* (pp. 555–576). Kluwer Academic/Plenum.

Cole, T. R. (1992). *The journey of life: A cultural history of aging in America.* Cambridge University Press.

Cruikshank, M. (2009). *Learning to be old: Gender, culture, and aging.* Rowman & Littlefield.

Gullette, M. M. (1997). *Aged by culture.* University of Chicago Press.

Horst, H. A., Herr-Stephenson, B. & Robinson, L. (2013). Media ecologies. In M. Itō, S. Baumer, M. Bittanti, d. boyd, R. Cody, B. Herr-Stephenson, H. A. Horst, P. G. Lange, D. Mahendran, K. Z. Martínez, C. J. Pascoe, D. Perkel, L. Robinson, C. Sims & L. Tripp, (Eds.), *Hanging out, messing around, and geeking out: Kids living and learning with new media* (pp. 29–78). MIT Press.

Journet, D. (2012). Narrative turns in writing studies research. In L. Nickoson & M. P. Sheridan (Eds.), *Writing studies research in practice: Methods and methodologies* (pp. 13–24). Southern Illinois University Press.

Kirsch, G. E. (2008). Being on location: Serendipity, place, and archival research. In G. E. Kirsch & L. Rohan (Eds.), *Beyond the archives: Research as a lived process* (pp. 20–27). Southern Illinois University Press.

Kirsch, G. E. & Rohan, L. (2008). Introduction: The role of serendipity, family connections, and cultural memory in historical research. In G. E. Kirsch & L. Rohan (Eds.), *Beyond the archives: Research as a lived process* (pp. 1–10). Southern Illinois University Press.

Micciche, L. R. (2014). Writing material. *College English*, *76*(6), 488–505.

Prior, P. & Shipka, J. (2003). Chronotopic lamination: Tracing the contours of literate activity. In C. Bazerman & D. R. Russell (Eds.), *Writing selves, writing societies: Research from activity perspectives* (pp. 180–238). The WAC Clearinghouse; Mind, Culture, and Activity. https://wac.colostate.edu/books/perspectives/selves-societies/.

Ray, R. E. (2000). *Beyond nostalgia: Aging and life-story writing*. University of Virginia Press.

Roozen, K. (2016). Reflective interviewing: Methodological moves for tracing tacit knowledge and challenging chronotopic representations. In K. B. Yancey (Ed.), *A rhetoric of reflection* (pp. 250–268). Utah State University Press.

Rosenberg, L. (2018). "Still learning": One couple's literacy development in older adulthood. *Literacy in Composition Studies*, *6*(2), 18–35. http://licsjournal.org/OJS/index.php/LiCS/article/view/200/248.

Rule, H. J. (2018). Writing's rooms. *College Composition and Communication*, *69*(3), 402–432.

Rumsey, S. K. (2018). Holding on to literacies: Older Adult narratives of literacy and agency. *Literacy in Composition Studies*, *6*(1), 81–104. http://licsjournal.org/OJS/index.php/LiCS/article/view/181/235.

Weinstein, G. & LaCoss, S. (1999). Literacy and older adults. In D. A. Wagner, R. R. Venezky & B. V. Street (Eds.), *Literacy: An international handbook* (pp. 318–323). Routledge.

CHAPTER 8.

TOWARD AN UNDERSTANDING OF THE MULTIDIRECTIONAL NATURE OF FAMILY LITERACY DEVELOPMENT

Yvonne Lee
Lehigh University

Over the last four decades, scholars have been working to uncover the nuances of family literacy learning. However, the discussion has often highlighted the impact that parents or adult family members have on the literacy development of children (Baker, 2013; Brandt, 2001; Cook-Cottone, 2004; Purcell-Gates, 1989; McDermott, 2004; Morrow et. al., 1993). In contrast, when scholars have examined a child's influence on the literacy development of older generations, this has typically been approached through a framework of bilingual literacy (Appleby & Hamilton, 2006; Auerbach, 1989; Baird et al., 2015), or the concept is mentioned but is not the focus of study (Barton et al., 2007; Barton & Hamilton, 2012; Brandt, 2001; Kress, 2003). The research I undertook for this project was intended to uncover how literacy development has moved forward and backward through the familial generations of my own Caucasian, English-speaking family who has spent generations in northeast Ohio.

In their influential text, Local Literacies, Barton and Hamilton (2012) claim, "Literacy practices can change, and new ones are frequently acquired through processes of informal learning and sense making" (p. 7). As one of the six tenets Barton and Hamilton (2012) outline as a framework for understanding literacy, this one highlights an understanding of literacy development as fluid, of literacy practices and beliefs as constantly in flux, and of literacy learning as happening in structured and non-structured environments. This is true not just for individuals, but, as this chapter will show, across living familial generations as well. Below, I draw together lived history narratives of six members representing four generations of my family (ages 20–85), whose literacy practices appear to have evolved from a reluctant or minimal participation in most literacy practices to a complete and purposeful immersion into multiple literacies that span community, family, and the academy. I examine how my own family's literacy practices and attitudes have traveled and changed across generations. Through a series of semi-structured interviews, I demonstrate ways that literacy development does indeed possess a multidirectional nature, moving back and forth along generational lines. Such an understanding of this multidirectional quality of literacy can likely inform the way scholars understand how literacy learning fluctuates and moves throughout one's lifetime by providing a broader frame for understanding literacy development and for promoting more inclusive practices in research and in classrooms.

THE MULTIDIRECTIONAL NATURE OF LITERACY DEVELOPMENT

Literacy scholars articulate the concept of literacy in increasingly broad ways as new technologies and practices have developed. Thomas and Takayoshi (2017) contend, "The substance of literacy increasingly involves a complex accumulation of reading and writing practices across all areas of human existence" (p. 4). They maintain a broad conceptualization of "writing" to include "print/alphabetic texts, digital media, and performed, embodied compositions" (2017, p. 4). Similarly, Barton and Hamilton (2012) argue, "[I]n literacy events people use written language in an integrated way as part of a range of semiotic systems; these semiotic systems include mathematical systems, musical notation, maps and other non-text-based images" (p. 9). These conceptions of literacy as social *and* beyond alphabetic text inform the definition of literacy I use in this chapter. I also draw heavily from the National Assessment of Adult Literacy's (NAAL) definition: "Literacy is the ability to use printed and written information to function in society, to achieve one's goals, and to develop one's knowledge and potential" (National Center for Educational Statistics, para. 3). This definition of literacy includes reading and writing alphabetic text, mathematics, and the languages of computer programming.

Literacy development, like literacy itself, often is described in unidirectional, accreting terms. In Literacy in American Lives, Brandt (2001) defines literacy development as the "accumulating project of literacy learning across a lifetime, the interrelated effects and potentials of learning over time" (p. 7). Brandt's focus throughout the chapter in which she discusses the evolving literacy practices of four generations of one Wisconsin family is on how each new generation builds and borrows from the literacy practices of the generation before, even as they construct their own. Brandt's findings demonstrate that individuals may never stop building and modifying their own literacy practices throughout their lifetimes. While I certainly don't deny the existence or the power of the kind of generational accumulation that Brandt describes, here I am more interested in uncovering other directions in which literacy may move and other ways that relationships foster literacy development. Earlier generations—parents, grandparents, etc.—continue to develop and accumulate literacy practices that are built and borrowed from later generations—children, grandchildren, and so forth—and from siblings or other generational peers.

The idea that literacy develops in multiple directions is not entirely new, however. Scholars have researched how children assist parental literacy learning (Auerbach, 1989), how siblings impact each other's literacy development (Gregory, 2001), and how children become "language brokers" for adult family members (Perry, 2009). However, most of these conversations are framed in discussions of second language learning (Appleby & Hamilton, 2006; Auerbach, 1989; Baird et al., 2017). For instance, Elsa Auerbach (1989), addressing the false assumption that the natural movement of literacy acquisition is unidirectional from parent to child, writes, "[W]ork with immigrants and refugees indicates that the distribution and sharing of language and literacy practices in families is complex and by no means unidirectional from parents to children . . . Clearly, a model [of family literacy development] that rests on the assumption of unilateral parent-to-child literacy assistance, with a neutral transfer of skills, misses important aspects of this dynamic" (p. 171). Appleby and Hamilton (2006) also work with bilingual learners but focus on relationships between teachers and children. They argue, "[S]ituated literacy and communication practices are complex, intergenerational, and multidirectional . . . Rigid boundaries between teacher and learner are challenged" (p. 205). For compositionists, the multidirectional nature of literacy development is similar to the recursivity of the writing process, wherein stages of writing such as inventing, drafting, revising, and editing are conceptualized as occurring in a nonlinear fashion. As Perl (2014) writes, "We go back in order to go forward" (para. 1) When creating a piece of writing, one stage may be revisited multiple times. Writers often do not move cleanly and discretely from one stage to the next but cycle forward and backward as needed. Likewise, literacy development is not stagnant but continues to move; relationships with literacy continue to grow and develop, being acted upon by the past, present, and future.

In this chapter I trace that movement through four generations of my own family. By conducting semi-structured interviews and examining the historical context of my participants, I suggest ways that literacies have developed in this family in multidirectional ways: from parent to child, child to parent, sibling to sibling, and more. I also argue that complicating our understanding of literacy development by identifying these multidirectionalities is vital for understanding writing development across the lifespan.

METHODOLOGY AND METHODS

For this project, I employed a feminist research methodology, purposefully working to disrupt the binary construction research methods can often take, i.e., researcher as powerful and participant as vulnerable (Wickramasinghe, 2009). Feminist research methodology pushes for researchers to be reflective of their practices (Burns, 2003; Cushman, 1996; Powell & Takayoshi, 2012) and self-reflexive, making parts of the self unfamiliar (Gorzelsky, 2012; Takayoshi et al., 2012). Feminist methodology is most applicable in this project because I am a member of the participant family, and the roles that I simultaneously inhabit—grand-daughter, daughter, niece, sister, mother, researcher—necessarily affected the interviews and the information provided by the participants. Should a researcher outside of the family conduct this research, it is highly likely that different memories would have come to the fore, and true but, nevertheless, alternate remembrances would have manifested.

My literacy memories represent the third generation of a family whose literacy practices have evolved from participating only enough to get the job done to a complete and purposeful immersion into multiple literacies that span community, family, and the academy. I did attempt to bracket my involvement by recording my own memories before recording the memories of others and by attempting to not interject my own memories into theirs. It is inevitable that my own interpretations of my family and their experiences have leaked through into this analysis. However, being a member of the participating family also helped me to know when to push on a certain topic. For instance, when I asked my grandmother about her memories of her own employment, she originally only mentioned work done with a publishing company. However, because I knew she had also worked for many years arranging weekly bingo trips, I knew to reiterate the question, adding that this could include self-employment. This jogged her memory, and she spoke about the activities she engaged in while arranging bingo trips. If I had not been familiar with the family history, I may not have known to clarify my question in such a way.

I audio-recorded semi-structured lifespan interviews with each of the six research participants. Each interview lasted between 1.5 and 2 hours, and most were conducted in the participant's home. Face-to-face interviews were used instead of electronic questionnaires or similar approaches because of the rich, collaborative meaning-making that is typical when people engage in face-to-face conversation. Selfe and Hawisher (2012) argue that "intimate and richly situated information emerges most productively from interviews, especially when such exchanges are structured or semi-structured" (p. 36). As the starting point for my interviews, I used the questions developed by Brandt (2001) for Literacy in American Lives because they seemed to fit my goal of triggering memory recall of past literacy events. I devised and added questions of my own that paralleled those but that centered on reading and writing practices involved with the participants' work lives. I also added questions regarding socioeconomic aims for children and literacy practices used in order to reach that desired status. These questions were added in order to understand connections participants made between their literacy practices and their current or desired socioeconomic status. One week prior to the start of my interview process, I emailed a copy of the interview questions to each participant so they could prepare for the interview.

After the interviews were completed, I transcribed the audio files and used open coding to uncover the literacies discussed. Once the first round of open coding was complete, I organized them into themes: academic—literacy practices tied to formal or informal schooling; private—literacy practices not shared with others or performed only when alone; and public—literacy practices that occur in public spaces, such as the workplace or organizational meetings. For each of these themes, I then fractured those codes into moments of personal literacy practices and moments about the literacy practices of others. From this, I identified instances of multidirectional literacy development. I also noted an affinity for literacy practices outside the realm of "English" or language arts, such as the language of computers and of mathematics.

Participants

My family's story is set within one Ohio city whose economic well-being rose and fell with the birth and decline of the industrial United States. In the mid-nineteenth century, Stark County became a center for the manufacture of farm equipment, and Ohio was the leading agricultural center of the country (Sterling, 1998). After the farm equipment industry began to move west, steel became a major industry in the area due to the abundance of water and it was during this time that the city reached the peak of its prosperity (Sterling, 1998). Since the late 1960s, the city has seen a continued decline in businesses and population (Sterling, 1998). Kenney (2003) notes

> In the latter half of the twentieth century, there was a national trend toward a service-oriented economy. Industrial jobs gave way to banking, retailing, insurance, medicine, law, and government. Manufacturing jobs have been consistently moving overseas. (p. 145)

causing the steady decline of population and prosperity in a once booming city.

The Stark County, Caucasian family represented in this study had four living adult generations on my maternal side at the time of my data collection. This offered a unique opportunity for a gaze into their literacy practices as they occurred across generations. For each of the four generations, I interviewed one or two representatives: Shirley, my grandmother (85); her daughters, Jeannette (my mother, 63) and Joyce (my aunt, 52); Jeannette's daughters, both me (42) and AnnMarie (my sister, 38); and finally, my son, Zane (20).

Shirley, my grandmother, was born in 1933, the second child of the family. She grew up in a household that included her mother, her father, an older brother, four younger brothers, and two younger sisters. In 1941, when Shirley was eight years old, the US launched into World War II. At that point

> rationing became a way of life as supplies were redirected to the war effort. In 1940, 68 local industries manufactured $140 million worth of products for the war effort. [A local manufacturer] was making bearings for the British and French before Pearl Harbor. It was the kind of increased production that pulled Stark County—and the nation—out of the grip of the Great Depression. (Kenney, 2003, p. 127)

Though the city in which they lived seemed to prosper from the manufacturing of wartime materials, Shirley's family did not benefit. Her father was in and out of work and her mother's job was caretaker of the home and children. Regarding her family's literacies, Shirley recalls very little reading and writing occurring in her childhood household.

Shirley's daughter and my mother, Jeannette, was born in 1954 and she describes the family of her youth as consisting of her mother, father, four sisters, and two brothers. Jeannette grew up in a city that was quickly declining economically. Jeannette's childhood family literacy memories focused on large family gatherings that occurred in December and July. These gatherings were meant to build comradery between family members who didn't see each other often and activities were always planned for the adults and children, such as the annual Christmas talent show, swimming, miniature golf, and sometimes board games like Scrabble and Pictionary. Often, however, the adults could be found sitting around the tables in small groups playing games of rummy or poker. Like Shirley, Jeannette recalls little reading and writing in her childhood home but her current household has full bookshelves and reading is a constant activity, in part due to her husband and mother-in-law's habits of passing time with a book.

Joyce, my aunt and the youngest of Shirley's children, was born in 1966. She reports that her father would come home from work and read the newspaper at the dining room table. This daily reading habit likely played a part in Joyce's own relationship to reading. Her earliest memory of using books on her own was when she was around four years old. Her parents had a set of encyclopedias that she used to build literal walls around herself when she played. By high school, due to divorce, Shirley could no longer afford the requisite tuition cost of the private, Catholic education that Joyce's older siblings had enjoyed. Subsequently, Joyce attended the area vocational high school where she studied data processing. Before Shirley's passing in 2019, she and Joyce lived in the same home in which there were multiple bookshelves overflowing with books because of the love of reading Joyce developed over the course of her life.

I am Jeannette's first child, born in 1976. My most vibrant early literacy memories are of reading time in elementary school and typing my own stories on an electric typewriter at our dining room table. AnnMarie, my younger sister, was born in 1979. When asked about her earliest literacy memories, she flippantly remarked, "I remember those lined papers that [we] had, and [we] would learn to write letters." However, as we talked further, she admitted that there was a time when reading and writing became an important activity for her. As she entered her teen years and the emotional rollercoaster than often accompanies them, she began journaling and writing poetry to work through her own feelings.

Currently, my household includes my husband and three children. Not only do we have overflowing bookshelves, but there are reading materials on tables, on countertops, and piled on the floor. AnnMarie's current household includes her husband and four children. She says she makes sure books are always available to her kids, remarking, "If they like to read then they will like learning and will seek out opportunities to learn more and go somewhere in life . . . If they like to read and learn then they will not find school so bad and will make it through college." She seems to have been correct, as higher education has played a major role in many of our lives over the last few decades, as will be shown below.

Zane, my eldest child, was born in 1997. When asked about his earliest literacy memories, he mentioned the nightly bedtime reading he and I engaged in from his birth through his sixth-grade year. The two books he mentioned by name from this time were Peter and the Star Catchers (Barry & Pearson, 2004) and Walk Two Moons (Creech, 2011). "Those I remember specifically," he said. When pressed as to why these two stand out to him, Zane reflected,

> It isn't so much the books themselves that mean much to me. It's the fact that it was a way for us to spend time together at a point in our lives when we didn't often have much time. Those memories really shaped my enjoyment of reading and storytelling because it is something I've always associated with spending time with you.

Not only was our quality time influential for Zane, but his father's video game activities and love of computers lent themselves to Zane's own interest in such pastimes, leading him to alphabet video games he could play on his own by the time he was three years old. Zane was recently working on his bachelor's degree, but realizing he was unhappy with his chosen major, he completed enough classes to earn his associate of science degree in general studies and is now taking a break from education to decide what he truly wants to do.

MULTIDIRECTIONAL LITERACY DEVELOPMENT IN ONE FAMILY

The experiences reported above suggest some of the ways in which literacy doesn't simply accumulate down through generations but that it instead has multidirectional impacts as one member's literacies reshape the literacies of other members of one's own generation, future generations, and even past generations. The literacies of younger generations are often the impetus for new literacy development among older generations. For example, my grandmother, Shirley, grew up and raised her children with the mindset that the skills of reading and writing were necessary to have, but she did not seek out multiple avenues for the use and development of these skills. When asked how much reading and writing were valued in her childhood home, Shirley's daughter, Jeannette, recalled, "I think it was more of a necessity than a value, really—[a necessity] for getting through school."

This seemingly apathetic relationship to literacy was likely influenced by the cultural climate in which Shirley grew up, the relationships generations before her had had with literacy, and her own personal interests in such activities. Shirley was born in 1933 and thus her early years were influenced by the Great Depression and the impact of the Second World War. Though she, herself, may not have been overtly aware of these events during her early childhood, her parents and the world around her certainly were. Not only was the nation suffering from financial declines and high unemployment rates, but these were lean years for the family. With an alcoholic father, a stay-at-home mother, and eight children in the home, there wasn't much time for literacy development. At one time, the living room in her childhood home was even turned into a bedroom for her grandfather, whom she watched pass away from leukemia. Add to such living conditions the fact that in 1930 4.3 percent of the US population 14 years and older was considered illiterate (National Center for Education Statistics, n.d.) and it can be imagined that for many like Shirley and her family, the ability to read and write may have been seen as a tool of necessity or an unaffordable luxury; there was likely less opportunity to develop particular literacies as hobbies or personal pursuits. Even so, as she grew and the world around her changed, so did Shirley's literacy development, which was later also influenced by her children's and grandchildren's relationships with literacy.

Both Shirley and Jeannette mentioned reading comprehension as something they had always struggled with. Of reading books, Shirley mentioned repeatedly how much she did not enjoy it. Jeannette, on the other hand, said of high school, "[The] reading part was fine. Comprehension—whenever I would get tested on that—I was average." This movement toward an acceptance of reading may have stemmed from Jeannette's father, whom she mentioned often reading the daily newspaper or a fishing magazine at the dining room table. In fact, when asked about her current reading practices, Jeannette laughed, "Reading has been a part of me now that I don't have kids." Now that she is retired and finds herself with more time on her hands, she enjoys the enlightenment she feels her religious texts bring her, so she engages in the activity more often.

Sisters Jeannette and Joyce do not recall ever seeing their mother, Shirley, reading for enjoyment, though they both recall seeing their father engaging in reading of many kinds. Though I only have vague childhood memories of my mother reading novels, reading fiction has always been something I loved; it offered me a glimpse into different lives and constantly offered new perspectives. Zane, my son, continues to build on such affinities as he has books in multiple formats—paper, electronic, and audio.

Across the generations of my family, there also seems to be a growing interest in and increased use of the language of mathematics and language interpretation. About compulsory education Shirley remembers, "I liked math. . . . I remember in my math class . . . the teacher would stand there and flash off numbers and you had to add them up as she goes along. And I used to raise my hand on all of them because I could add them really fast no matter what." With pride in her voice, Jeannette also recalls a math-related school memory,

> In third grade we had a math teacher and she had a contest . . . [and] there was going be first and second place. She had a section [of the math textbook] that if you completed within a certain period of time . . . she took you on an outing . . . I think Brown Derby. I came in second and had a boxed lunch with her.

She said this lunch was a highlight of her schooling because she never felt above average in any other academic area. Shirley used her inclination toward math to help her arrange and run bingo games, while Jeannette put hers to use in a career working in payroll departments.

Younger generations have also demonstrated increasing affinity for language interpretation. Of her position in medical coding, AnnMarie remarked,

> I have to understand the doctor's language. Not all doctors use the same abbreviations or the same language, so it's not just you sit here and you punch this code in. It's a lot of using your thought process and then you have to read the codes because each code has a description and you have to make sure that you pick the right one.

During his interview, Zane talked about needing to understand various student needs in his recent position as a computer science tutor.

> Normally the question [that students visit with] is that "I have a problem with my code, can you look at it, can you read it for me? Comprehend what is going on and maybe tell me where the problem is?" . . . So I have to both know how to read it and understand it on a very deep level and then I also have to understand how to write it so that I can give an answer for, like "This is why it's broken. Here's how to fix it."

His description of the work of tutoring a subject such as computer science is thus similar to AnnMarie's description of interpreting the language use of various doctors.

From a multidirectional perspective of literacy development, faint lines can start to be seen crisscrossing among and between generational lines. Shirley, Jeannette, and AnnMarie all talked about their children when asked about people in their lives they associate with reading and writing. Shirley remarked on Joyce's journaling, a practice that has followed her into adulthood; Jeannette mentioned my pursuit of an advanced degree in the field of writing studies; and AnnMarie's first thought was of enrolling her daughters in a pre-school literacy program. The fact that the general question about who they associate with literacy consistently elicited primary responses about children suggests the literacy practices, values, and beliefs of one generation may be both affecting and being affected by their children.

Perhaps more clearly related to the concept of the multidirectional nature of literacy development is when Joyce, my aunt, recalled, "I remember when we were both very young, realizing that we both had an interest in writing. So maybe you should write you on there as being one of the people I associate with reading and writing because of all the conversations we had when we were younger." Joyce and I have had many discussions throughout the years about book recommendations and creative writing we were working on. Our sharing prompted our literacy practices to influence each other. For example, when I discovered and read The Hunger Games trilogy (Collins, 2010), she was the first person I talked to about it and our conversation prompted her to read the books. Hence, the literacy practices of a later generation influenced those of an earlier generation.

The most interesting suggestion of later generations influencing earlier generations' literacy is that four of the six participants discussed entering or returning to a higher education environment at a non-traditional age—my mother, Jeannette; my aunt, Joyce; myself; and my sister, AnnMarie. In 2001 at the age of 47, after both my sister and I had graduated from high school and were no longer a time or financial burden, my mother earned an associate of applied science in business management. At 64 years old she made the decision to retire from the daily grind, to earn her State Tested Nurse Aide certification, and to stay home and care for her elderly mother-in-law who needed around-the-clock care.

Joyce also returned to school in her 40s. Though she did try a semester at a local community college in 1985, she decided it wasn't for her. She didn't try again until 2005, when she spent the next five years taking various classes at a few of the local campuses, all while maintaining a full-time job. Eventually, in 2010, she took all the credits she had acquired throughout the years, enrolled at the university regional campus, took two classes, and earned her associate of science degree. After that success, she remained enrolled, eventually earning a bachelor of arts in general studies in 2013. When asked what her family thought of her scholastic endeavors, she explained that they were mostly ambivalent, but that her brother-in-law "was the only one that questioned" why she was "spending money" and "to make sure that I get something from that education. It's a lot of money to spend."

Like my mother and my aunt, I, too returned to education later in life. For me, the difficulty was that I was a mother and a wife by the age of 21, so my young family had to come before my educational goals. However, in 2009 at the age of 33, then divorced and living as a single mother with three children and working part-time waiting tables, I earned my Bachelor of Arts in English. When I was on my own, it became important for me to show my children, who were then 9, 5, and 4, that there was more to life than living a shift-to-shift existence. The best way I knew how to do this was to return to school. Hence, though I was consciously attempting to influence their current literacy beliefs by showing them the value of school, it was, essentially, their possible future literacy attitudes influencing the choices I was making at that time.

After earning my bachelor's, I worked for a couple of years as a part-time writing tutor and an adjunct, student success instructor. Realizing that I had only gone from living shift-to-shift to paycheck-to-paycheck, I sought out and was awarded a graduate assistantship, enabling me to spend the next two years completing a Master of Arts in Rhetoric and Composition. One year after graduation, I married a man who offered mutual support for our children and our dreams. Four years of adjunct work later, I knew the writing classroom was where I wanted to be, but I craved the stability of full-time employment so I returned to school, once again earning a graduate assistantship, and I have now earned a doctorate in rhetoric and composition.

On a slightly different track, my sister, AnnMarie, returned to school, earning her Associate in Applied Science with Health Information Management at the age of 34. She, too, was separated from her husband and finding the freedom to pursue her own dreams. By the time she had earned her associate's degree, she had met a man who provided the stability she and her three young children had been lacking. That stability opened the opportunity for her to work full-time and to complete an online Bachelor of Science in Health Information Management.

Each generation's encouragement and success in a higher education environment likely impacted the decisions of the others to continue to engage in academic endeavors of their own. Also implicit in the arguments of AnnMarie's and my own return to school is an influence not only on, but *from* the literacy practices of our children. We have both at one time or another mentioned that one of the major reasons for returning to school was to impress upon our children the importance and difficulty of higher education, hopefully encouraging them to put in the hard work necessary to earn a degree before starting a family. AnnMarie stated, "I want them to go to college and finish with a degree—whatever degree they want—if it's at least an associate degree or if they want to take it all the way. I mean whatever one they want in the best field that fits them." AnnMarie's push for her children to complete some level of college is built upon a belief shared by each of the family members mentioned here—a belief that education is the path out of a hand-to-mouth existence. Each family member in this chapter has first-hand knowledge of the difficulties that come with living in poverty and many of us have used education to pull ourselves, our children, and our world views through that life and into financial and emotional stability.

DISCUSSION

Scholars have argued for a social-contextual model of family literacy and have pointed out that we all already inhabit multiple literacy worlds that differ from generation to generation (Appley & Hamilton, 2006; Auerbach, 1989; Kress, 2003). My study indicates this concept is important for all literacy learners and all aspects of literacy learning. Auerbach (1989) argues that more purposeful connections must be made between family literacies and academic literacies. As can be suggested from my brief portrayal here of my family, our literacy practices seem to have evolved from a rather ambivalent approach to literacy to complete and purposeful immersion into multiple literacies. Understanding the multidirectional literacy movement within families can help literacy scholars and compositionists better understand the needs of the writers they study or those who enter their classrooms. As was mentioned earlier, many of these discussions of the multidirectional nature of literacy practices, attitudes, and beliefs are happening within the framework of English language learners and their family literacy dynamics. Without taking away from the importance of those conversations, helping to move such an understanding of literacy into the broader pedagogical realm of Composition Studies would help practitioners and scholars gain important insight into some of the invisible struggles so many of their students encounter as they try and fail and try again.

While the accumulation of literacy practices (e.g., Brandt, 2001) by later generations is an important and worthy focus, it is equally important to understand the multidirectional ways that literacies continue to develop among individuals throughout their lifespans. Though it is important for later generations to be flexible enough to reposition their literacy practices, so, too, must earlier generations. In fact, an argument may be made that for later generations to wholly embrace new literacies and literacy practices, earlier generations must provide a space in which such flexibility is modeled, making it necessary for parents' literacy practices to be influenced by their children.

To truly develop a "multidimensional understanding" of literacy development, as the Writing through the Lifespan Collaboration has called us to do (Lifespan Through the Lifespan Collaboration, n.d.), scholars throughout the disciplines of writing studies must continue to find ways to study both the explicit and implicit movements of literacy across generations, cultures, and eras. This is a big ask. As my study suggests, one way we can add to such multigenerational research is to build a better understanding of the multidirectional nature of literacy learning through the examination of the ways literacy practices move among generations. This research with my own family has provided an interesting glimpse into literacy development amongst family members and across generations. However, further study is needed to continue to tease out more nuanced examples of this phenomenon and its pedagogical implications. Additional, purposeful research on the multidirectional processes of literacy development across generations beyond the realm of bilingual literacy can help researchers and practitioners better understand this phenomenon and to continue moving the field forward.

REFERENCES

Appleby, Y. & Hamilton, M. (2006). Literacy as social practice: Travelling between the everyday and other forms of learning. In J. Crowther & P. Sutherland (Eds.), *Lifelong learning: Concepts and contexts*. Routledge.

Auerbach, E. R. (1989). Toward a social-contextual approach to family literacy. *Harvard Educational Review, 59*(2), 165–181.

Baird, A. S., Kibler, A. & Palacios, N. (2015). "'Yo te estoy ayudando; estoy aprendiendo también/I am helping you; I am learning too:'" A bilingual family's community of practice during home literacy events. *Journal of Early Childhood Literacy, 15*(2), 147–176. https://doi.org/10.1177/1468798414551949.

Baker, C. (2013). Fathers' and mothers' home literacy involvement and children's cognitive and social emotional development: Implications for family literacy programs. *Applied Developmental Science, 17*(4), 184–197. https://doi.org/10.1080/10888691.2013.836034.

Barry, D. & Pearson, R. (2004). *Peter and the starcatchers*. Disney Press.

Barton, D. & Hamilton, M. (2012). *Local literacies: Reading and writing in one community*. Routledge.

Barton, D., Ivanič, R., Appleby, Y., Hodge, R. & Tusting, K. (2007). *Literacy, lives and learning*. Routledge.

Brandt, D. (2001). *Literacy in American lives*. Cambridge University Press.

Burns, M. (2003). Interviewing: Embodied communication. *Feminism and Psychology, 13*(2), 229–236.

Collins, S. (2010). *The hunger games*. Scholastic Press.

Cook-Cottone, C. (2004). Constructivism in family literacy practices: Parents as mentors. *Reading Improvement, 41*(4), 208–216.

Creech, S. (2011). *Walk two moons*. Harper Collins.

Cushman, E. (1996). The rhetorician as an agent of social change. *College Composition and Communication, 47*(1), 7–28.

Gorzelsky, G. (2012). An experiential approach to literacy studies. In K. M. Powell & P. Takayoshi (Eds.), *Practicing research in writing studies: Reflexive and ethically responsible research* (pp. 349–371). Hampton Press.

Gregory, E. (2001). Sisters and brothers as language and literacy teachers: Synergy between siblings playing and working together. *Journal of Early Childhood Literacy, 1*(3), 301–322.

Kenney, K. A. (2003). *Canton: A journey through time*. Arcadia.

Kress, G. (2003). *Literacy in the new media age*. Routledge.

McDermott, R. (2004). Putting literacy in its place: From ordinary to special to treacherous—a story of literacy in three generations of an American family. *Journal of Education, 184*(1), 11–30.

Morrow, L. M., Paratore, L., Gaber, D., Harrison, C. & Tracey, D. (1993). Family literacy: Perspectives and practices. *The Reading Teacher, 47*(3), 194–200.

National Center for Education Statistics. (n.d.). *120 years of literacy*. https://nces.ed.gov/naal/lit_history.asp.

Perl, S. (2014). Research as a recursive process: Reconsidering "The composing processes of unskilled college writers" 35 years later. *Composition Forum, 29*. https://compositionforum.com/issue/29/perl-retrospective.php.

Perry, K. H. (2009). Genres, contexts, and literacy practices: Literacy brokering among Sudanese refugee families. *Reading Research Quarterly, 44*(3), 256–276.

Powell, K. M. & Takayoshi, P. (Eds.). (2012). *Practicing research in writing studies: Reflexive and ethically responsible research*. Hampton Press.

Purcell-Gates, V. (1988). Lexical and syntactic knowledge of written narrative held by well-read-to kindergarteners and second graders. *Research in the Teaching of English, 22*(2), 128–160.

Selfe, C. L. & Hawisher, G. E. (2012). Exceeding the bounds of the interview: Feminism, mediation, narrative, and conversations about digital literacy. In L. Nickoson & M. P. Sheridan (Eds.), *Writing studies research in practice: Methods and methodologies* (pp. 36–50). Southern Illinois University Press.

Sterling, R. E. (1998). *Images of America: Canton, Ohio*. Arcadia.

Takayoshi, P., Tomlinson, E. & Castillo, J. (2012). The construction of research problems and methods. In In K. M. Powell & P. Takayoshi (Eds.), *Practicing research in writing studies: Reflexive and ethically responsible research* (pp. 97–121). Hampton Press.

Thomas, P. & Takayoshi, P. (2016). Introduction: Methodological matters and the invisibility of literacy. In P. Thomas, P. Takayoshi, S. Pigg, S. Moody, Y. R. Teems, J. Cunningham, A. M. Buck, M. B. Ressler, M. Blackburn, T. Bogard, J. E. Haan, K. E. Mallett, N. Caswell, E. Tomlinson, U. Krishnan, L. B. Steiner, J. Hill, J. Cushman & P. Sullivan (Eds.), *Literacy in practice: Writing in private, public, and working lives* (pp. 1–14). Routledge.

Wickramasinghe, M. (2010). *Feminist research methodology: Making meanings of meaning-making*. Routledge.

Writing Through the Lifespan Collaboration. (n.d.). *Our mission*. https://www.lifespanwriting.org/.

CHAPTER 9.

WRITING AS A MATTER OF LIFE AND DEATH: WRITING THROUGH THE TRANSITION BETWEEN EMPLOYMENT AND RETIREMENT IN THE USA

James T. Zebroski
University of Houston

"Jim, don't ever retire." It was September, the start of a new academic year, and I hadn't seen John since the previous spring. He was in the hall as I was going down to the University of Houston English Department offices to use the printer, and we chatted briefly. John was the grand old man of the department whom everyone, including me, loved, and he had continued teaching Anglo-Saxon and medieval literature courses well through his seventies. He had just decided to retire and this seemed an odd thing for him to say. The sense that I got from our chat was that John was struggling with the bureaucracy of retirement, but I thought to myself, "How hard could it be?" Academics do a great deal of bureaucratic writing during our careers and in our role as guardians of the paperwork empire. So retirement asked for a bit more of that? Surely, we could handle that with aplomb.

This chapter is part of a year-long autoethnographic study that makes visible some of the literacy practices that one worker, a professor of English—me—deployed in the transition from employment to retirement. What I discovered is that John was right; the successful uses of very specific kinds of writing (and reading and speaking) during the retirement process are a matter of life and death and very overwhelming. These literacy practices are nearly universally required in some form in the U.S. system of retirement. They are also complex and understudied in composition studies. Because they are largely invisible and "disappear" if they are ultimately successful, such practices are difficult to see. This study tracks these literacies, makes them visible, and tries to preserve them for further research.

Throughout the remainder of this chapter I consider (1) The Life Narrative: The Process of Applying for Retirement, and (2) The Autoethnographic Method and an Analysis of the Findings, and finally offer (3) a Marxist Conclusion that zooms out to the larger forces which construct retirement and ageing in our society in this moment in history.

THE LIFE NARRATIVE: THE PROCESS OF APPLYING FOR RETIREMENT

I really did not want to retire. I wrote in my journal on May 17, 2018 that "In a different world it is conceivable I wouldn't even be retiring. If I didn't fear for my health, if the loads were reasonable, if composition were treated with respect—if, if, if . . . Never will happen . . . isn't going to happen now" (Journal, p. 75). I would have been happy to stay employed. Pfeffer (2010) shows how U.S. workplaces are increasingly toxic and hurting the health of workers. Given serious arthritis and infections that were worsening combined with the annually increasing workloads, staying employed was simply not an option. I felt the department had "forced" me out simply by piling more and more work on me to the detriment of my health. Yet the once-for-all-time quality of retirement in twenty-first century USA was scary. Retirement in the US is essentially all or nothing; it's difficult to *un*retire because the bureaucratic paperwork both with the government and with pension companies tends to be final and irreversible. I began the process with strong ambivalence.

Still, one theme going through this entire chapter is how privileged academics like me are compared to other workers. As challenging as it was to use literacies (and oralities) to navigate the applications for retirement successfully, I had the privilege of having the summer "off" and no official workload, though I was meeting weekly with a half dozen students, so I could make time for this crucial work which took 40 to 50 percent of my work time during the week.

On May 15, 2018, I met with the University of Houston Human Relations (HR) director (I had met with her in September 2017 and January 2018 as well) and that day we collaborated to fill in and submit the four key forms that officially initiated the process at the university, state, and federal levels. The process included transactions with the state retirement system (Employees Retirement System of Texas), the private healthcare companies (Humana and United Healthcare), and the federal government (Social Security and Medicare). These forms included (1) ERS TRS/ORP Retiree Insurance Enrollment Form, (2) ERS Automatic Withdrawal/Cancellation of Insurance Premiums for Texas Employees Group Benefits Program (GBP), (3) Department of Health and Human Services in the federal government Request for Employment Information (for Medicare Part B), and (4) Department of Health and Human Services Application for Enrollment in Medicare B (i.e., medical insurance). Then on

May 17, on the recommendation of the Human Relations director, I went to the Houston Social Security office to continue the application for Medicare B. Arriving about 8:00 am, thanks to the ride offered by a colleague, I joined a line that wound around the building an hour before the office opened. The line was well-organized and it was triaged right before the doors opened. Within about ten minutes of entering the office I was talking to the Social Security agent who informed me that I was too early and that I needed to apply in July. She also noted that I could do so by simply mailing in the signed forms from HR which I brought with me and she provided an addressed envelope for that. This proved to be the first instance of a recurring process. No one had told me there was a pre-deadline for applying for Medicare; it was, in the parlance of Patrick Hartwell (1985), COIK—clear only if known.

I also did not know that Medicare B, the retirement health coverage which is paired with private health coverage (for me, Humana Corporation healthcare) was the portal to everything else. Through May and June I had received bulk mailings about the Humana healthcare plan that I had applied for but Humana sent me a letter dated July 4, 2018 saying:

> Thank you for your interest in a Humana Medicare Plan. We are sorry we can't accept your request for enrollment. You're not eligible for a Medicare Advantage plan. You need both Medicare Part A and Part B to enroll in a Medicare Advantage plan.

So I could not get approval for retirement healthcare without getting Medicare B, but I also couldn't even apply for, let alone get approval for Medicare Part B until July 1. It was an interesting Catch-22.

I had decided in late June to apply for Social Security since I had reached the mandatory minimum age for my cohort's full benefits. That nine-page application was provided online and could be downloaded and printed as a hard copy. The Social Security website, unlike most of the others, allows one to enter the site, partially fill in the form, and come back later to complete or revise it. The Social Security "My Account" tool is secured not just with passwords, but by using a simultaneous and changing cellphone number code. There was also a toll-free number that featured knowledgeable and courteous agents. None of these options were available in the corporate or state realms.

After I had received the Humana letter that in effect said I had no healthcare starting September 1—that got my attention in a panic-y kind of way—I had both an email and a phone call from a Social Security case worker in Alabama who was processing my application there. It is hard to emphasize how crucial this was in this complex process—to have a real person who knows what they are doing and to whom one can ask specific questions during this process. None of the toll-free corporate numbers were very good at doing this and the ubiquitous "My Accounts" that were required by every separate agency for the simplest matters, were, for me, universally worthless. The "My Accounts" offered no parallel options, there was no easy way to reset the codes (I was frozen and locked out often), and there was no face-to-face transaction in which one could ask questions or even ask for help. There was also no hard-copy, paper option with any of these agencies. By the end of the process, one suspected that several of these tools were as much about discouraging consumers as helping them. They certainly were invested in cutting the labor costs of having real, knowledgeable people helping the applicants.

Social Security, though, was different. The form was a bit challenging (one form for all, so therefore many options which I learned mostly did not apply to me), but when Agent Y phoned me the afternoon of the day before I planned to train, bus, and hike to the Social Security office (there was no direct public transport to the office in Houston), I was delighted to have someone I could ask about this process. Let me stress that she called me on July 2, 2018. Not one of any of the other agencies ever phoned me. Agent Y not only saved me from a dangerous and torturous trip to the Houston office in 100-degree heat, but when I told her about the letter from Humana which indicated that my coverage ended on September 1, she told me that the process of applying for Medicare B (which was the linchpin) would likely be done by then and that she would help me with it. She asked me when I wanted to start collecting Social Security and the details about having my benefits deposited. She also noted that if I could email her the four HR documents as PDFs (or equivalent) that I would not have to go to the local Houston office or use the mail. Immediately the next morning, July 13, I used my smartphone to take photos of the hard copies of the four documents generated by me and the director of HR back in mid-May and sent them to my email. I then sent the email attachments to Agent Y and waited.

Through this period, I was also juggling transactions with United Health Care which I learned (COIK again) was my Medicare D for drug coverage. For that I needed to get information from the Employee Retirement System (ERS). ERS is the pension and retirement healthcare system for public employees of Texas. Because I had moved six times in my career, I had opted for a national retirement pension system. I only needed Texas' ERS for the retirement healthcare. ERS was notorious in my experience for understaffing its toll-free number. It was not unusual to have to wait forty minutes or more. When I waited and did get a real person, they tended to be quite helpful, knowledgeable, and courteous; however, I gave up on ERS' toll-free line. I was able to set up a "My Account" to get the name of my previous drug coverage provider which was required for the United Healthcare application.

This was a very stressful moment in a process on which I had been diligently working for two months. As my journal records, I was feeling overwhelmed, fearful, frustrated, depressed, and, finally, angry. Several quotations from my journals render the way this process was experienced. Early in this process I am already writing "I really want to get out of this triage way of living. I hate this. But I'm not there yet." (Journal, May 9, 2018, p. 35). I was learning: "Retirement is a series of half dozen processes/events. So retirement will take place for weeks until September" (Journal, May 10, 2018, p. 42). In response to yet another "My Account" I noted, "So I registered. Yet again a horror. I hate these 'easy' online registrations which require accounts, passwords, etc. Awful. Not easy. Not user friendly. PITA—pain in the ass" (Journal, May 11, 2018, p. 51). And on the continual, months long, liminal nature of the transition—"Ambiguity? Yes, but much more. *Overwhelmed and alone*" (emphasis in text; Journal, May 18, 2018, p. 82). At the very moment when I was being kicked out of an identity I had constructed and lived in for thirty-five years or more, when I was trying to imagine what kind of life and identity I would compose if I were successful in retiring, I was caught in a Catch-22 set of processes that I felt had it in for me, despite my knowledge that millions retire every year.

Writing helped me every step of the way but what really helped was the assistance of Agent Y, my Social Security caseworker who phoned me again on July 12 and reminded me that we were approaching the deadline for both Social Security and Medicare B applications. She asked about my four forms which were needed to process the requests. At first, I was terror stricken because I had sent them on July 3, but she kept calm and quickly found the forms in her junk mail. The relief is hard to describe. By Friday, July 13—the next morning!—I had my first Social Security check in my bank account. A week or so later I had Medicare B and the logjam with Humana, United Health Care, and the rest was broken. I received my membership cards by mid-August. Because I knew how I would pay bills and moving expenses and that I would have healthcare, I put in my resignation on August 1, 2018. I had been raised in a working-class culture and learned the lesson as a teen that one never resigned one job until one had another job or the equivalent: an income and healthcare.

Writing had been a matter of life and death—a matter of successfully receiving an income and healthcare by the September deadline when both ended at my place of employment. Writing (and friends) had successfully helped me navigate a morass of agencies. Writing had been the mediated means of navigating agencies, but also of regulating my own progress in the applications and forms. Writing had also helped me to navigate my emotional state throughout the process. Writing was both social and individual. Social Security, especially the intervention of Agent Y, had saved me.

But I was not finished yet. Far from it. Later in the summer, I had to meet with my pension company advisor on June 12 and July 10. On July 25, I met again with my advisor and another pension employee who served as a witness as I signed a dozen documents giving permission to transfer half of my accumulated pension funds into an IRA from which I would receive my monthly pension deposit. At the end of August, I phoned yet another pension employee in Colorado who was in charge of setting up the deposit of the pension into my bank on the 21st of each month. By September 21, 2018, my pension check joined my monthly Social Security deposit.

And I still was not finished. To attend to all the details of the retiring process takes about a year and, as I write this, I am winding up some of what I hope are the final income and healthcare bureaucratic details of this transition. And just as the major income and healthcare hurdles seemed to be overcome, in September there arose a new set of bureaucracies and obstacles which were in many ways as challenging as the earlier ones, as I went on to find a new home, pack, move, and begin to more fully compose a further life.

THE AUTOETHNOGRAPHIC METHOD AND AN ANALYSIS OF THE FINDINGS

Having described my retirement experience, in this section I pull back and discuss autoethnography as a method, both broadly and the ways that I applied it for this particular study. I also consider implications for the field of composition studies before offering a Marxist conclusion.

METHOD: USING CAROLYN ELLIS'S WRITERLY AUTOETHNOGRAPHY APPROACH

I came both early and late to autoethnography. As described by Adams et al. (2015), "autoethnography is a qualitative method —it offers a nuanced, complex, and specific knowledge about particular lives, experiences, and relationships rather than general information about large groups of people" (p. 21). They also note that autoethnography is a research method that:

- Uses a researcher's personal experience to describe and critique cultural beliefs, practices, and experiences.
- Acknowledges and values the researcher's relationships with others.
- Uses deep and careful self-reflection—typically referred to as "reflexivity" to name and interrogate the intersections between self and society, the particular and the general, the personal and the political.

- Shows people in the process of figuring out what to do, how to live, and the meaning of their struggles.
- Strives for social justice and to make life better. (2015, pp. 1–2)

My early experience with autoethnography was more ethnographic and began with my Ph.D. studies in 1978 when I began to read Vygotsky and was struck by the contrast between the individualistic nature of most contemporary U.S. research in literacy and the research done in a Vygotskian framework in the Soviet Union. Among many others, Leontiev & Leontiev (1959) had argued for putting the social and individual together in research. The very separation of the individual from the social—and from the capitalist society it was part of—seemed to be nearly universal in the US. My chair advised me to take some courses from a cultural anthropologist, Ojo Arewa and a folklorist in English, Patrick Mullen, to begin to understand the social foundations of literacy. I learned ethnography from them and discovered that ethnographic work was under critique for being complicit with colonialism and that ethnographers were in the process of discovering alternative venues and experimenting with alternative methodological approaches (Geertz, 1973; Hymes, 1972; Spradley & McCurdy, 1972). For over 35 years I worked within this domain (see Zebroski [1986] for one of the first articles on using ethnographic writing in rhetoric and composition).

Time passed. Then around 2015 at the University of Houston, I began working with Soyeon Lee, a doctoral student from South Korea who wrote about her experience learning U.S. academic writing both in Korea and then in the US (Lee, in press). She drew extensively on autoethnography, re-introducing me to the method, which I came across again in Thomas Gorman's (2017) critical new autoethnography of his experience growing up in the U.S. working class. In it, Gorman uses his knowledge as an individual and as a sociologist to analyze his experience in sociological terms.

It is this bringing together of social and individual that I found attractive. That this synthesis happened in (the process of) writing is the other aspect of autoethnography which I liked. I discovered this writerly approach in the work of Carolyn Ellis and her students (Adams et al., 2015), whose autoethnography almost eerily reflected what I had been doing for 40 years but did not have a legitimate name for. Her stress on constant writing, drafting, and storying, with continual reflection as an instrument for synthesizing data appealed to me. Her methodological advice for advancing the writing research also resonated with my decades of writing experience—"Keep butt in chair" (Adams et al., 2015, p. 69). Adams et al. (2015) further argue that "Autoethnographic stories are artistic and analytic demonstrations of how we come to know, name, and interpret personal and cultural experience" (2015, p. 1). Since the processing of data is done in the writing, autoethnography is an excellent fit for those of us in composition studies.

The Emergence of Categories: Thematizing the Texts

Now how does autoethnography work in practice? Autoethnography is radically inductive. The categories and the themes of the study emerge from the writing explorations. Written reflection emerges in a dialectic that alternates between the collection of data (written fieldnotes, documents, journals, other written ephemera) and the theorizing of that data on its own terms. Adams et al. (2015) call this theorizing of data *thematizing* (p. 77). It entails a continual rereading of this mass of writing, and then reflecting in writing that looks for themes, which may be signaled by repeated words, "images, phrases, and/or experiences" (Adams et al., 2015, p. 77).

In my autoethnography of retirement, the dissonance I felt and wrote about went something like this: here I am, both a person who has used literacy well for decades and an expert on literacy, and I am finding the experience of literacy in the employment-retirement transition to be overwhelming. At first, I tried coding my fieldnotes and journals but when I reflected on this, I noted that more was involved than just the language. I needed to go deeper. For instance, in one journal entry I wrote in my fieldnotes in January 2019:

> Why am I—*still*—overwhelmed. Here I am, a competent if not very successful writer with a Ph.D. in writing for crying out loud and I am, for the first time since I took freshman composition, constantly feeling overwhelmed. At bottom, it is only writing. So what is the problem? Why is this the hardest thing I have done since writing the dissertation? Or being a physics major my freshman year? What is going on here? What are the cultural forces that I am encountering that are making a literate person—one might argue an extremely literate person—into nearly a nonliterate?

Afterward, I noted the following reflections/ideas about my experiences with taking freshman composition, writing the dissertation, and being a physics major my freshman year. Each of these ideas came in a flash, spontaneously, after extensive pondering, probing, study, and writing as I reflected on these experiences from fifty years ago. If you would have asked me before I wrote them, was freshman composition overwhelming? Was your dissertation hard? Was being a physics major freshman year difficult? My immediate and truthful first response would be to say no, not really. I was—and am—surprised by this. After further thought, I decided that, yes, back then, I guess these were crises. I guess I was overwhelmed. That they all come from school bureaucratic experience is significant too—the interplay of the social and individual again. These experiences were also complicated by social class since I am a first-generation college student and first-generation Ph.D.

After this realization I began to question my initial plan to study this transitional process by collecting the written bureaucratic forms I had to fill out in order to receive a retirement income and retirement healthcare. Literacy initially was delimited by the institutional bureaucratic forms since that was the new material that might account for my dissonance. But in my ongoing research, it became clear that the focus on the forms which I was required to fill out was not accounting for what I was experiencing. It was not really simply the strangeness of the forms alone, but also the high stakes, under-the-gun deadlines (like being a first-generation college student from the working class). It was the entire culture of using literacy to navigate the bureaucracies at the same time as I was trying to imagine a new way of life and a new identity (like being a first-generation college student). It was navigating the social and individual through language—perhaps the primary theme of my work on the Vygotsky school over four decades (Leontiev & Leontiev, 1959; Zebroski, 1994). In this case that theme of being overwhelmed was embodied not only in my felt sense, but also in the almost ontological categories at work in the study—the individual (me) and the social (many bureaucracies both private and public, for-profit and for-service). Language connected and reconstructed both.

I also discovered the need to expand my literacy categories to include the copious marginalia I made on documents to try to get the forms right. Marginalia, notes, to-do lists, reminders, even calendars (I had three) were often crucial in my understanding of this culture of bureaucracies as well as for supporting my plans to go forward. But those ephemera were part and parcel of the reading I was doing of the overwhelming and confusing forms, websites, documents and materials about retirement being sent to me. That marginalia was also part and parcel of the phone calls I made. So then to my analysis of writing and reading, I had to add oralities such as navigating numerous toll-free numbers. Thus, the literacy categories for this autoethnography came out of the developing writing I did and the sense of whether those categories were addressing the original and ongoing dissonance.

FINDINGS: AGENTS, AGENCIES, LITERACY GENRES

What follows are some of the findings that resulted from the autoethnographic process described in the last section. From these data and by linking this study with the work in rhetoric and composition on literacy, one can tentatively draw the following conclusions.

1. The literacies were addressed to multiple organizations simultaneously. As Naftzinger (this volume) argues, what is "named" as literacy by the participants in this process—both the individual applying for retirement and the organizations to which he is applying—becomes critical, and is often a site of confusion which disrupts the successful end of the process.

2. There was collaborative writing only twice in the process, when the HR director and later the Social Security agent filled out crucial forms with me. This lack of collaboration is distinctly different from much professional writing which is multi-authored or authored under the authority of a committee or team or agency. This anti-collaborative writing seems to be linked to the push by corporations to cut labor costs by Taylorizing all functions to "machines"—that is cutting human labor by reducing it to small, lock step operations that can be digitized by software, hardware, online sites, "My Accounts," and toll-free numbers. Cutting out human labor—by automating labor—puts all of the burden on the consumer. Through Taylorization, we are essentially doing for free what had been the corporation's job.

3. The literacies were all nonfiction, prosaic, and mostly ephemeral. This study, then, provides evidence that the view that the primary literacy of senior citizens is creative writing about their lives is inaccurate.

4. The literacies were radically determined by the imperatives of late capitalism. I shall have more to say about this in my conclusion. For now, let me note that these literacies are situated in a specific time in history and in a specific culture. These locations largely shape what we see as and call "literacy" (see Naftzinger, this volume). Even within a short period—say, since the 1970s—literacy under influence of changing sociohistorical forces has become a radically different activity than it was. From a Marxist view, the changing mode of production changes literacy.

5. The literacies were highly interdependent. There was no Humana care without Medicare B. There was no Social Security without the four HR documents, etc. This interrelatedness made it extremely difficult for *the writer alone* to intervene successfully in the cycle without another person's help (in this case, Social Security Agent Y.)

6. The most frequent mode of writing, reading, and speaking involved a constant, dialectical shifting between handwriting and electronic writing. This is strong evidence of the multi-modal nature of literacies, but also of the socially and historically specific nature of that multi-modality. I would also suggest this study points to one source of inequality in the US in 2020. Multi-modal literacies are classist in that such literacies almost always assume possession of and training in not only high-tech machines like smart phones, laptops, and inter-

net access, but also in the creative workarounds required to make any of these multi-modal-ist, machine-centric literacies work. A person who does not have the money to buy and use the newest of these machines and services—smart phones go for up to $1000 with each new model/edition—is simply out of the loop and out of luck.

7. The literacies in the bureaucracies were mostly unsupported by alternative tools and redundancy in the systems. (Again, Social Security and Medicare were exceptions.) There was little help aside from the toll-free numbers, some of which were very difficult to access. The online literacies with the exception of Social Security were one-shot, product based, and did not allow for saving and later revision. In this respect, the corporate online literacies were a lot like the so-called literacies of high stakes testing used in the public schools. By radically restricting help in the process, by making literacy into a one-shot, no revision, lock step, high stakes act—again, high stakes defined in this case as a matter of life (income) and death (healthcare), these corporate pre-retirement literacies are anti-democratic and anti-egalitarian.

8. Personal journals, informants, and face-to-face speech were essential in the regulation of the process over four months and in my own self-regulation of life over a much longer period in the transition. My personal journals were especially crucial and were, in fact, a matrix of the other writing—i.e., they were expressive in the original sense of that term (Britton et al., 1975). My journals in this period changed from a focus on identity to a focus on self-regulation and success in completing the literacy and retirement goals.

9. As Nancy Mack (personal communication) importantly notes, at the very moment that senior citizens are forced to narrow their activities—mostly by institutions and cultural conventions but also by physical limitations—they are also required by the collectives (mostly corporate) that govern our lives (income, healthcare, economic transactions, and social media) to use entirely new (and unsupported) technologies and literacies. Even for academics, I would add that the very electronic media on which this process is so reliant are designed by large, profit-making, unregulated technology giants for younger people who rarely have to deal with issues of arthritis or failing eyesight as they engage technologies which are hypersensitive to touch and hard to see. I bought a brand-new laptop six months before this entire retirement process began and it was not in any way designed to be sensitive to these or other age-linked ability/disability issues.

A MARXIST CONCLUSION

This study is a both Vygotskian and a lifespan developmental contribution to literacy. Of course, Vygotsky himself did not do any studies that we can now call lifespan development psychology. Yet in his classic work, *Thought and Language*, Vygotsky (2012) puts forward a genetic, that is an historical psychology which studies both the social and individual histories. This is one reason he chose the term *sociohistorical*. Vygotsky says that

> [o]nce we acknowledge the historical character of verbal thought, we must consider it subject to all the premises of historical materialism, which are valid for any historical phenomenon in human society. It is only to be expected that at this level the development of behavior will essentially be governed *by the general laws of the historical development of human society*. (p. 101; my emphasis)

What this means is that individual human capacities, in dialectic with social development, are in lifelong or life span development. Markova (1979) later acknowledges this and uses it to critique the lack of Vygotskian studies on later life development. She notes that:

> Almost no studies have been carried out on the dynamics of speech development in the young person after he has finished school. . . . As B.G. Aman'ev (1972) has justifiably noted, until recently, maturity was regarded as the opposite to developmental, as a period of stabilization. But there is no doubt that the aspect of the individual's psychology undergoes fundamental changes during the period from 18–60 and beyond. [I]n later maturity language activity becomes a tool of the individual in his endeavors to articulate his own experience, remember it, and pass it on to others (the writing of memoirs, conversations with younger people). (p. 26)

Clearly Markova (1979), working in a Vygotskian framework, is calling for the study of life-long development here. While she does not use the term lifespan development per se, her critique, based on Vygotsky's theory, suggests that research throughout the lifespan is the next step. The history of the term lifespan development in U.S. research seems to go back to a series of the West Virginia Conferences on lifespan development which were held in the late 1960s and 1970s (Goulet & Balthes, 1970; Hooper 1970), when Markova's work was just occurring. Further, Urie Bronfenbrenner's (1974) work anticipates lifespan development research and links Vygotskian theory with U.S.S.R. schooling through the person of A. N. Leontiev. Finally, we see a later moment of this trajectory of "Vygotskian life span" research in an explicit "neo-Vygotskian approach" to lifespan development in Y. Karpov's (2003, p. 238) work.

Vygotsky would argue that literacy study has to begin with historicized individual and social experience. This means that we must begin with the fact that my writing was for retirement, in Texas, in the US, in 2018. The exigence of late capitalism is necessarily part of the study. One crucial change from the generation immediately before me is the absence of retirement options for many of the generation now working. During high Fordist capitalism, 80 percent of employers offered retirement pensions and retirement healthcare; now only about 50 percent of workers have such options (Pew Trusts, 2018). Retirees are then forced to develop new retirement literacies in response.

Vygotsky built his psychology on Marx (Ratner & Silva, 2017). Perhaps the central concept for Marx is labor, by which he means all human activity that creates the world. Over the ages, labor has been organized radically differently. In the capitalist era, labor in the workplace (especially) is appropriated, that is, part of the worker's labor in the workplace is taken (invisibly) by capital. Marx shows and recent empirical research (e.g., Picketty, 2015) supports the fact that unregulated capitalism creates increasing inequality because it must increasingly cut labor or appropriate more surplus value from all workers. And capital must increasingly cut labor to maintain profits in competition in the market. The post-Reagan years from 1980 to the present are classic in this process of cutting labor, in this case mostly through deregulation and privatization.

My deployed literacies all occur in the context of this late neoliberal capitalism; these cuts in and appropriation of labor have large effects on the tools, process, and embodiment of the literacies of pre-retirement. The universal use of "My Accounts" and toll-free numbers, as well as the Taylorization (i.e., dividing labor into small, lock-step tasks that are automated by machines) of all digital transactions and of the entire process, and the relative lack of backup or face-to-face options all of which add to the costs of labor, are part of Post-Fordist late capitalism. The fact that only the public-sector agency—Social Security—actually offered options for interaction underscores the role of capitalism in this study. The public, through their elected representatives, has made it clear that they want access to Social Security to be easier and universal; corporations respond first to the extraction of surplus value from labor—or simply profit. In contrast, Social Security has some leeway to add labor power—to add workers to respond to the public's needs. Corporations will only add labor power if there is a looming consequence of a drastically reduced profit if they do not. In a wider perspective, the idea pervasive in current research that increasing longevity is a fact across the globe is only one pole of the dialectic; the fact is that although there have been some advances in science and health for the privileged few, the Centers for Disease Control notes at this very moment the average number of years most Americans live has actually decreased for the first time in a century—not unrelated to the increasing economic inequality created by forty years of Post-Reagan, Post-Fordist economics (Bernstein, 2018; Devitt, 2018). Further, average workplaces (including academic workplaces) are increasingly toxic, killing or sickening environments (see Pfeffer, 2010, who is not a Marxist, but a corporate adviser who works at Stanford Business School). At some level workers are well aware of all of this. But they are also so overworked—worked to death—they have no time to reflect on these changes. At least until it is too late, or they have the privilege to retire.

As I exit from the capitalist appropriation in workplace labor, I do have the privilege and luxury of writing and studying and doing other things outside of the paperwork empire and dysfunctional workplace. The literacy practices that have made this possible must always be remembered as products of the concrete history described above, shaped in the last instance by a virulent capitalism. I look forward to more study of writing under capitalism.

REFERENCES

Adams, T., Jones, S. & C. Ellis (Eds). (2015). *Autoethnography: Understanding qualitative research*. Oxford University Press.
Bateson, M. (2010). *Composing a further life: The age of active wisdom*. Vintage Books.
Bernstein, L. (2018, November 29). U.S. life span expectancy declines again, a dismal trend not seen since World War I. *Washington Post*.
Boyland, R. & Orbe M. (Eds.). (2014). *Critical autoethnography: Intersecting cultural identities in everyday life*. Routledge.
Britton, J., Burgess, T., Marin, N., McCleod, A. & Rosen, H. (Eds.). (1975). *The development of writing abilities (11–18)*. Macmillan Education.
Bronfenbrenner, U. (1974). *Two worlds of childhood*. Penguin.
Charmaz, K. (2005). Grounded theory in the 21st Century: Applications for advancing social justice studies. In N. Denzin & Y. Lincoln (Eds.), *Handbook of qualitative research* (3rd ed., pp. 507–535). Sage.
Devitt, M. (2018). CDC data show U.S. life expectancy continues to decline. *American Academy of Family Physicians*. https://www.aafp.org/news/health-of-the-public/20181210lifeexpectdrop.html.
Geertz, C. (1973). *The interpretation of culture*. Basic Books.
Gorman. T. (2017). *Growing up working class. Hidden injuries and the development of angry white men and women*. Palgrave Macmillan.
Goulet, L. R. & P. B. Balthes (Eds.). (1970). *Life-span developmental psychology: Research and theory*. Academic Press.
Hall, D. & M. Harker. (2018). Coming of age in the era of acceleration: Rethinking literacy narratives as pedagogies of lifelong learning. *Literacy and Composition Studies, 6*(2), 151–169.
Hartwell, P. (1985). Grammar, grammars, and the teaching of grammar. *College English, 47*(2), 105–127.

Hermann, A. (Ed.). (2017). *Organizational autoethnographies: Power and identities in our working lives.* Routledge.

Hooper, F. H. (1970). The West Virginia University conference on life-span developmental psychology. *Human Development, 13,* 53–60.

Hymes, D. (Ed.) (1974). *Reinventing anthropology.* Vintage Books.

Karpov, Y. (2003). Development through the lifespan: a neo-Vygotskian approach. In A. Kozulin, B. Gindis, V. Ageyev & S. Miller (Eds.), *Learning in doing: Vygotsky's educational theory in cultural context* (pp. 138–155). Cambridge University Press.

Lee, S. (in press). Constructing a transnational-multilingual teacher subjectivity in a first-year writing class: An autoethnography. In R. Jackson & J. Grutsch McKinney (Eds.), *Self+culture+writing: Autoethnography for/as writing studies.* Utah State University Press.

Leontiev, A. N. & A. A. Leontiev. (1959). The social and individual in language. *Language and Speech, 2,* 193–204.

Lockenhoff, C. E. (2012). Understanding retirement: The promise of life-span developmental frameworks. *European Journal of Ageing, 9*(3), 227–231.

Markova, A. (1979). *The Teaching and mastery of language.* M. E. Sharpe.

Mlynarczyk, R. (2018). Making meaning in (and of) old age: The value of lifelong literacy. *Literacy and Composition Studies, 6*(2), 36–58.

Park, J. & B. Brenna. (2015). The value of writing for senior citizen writers. *Language and Literacy, 17*(3),100–114.

Pew Trusts. (2018). Retirement plan access across the generations. https://www.pew trusts.org/en/research-and-analysis/issue-briefs/2017/02/retirement-plan-access-and-participation-across-generations.

Pfeffer, J. (2010). *Dying for a paycheck.* Harper Collins.

Phelps, L. (2018). Afterward—horizons of transformation: When age, literacy, and scholarship meet. *Literacy and Composition Studies, 6*(2), 170–182.

Piketty, T. & A. Goldhammer. (2014). Capital in the twenty-first century. Harvard University Press.

Ratner, C. & D. Silva (Eds.) (2017). *Vygotsky and Marx: Towards a Marxist psychology.* Routledge.

Spradley, J. & D. McCurdy. (1972). *The cultural experience: Ethnography in complex society.* Science Research Associates.

Volosinov, V. (1986). *Marxism and the philosophy of language.* Harvard University Press.

Vygotsky, L. (2012). *Thought and language.* MIT Press.

Winterowd, R. (2007). *Senior citizens writing.* Parlor Press.

Zebroski, J. (1986). The uses of theory: a Vygotskian approach to composition. *The Writing Instructor, 5*(2), 57–65.

Zebroski, J. (1994). *Thinking through theory: Vygotskian perspectives on the teaching of writing.* Boynton Cook/Heinemann.

Zebroski, J. & N. Mack. (1992). Ethnographic writing for critical consciousness. In C. M. Hurlbert & S. Totten (Eds.), *Social issues in the teaching of English* (pp. 196–205). National Council of Teachers of English.

CHAPTER 10.
THE RELATIONS AMONG THE DEVELOPMENT OF WRITTEN LANGUAGE AND EXECUTIVE FUNCTIONS FOR CHILDREN IN ELEMENTARY SCHOOL

Lara-Jeane C. Costa
Jeffrey A. Greene
Stephen R. Hooper
University of North Carolina at Chapel Hill

Writing is a critical skill that is necessary for success in school, the workplace, and within society (Bazerman et al., 2018; Graham & Harris, 2005)—across the lifespan. Unfortunately, writing problems for students in the US are significant. According to the 2011 National Assessment of Educational Progress (NAEP) writing report, a mere 27 percent of eighth and 12th grade students scored at or above the proficient level (NAEP, 2012). Furthermore, this percentage has not changed significantly from previous reports in 2007 and 2002.

The NAEP data are indicative of a number of potential concerns including the nature and quality of writing instruction, the developmental appropriateness of that instruction, and trends in students' cognitive capabilities. The unsettling fact is that a student who cannot write at the proficient level cannot create a text that clearly accomplishes its communicative purpose, that is coherent and well structured, or that includes appropriate connections and transitions (National Center for Education Statistics, 2012). This difficulty may be attributable to the fact that writing is complex (Bazerman et al., 2018) and, as such, it requires the coordination of multiple skills including organization, transcription, orthographic and mechanical knowledge, understanding of audience, executive functions (EF), and social context (Graham, 2018; Kim & Schatschneider, 2017). Further complication comes from the fact that writing develops across the lifespan with variations among people and the nature of the communication demanded by a particular task or situation. To study these complex skills

DOI: https://doi.org/10.37514/PER-B.2020.1053.2.10

and developmental trajectories, researchers must gather data regarding children's writing in environments that are easily accessible with an abundance of data collection opportunities where the phenomena of interest play a central role in children's cognitive, social, and identity development (i.e., strategic research sites; Bazerman, 2008).

The primary purpose of this study was to investigate the complexities of writing development, specifically the individual and interactive developmental trajectories of EF and writing performance, by using longitudinal methodology and associated statistical strategies in a strategic research site: elementary classrooms where educators were focused upon initiating children into the practice and identity of writing. The elementary school developmental period for children is fraught with demanding changes in skills and processing (Zins & Hooper, 2012), which in turn affect children's later performance and identification as a "writer." For instance, children in kindergarten are asked to generate simple sentences, whereas by fifth grade these same children must be able to write reports and make arguments. How these functions evolve over time and how the various factors interact with one another at different developmental time points remain challenging to understand and study.

WRITING

As noted in the chapters in this volume, when writing a person must have an idea, understand the meaning of symbols used to express the idea (e.g., hieroglyphics, Roman alphabet), translate the idea to symbols, and have the capability to produce the symbols. As children develop the ability to hear and manipulate units of sound (e.g., phonemes) and acquire knowledge that letters and letter groups are used to represent sounds (i.e., alphabetic principle), they apply this knowledge to writing. To write successfully, writers need to comprehend the structure (i.e., sentence, paragraph, and text), content (i.e., ideas and their relationships), and purpose (i.e., writer's goals and audience) of the writing process (Collins & Gentner, 1980).

Hayes and Flower (1986) described planning, translating, and reviewing as the three most important cognitive processes used to produce written output. Specifically, the writer generates and organizes ideas, and then sets goals during the planning process, followed by sentence generation (i.e., translating ideas into sentences), reviewing, and editing. Whereas later in development students can self-regulate their own writing, in early years students rely on support from others to enact basic cognitive processes necessary for writing, such as EF (e.g., attention, planning; Berninger & Amtmann, 2003). At the elementary age, educators have the optimal opportunity to provide instruction and interventions for students who need assistance in developing effective writing skills, including those related to EF. In later grade levels, it is assumed that students have internalized these skills; therefore, those students who have acquired ineffective skills must not only acquire skills that are more effective but, perhaps, also unlearn ineffective ones.

EXECUTIVE FUNCTIONS

Numerous definitions of EF have been proposed as well as several models, theories, and frameworks (e.g., Miyake et al., 2000; Pennington et al., 1996; Zelazo et al., 1997). Researchers have advanced theory and empirical evidence for a variety of EF related to writing including working memory, sustained attention, inhibitory control, and planning (Pennington et al., 1996; Roberts & Pennington, 1996; Zelazo et al., 2003; Zelazo et al.; 2010). Even though none of these researchers explicated sustained attention in their models, Pennington suggested that attentional control is an executive function behavior as well. They posited the purpose of executive functioning was to enable a process to solve a problem, and explained that success occurs through creating an accurate mental representation of the task and then generating a plan to execute that task.

RELATIONS AMONG EXECUTIVE FUNCTIONS AND WRITING

As Bazerman et al. (2018) highlighted, writing development influences and is influenced by the development of a range of factors, including EF, perhaps implicating a bidirectional relationship for these factors, as well as developmental interactions. Research to date has demonstrated various relations between written language and cognitive (McCutchen, 2006), perceptual-motor (Graham & Harris, 2005), and linguistic functions (Berninger et al., 2006). Based on the Not-So-Simple View of Writing model (Berninger & Winn, 2006), and earlier work (Kellogg, 1996), EF are important contributors to the development of written language. EF are associated with handwriting automaticity, which requires orthographic-motor integration and processing speed, as well as with high-level composing (Altemeier et al., 2008). In particular, the EF components of attention, inhibitory control, planning, and working memory have been linked to writing (Hooper et al., 2011).

Altemeier et al. (2008) examined how performance changed on three EF tasks in elementary-aged students using a cross-sectional design. They found that typically developing writers showed steady improvement on an inhibition task from first to fifth grade, but switching and inhibition performance scores increased from first to fourth grade and then leveled off. In addition, their results suggested EF tasks contributed to spelling and written language. Hooper et al. (2011) also addressed the relations between writing and EF and concluded that language-related functions and EF were more highly associated with written language and spelling than fine-motor functions. Both of these studies found strong relations between EF and written language, but more research is needed regarding how the relationship between EF and writing performance changes over time. In particular, more research is needed regarding the trajectory of EF growth and writing performance over time. Most researchers have posited a consistent linear growth trajectory for both EF and writing performance, but Altemeier et al.'s (2008) findings regarding a leveling of development suggest it is important to investigate whether that growth is more curved than linear. A clear understanding of the trajectory of growth in EF and writing over time (i.e., linear versus curved) is necessary to subsequently examine how the growth in one might relate to the growth in the other.

CURRENT STUDY

Given the apparent importance of EF to written language in school-age children (Altemeier et al., 2008; Hooper et al., 2011), for this study we aimed to examine one key gap in the literature; namely, the relations among EF, writing skills, and their development over time. We used longitudinal data and contemporary statistical strategies, including latent growth curve analysis, to answer the following research questions: (1) Does EF performance over time grow in a linear or curvilinear manner? Does writing performance over time grow in a linear or curvilinear manner? (2) How do EF and writing performance relate to each other at each time point, as well as across time points?

METHODS

Participants

Two hundred five students from seven elementary schools in one suburban-rural school system in the southeastern US participated in this study. Each of these students had a primary placement in the regular education setting, completed kindergarten, and spoke English as a primary language. Of these students, 117 (57%) were male and 88 (43%) were female, and their ages ranged from 6 years 3 months to 7 years 4 months at the time of recruitment (i.e., first grade). Almost three-quarters (74%) of the students were of European American ethnicity, 20 percent were African-American, 4 percent were multi-racial, and 1 percent were Native American and Asian American (see Table 10.1). The students participated in the study from first to fourth grade. Of the 205 students, 67 were typically developing writers, and 138 struggled with written language. As part of the larger study, the participants who were identified as struggling writers were randomly assigned to either a treatment group ($n = 68$) or control condition ($n = 70$). It is important to note that all of the classrooms were following the state curriculum for writing instruction such that all students were receiving the same type and amount of instruction for writing skills development in the regular classroom setting, thus making this an effective strategic research site.

Table 10.1. Participants' Demographic Profile

	Sample f (%)	SWC f (%)	SWT f (%)	TDW f (%)
1st graders ages[a]	205	70	68	67
6	46 (22.4)	17 (24.3)	14 (20.6)	15 (22.4)
7	149 (72.7)	49 (70.0)	52 (76.5)	48 (71.6)
8	10 (4.9)	4 (5.7)	2 (2.9)	4 (6.0)
2nd graders ages[a]	200	68	67	65
7	44 (22)	15 (22.1)	14 (20.9)	15 (23.1)
8	145 (72.5)	49 (72.1)	50 (74.6)	46 (70.8)
9	11 (5.5)	4 (5.9)	3 (4.5)	4 (6.2)
3rd graders ages[a]	189	64	65	60
8	46 (24.3)	16 (25)	14 (21.5)	16 (26.7)
9	132 (69.9)	44 (68.8)	48 (73.9)	40 (66.7)
10	11 (5.8)	4 (6.3)	3 (4.6)	4 (6.7)
4th graders ages[a]	179	62	60	57
9	40 (7.1)	14 (22.6)	11 (18.3)	15 (26.3)
10	129 (72.1)	44 (70.1)	46 (76.7)	39 (68.4)
11	10 (5.6)	4 (6.5)	3 (5.0)	3 (5.3)
Female	88 (42.9)	27 (38.6)	27 (39.7)	34 (50.8)
Ethnicity 1				
Asian	2 (1.0)	0 (0)	0 (0)	2 (3.0)
Black	40 (19.5)	14 (20.0)	17 (25)	9 (13.4)

163

	Sample f (%)	SWC f (%)	SWT f (%)	TDW f (%)
Ethnicity 1 (Continued)				
2 or More Races	9 (4.4)	3 (4.3)	4 (5.9)	2 (3)
Native American	2 (1.0)	1 (1.4)	1 (1.5)	0 (0)
White	152 (74.1)	52 (74.3)	46 (67.7)	54 (80.6)
Ethnicity 2				
Hispanic or Latino	36 (17.6)	7 (1.0)	12 (1.8)	7 (1.0)
School				
School 1	37 (18.1)	15 (21.4)	9 (13.2)	13 (19.4)
School 2	17 (8.3)	6 (8.6)	7 (10.3)	4 (6.0)
School 3	48 (23.4)	19 (27.1)	16 (23.5)	13 (19.4)
School 4	24 (11.7)	9 (12.9)	10 (14.7)	5 (7.5)
School 5	29 (14.2)	10 (14.3)	10 (14.7)	9 (13.4)
School 6	24 (11.7)	8 (11.4)	8 (11.8)	8 (11.9)
School 7	24 (11.7)	2 (2.9)	8 (11.8)	14 (20.0)
Out of County	2 (1.0)	1 (1.4)	0 (0)	1 (1.5)
Retained	15	6	7	2
Retained 2nd grade	5	5	0	0
Retained 3rd grade	7	1	4	2
Retained 4th grade	3	0	3	0
Mother's Education				
No HS diploma	18 (10.1)	6 (10.7)	9 (14.5)	3 (5.0)
HS diploma	77 (43.3)	18 (32.1)	36 (58.1)	23 (38.3)
Associates or College Degree	83 (46.6)	32 (57.1)	17 (27.4)	34 (56.7)

Note: SWC = struggling writers control group; SWT = struggling writers treatment group; TDW = typically developing writers group.

[a] *ages rounded to the closest year.*

Procedure

For the initial screening into the study, students in each of the first-grade classes were administered the Wechsler Individual Achievement Test (WIAT II) Written Expression Subtest and, once enrolled in the study, they participated in a battery of cognitive measures. The measures were divided into two administration blocks to minimize order effects (e.g., fatigue, learning). After the first year of the project, three assessments were changed per school system request because their school psychologists were using the measures. After the initial screening, all participants were administered a battery of neuropsychological and cognitive assessments by trained research assistants and graduate students. All of the measures can be seen in Table 10.2.

Table 10.2. Measures

Construct	Measure	Task
Written Language	Wechsler Individual Achievement Test—Second Edition form A (WIAT-II; Wechsler, 2002)	Written word fluency from the Written Expression subtest Spelling Subtest
	Process Assessment of the Learner: Test Battery for Reading and Writing (PAL; Berninger, 2001)	Timed Alphabet-writing
EF: Planning	Woodcock Johnson-III Test of Cognitive Abilities (WJ-III; Woodcock et al., 2001)	Planning subtest
EF: Sustained attention and Inhibitory control	Vigil Continuous Performance Test (Vigil CPT; Psychological Corporation, 1998)	Errors of Omission Errors of Commission
EF: Working Memory	The Wechsler Intelligence Scale for Children IV Integrated (WISC-IV I; Wechsler et al., 2004)	Spatial Span Backward

The results from the initial assessments were used to group students as typically developing writers (TDW) or struggling writers (SW), the latter group defined by scores falling in the bottom quartile for grade placement. Then, SW students were randomly assigned to either a treatment or control condition. Therefore, group status (GS) consisted of three categories: TDW, struggling writers in the treatment group (SWT), and struggling writers in the control group (SWC). For this study, we were not interested in testing differences across group status or school, therefore we controlled for these covariates in our analyses.

Data Analysis

We used latent growth curve analysis to investigate our research questions. Our models included summed scores of the observed variables (i.e., raw scores) to represent written language and EF, with latent factors (i.e., unobserved variables) representing initial starting point (i.e., intercept) and growth over time (i.e., slope). Figure 10.1 shows our hypothesized model. All results were examined for outliers, influential cases, and normality.

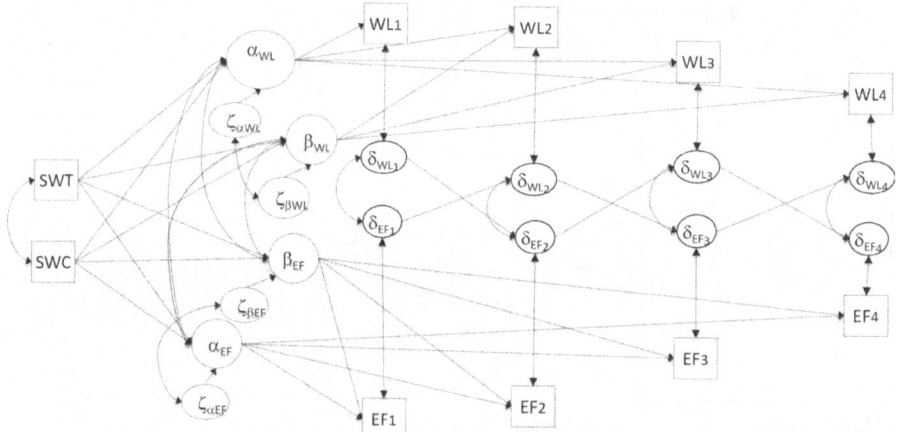

Figure 10.1. Final model. WL = Written Language, EF = Executive Functions, SWT = struggling writers' treatment, SWC = struggling writers control.

Research Question 1. Does EF performance over time grow in a linear or curvilinear manner? Does writing performance over time grow in a linear or curvilinear manner?

Our longitudinal design allowed us to model each participant's specific, individual growth in both written language and EF over multiple time points, as opposed to inferring such growth using different participants at different time points, as in a cross-sectional design. The former captures actual intraindividual change in writing performance and EF over multiple time points, whereas the latter requires the unlikely assumption that different participants' scores at each time point accurately represent actual intraindividual change.

Following accepted methods for quantitative analysis of writing phenomena (see Zajic et al., this volume), we conducted latent growth curve analyses in a structural equation model (SEM) framework to examine the change over time of written language and EF scores. We chose to estimate latent growth curve models (LGCMs) over other traditional repeated measures statistical techniques (e.g., Analysis of Variance) for several reasons. First, ANOVA techniques require unlikely assumptions regarding the equivalence of change over equidistant multiple time points, cannot account for missing data at any time point, and do not account for the error inherent in any measure. On the other hand, LGCM analyses do not have these restrictive assumptions, can accommodate missing data, and allow for better measurement of the latent constructs by disattenuating measurement error (Hancock et al., 2013). LGCM analyses estimate an initial starting point (i.e., intercept), growth over time (i.e., slope), and residuals. LGCM analyses are a good option for modeling growth as they capture intra- as well as inter-individual variability in EF and writing performance from a quantitative perspective.

We evaluated the adequacy of model fit with the data using the chi-square test statistic and other fit indices. The chi-square test statistic is the oldest fit measure in SEM, although many researchers do not rely exclusively on this measure because this statistic is sensitive to sample size and excessive kurtosis (i.e., multivariate distributions of observed variables; Bollen & Curran, 2006; Hox, 2010). Thus, model fit was evaluated based upon several criteria including the chi-square test statistic, as well as several data-model fit indices including the Comparative Fit index (CFI), the root mean squared error of approximation (RMSEA), p of close fit (PCLOSE), and the standard root mean square residual (SRMR). A statistically non-significant chi-square test statistic indicated adequate data-model fit. CFI values greater than .90 were considered adequate and values greater than .95 were considered good. RMSEA values were examined using a 90 percent confidence interval (CI). Confidence intervals whose lower value was no higher than .05 and upper value was less than .08 were considered good. PCLOSE is a measure that provides a one-sided test that the RMSEA is less than 0.05. If the PCLOSE value was greater than .05 the data-model was considered good. SRMR values less than .08 were considered indicators of good fit (Hu & Bentler, 1999).

Unconditional LGCMs. As an initial attempt to model participants' writing performance and EF growth trajectories, we estimated models without covariates (i.e., unconditional LGMs). First, an intercept-only model and a linear LGCM were estimated and compared. When the linear model demonstrated better fit to the data than the intercept only model, then the linear model was compared to a curvilinear model. Per Zajic et al., (this volume) models that resulted in the best fit to the data were used in subsequent analyses.

Conditional LGCMs. Next, we included covariates in the LGCMs to control for differences in the growth parameters of the latent factors as a function of school and GS, treating both as time-invariant covariates (TIC), given each was a person-specific variable that did not change over the course of the study. Both were used as control variables, thus differences in GS and school were not interpreted. Specifically, we modeled school and GS as predictors with equal factor variances, factor covariances, and time-specific error variances, where the functional forms of the model were equal across groups (Bollen & Curran, 2006).

Research Question 2. How do EF and writing performance relate to each other at each time point, as well as across time points?

To answer our second research question, we conducted several analyses. First, we regressed the constructs on each other across time points to determine whether scores at one time point on a construct predicted scores on the other construct at the subsequent time point. Next, we correlated the latent growth parameters (e.g., written language intercept with EF slope) to determine the relations between written language and EF. In addition, we estimated a "nonstandard effect" (Curran et al., 2012, p. 243) by correlating the time-specific residual of written language with the time-specific residual of EF (Figure 13.1) to determine if there were within-person effects.

With this plan, we were able to determine the relations between written language and EF beyond systematic growth from first to fourth grade. The interpretation of these effects can be problematic given it is conceivable that the constructs could exert a within-person and a between person effect, only a between person effect, only a within person effect, or none of the above (Curran et al., 2012). Thus, we reported the results for each effect as necessary. For instance, EF may influence the rate of growth for written language for a participant, and simultaneously influence differences in the growth trajectories across individuals.

RESULTS

Descriptive Statistics

The results presented in Table 10.3 suggested that the means and standard deviations were as expected for this sample. However, a few of the skewness and kurtosis values for the individual measures (see Costa, 2014) were out of normal range (i.e., skewness values whose absolute values were less than two and kurtosis values less than seven; Kline, 2005). Based on the results of the Shapiro-Wilk W test, we rejected the null hypothesis that all of the variables were normally distributed. After consideration of the initial descriptive statistics and tests of univariate normality, we decided to use robust estimation techniques in our analyses. We used a resampling method (i.e., bootstrap) to estimate standard errors and confidence intervals that are robust to non-normality (Kolenikov & Bollen, 2012). This is beneficial because the bootstrapped distribution (i.e., sampled from the empirical distribution of the observed data) of each parameter estimate is used to determine the confidence intervals. These values take the non-normality of the parameter estimate distribution into account. The descriptive statistics for the individual measures comprising the summed scores and correlation matrix of all the continuous variables can be found in Costa (2014).

Table 10.3. Sample Statistics for Summed Variables

Construct	Time point	N	M	SD	Min	Max
Written Language	1	205	17.61	7.40	0	36
	2	200	26.31	7.15	3	44
	3	189	31.99	7.87	6	53
	4	179	36.28	9.64	3	59
Executive Functions	1	202	11.07	2.26	6.82	19
	2	200	12.64	2.20	6.83	18.17
	3	188	14.18	2.18	6.16	19.37
	4	176	14.94	2.24	7.32	19.42

Research Question 1

First, we tested several models to determine the type of growth over time (i.e., linear or curvilinear) in both written language and EF. Once this was determined for written language and EF, we conducted additional analyses to control for group status and school. Here we provide a summary of this modeling; detailed results can be found in Costa (2014).

Written language. We found the written language linear model had the best fit with the data [$\chi^2(df)$ = 228.58 (121), bootstrap p-value = 0.06, CFI = 0.92, SRMR = 0.06]. The parameter estimates and p-values for the unconditional model suggested that participants' initial written language scores significantly differed ($p < 0.001$), but not their rate of growth (i.e., slope variance; $p > 0.05$). Group and school differences were not the focus of this study, but they were included in the models as covariates to control for their effects. Overall, we did not find school effects, but the groups did differ in their initial scores and growth trajectory. We controlled for these differences in all subsequent models.

Executive functions. After removing some of the modeling restrictions, the preponderance of evidence (i.e., data-model fit results) supported a nonlinear LGCM. Thus, we concluded that a positive nonlinear model best represented the growth trajectory of EF for students from first grade to fourth grade after controlling for school [$\chi^2(df)$ = 305.59 (203), bootstrap p-value = 0.24, RMSEA (PCLOSE) = 0.05 (0.51), RMSEA CI = 0.04–0.06].

Group and school differences were included in the models as covariates to control for their effects. Overall, we did not find school effects. The groups did differ in their initial scores but not in their growth trajectory. We controlled for these differences in all subsequent models.

Research Question 2

Final LGCM. We estimated several models, none of which we deemed to have good fit with the data (Costa, 2014), thus any interpretation of these results should be done with caution. The final model was selected as the most interpretable model [$\chi^2(df)$ = 132.70 (29), bootstrap p-value <0.001, RMSEA (PCLOSE) = 0.132 (<0.001), RMSEA CI = 0.11–0.15, CFI = 0.90, SRMR = 0.09].

A diagram of the final model can be seen in Figure 10.1. The majority of the parameter estimates for the structural paths were not statistically significantly different from zero, which revealed that there is no evidence to support within-person (i.e., intraindividual) effects among written language and EF. Therefore, EF did not predict written language scores across time, nor did written language predict EF scores across time. That said, there were statistically significant positive relations (all p-values < 0.001) between written language intercept and written language slope as well as written language intercept and EF intercept. These results provided evidence to support between-person effects among written language and EF, and suggested that individual variability in written language at grade 1 was positively related to the individual variability in rate of change over time of written language and the individual variability in EF at grade 1.

DISCUSSION

In this study, we investigated a component of writing development and provided one of the first longitudinal examinations of both written language and EF in elementary-aged children. Specifically, we examined how to best model the development of written language and EF as well as the relations between written language and EF from first to fourth grades. At a minimum, the results of this study are a testament to the complexity of the relationship of writing to EF over time, and perhaps to the complexity inherent in the development of any academic skill.

Written Language and Executive Functions Summary

Based on the work of Curran et al. (2012), we decided that the most comprehensive way to understand the relations between written language and EF was by modeling the between-person (i.e., directly predict growth parameters), within-person (i.e., directly influence the repeated measures), and across-time differences in growth. We discovered that EF did not predict written language scores across time, nor did written language predict EF across time. On the other hand, on average, individual variability in written language at grade 1 was positively related to the individual variability of growth in written language and the individual variability in EF at grade 1. Thus, scores of written language in first grade were positively related to scores of EF in first grade. In general, written language performance in first-grade predicted growth in written language over time, and therefore first grade seems like a good place to intervene to improve performance (e.g., increase the growth trajectory).

Limitations

Model diagnosis is not an exact science, thus there are several possible reasons why our models did not converge or have good fit with the data (e.g., Heywood cases, variables were not normally distributed). The current study was a secondary data analysis of a more comprehensive longitudinal study designed to examine the many factors shown to influence the development of written language as well as to investigate the effectiveness of an intervention. The presence of an intervention complicated the analyses, and potentially could have led to issues with power. It is plausible that the model did not include enough information to explore the relation between written language and EF. For example, other cognitive functions, such as language skills, as well as environmental variables, such as teacher quality and gender, may be necessary to understand the developmental interplay of writing and EF, and their longitudinal relations.

Further, the models may have had a better fit if we had employed different measures of written language and EF; i.e., the full range of components used to indicate written language and EF may not have been represented in this study. In addition, the lack of specifically developed measures to assess writing and EF for struggling writers may have been problematic. This is limiting because it is possible that the measures did not assess the full range of performance for the population. Restriction of range can be problematic because the true range of ability for the participants may not be captured by the measures used. In this case, a participant's ability may be lower than the score reflects, but a lower score was not possible given the measure. For instance, 33 percent of the sample received a score of zero for alphabet writing in first grade. This suggests that these participants did not write one legible letter of the alphabet in 15 seconds. Perhaps our chosen measure was not able to capture the full range of written language performance at first grade. Overall, the limitations discussed above should not be used to disregard the results of this study, but are reasons for caution when interpreting the results. The limitations also provide ideas for improvement of future writing development research.

Implications and Future Directions

This study illustrated how latent-variable statistical techniques can be used to model longitudinal data in educational research. Future researchers should continue to explore the use of latent variable statistical techniques in education research given their advantages over traditional ANOVA repeated-measures techniques (see Zajic et al., this volume). Even though the current study did not provide definitive answers regarding the relations between written language and EF, the questions are nonetheless important to understanding the factors associated with the development of written language in younger children. Theorists who have described the relations between written language and EF suggest that there are overlapping components between the two constructs, including planning and working memory (Berninger & Winn, 2006). Indeed, researchers who have studied written language and EF in a cross-sectional fashion have found relations among these constructs (Altemeier et al., 2008; Hooper et al., 2011). More longitudinal research is needed to examine actual change over time in these constructs, and their commonalities and differences.

This study provided new ways for researchers to think about the relations between writing and EF, and perhaps other cognitive functions. Researchers can begin to think of new interventions that could be used to test the proposed causal relations between EF and written language. For instance, it is likely that a student who has weak EF also has weak writing skills. Therefore, an intervention for this type of student may need to include writing instruction along with strategies to improve selected EF components. It is also possible that new writing interventions could be developed that embed EF training (e.g., Self-Regulated Strategy Development Model; Graham & Harris, 2005). In this type of intervention, students would be taught writing skills and EF strategies simultaneously. Educators and researchers need to continue to collaborate to discover effective methods of teaching writing to all children, and such methods require additional scientific inquiries into the relationship between the development of written language skills and other key factors such as EF. Further, how these cognitive factors relate to other environmental facilitators and barriers to the development of written expression remains a fruitful avenue for future exploration.

EF and writing are both complex and dynamic constructs that change across the lifespan with a range of variability between people in the amount and rate of growth. This variability likely is influenced by a large number of potential factors (e.g., classroom instruction, lifespan experiences), and how these factors contribute to the evolution of written language skills over the course of development remain largely unexplored to date. Indeed, as Bazerman et al. (2018) have noted, this relation may be bidirectional, but when that bidirectionality occurs and under what conditions (e.g., one factor may be more influential than another) remains unknown. Consequently, the field is in need of increased examination of this interrelationship, with additional factors including different disorders, different conditions, and different ages, in an effort to increase our understanding of the development of written language and this overall developmental interplay. Such findings might be helpful in guiding future research on intervention and classroom instruction. In that regard, we echo Charles Bazerman's plea (Bazerman et al., 2018) for writing researchers to conduct longitudinal studies of writing development as exemplified in this chapter.

REFERENCES

Altemeier, L. E., Abbott, R. D. & Berninger, V. W. (2008). Executive functions for reading and writing in typical literacy development and dyslexia. *Journal of Clinical and Experimental Neuropsychology, 30*, 588–606.

Bazerman, C. (2008). Theories of the middle range in historical studies of writing practice. *Written Communication, 25*, 298–318.

Bazerman, C., Applebee, A. N., Berninger, V. W., Brandt, D., Graham, S., Jeffery, J. V., Matsuda, P. K., Murphy, S., Rowe, D. W., Schleppegrell, M. & Wilcox, K. C. (2018). *The lifespan development of writing*. National Council of Teachers of English.

Berninger, V. (2001). *The process assessment of the learner: Test battery for reading and writing*. The Psychological Corporation.

Berninger, V., Abbott, R., Jones, J., Wolf, B., Gould, L., Anderson-Youngstrom, M., Shimada, S. & Apel, K. (2006). Early development of language by hand: Composing, reading, listening, and speaking connections; three letter-writing modes; and fast mapping in spelling. *Developmental Neuropsychology, 29*(1), 61–92.

Berninger, V. & Amtmann, D. (2003). Preventing written expression disabilities through early and continuing assessment and intervention for handwriting and/or spelling problems: Research into practice. In H. Swanson, K. Harris & S. Graham (Eds.), *Handbook of learning disabilities* (pp. 323–344). The Guilford Press.

Berninger, V. & Winn, W. (2006). Implications of advancements in brain research and technology for writing development, writing instruction, and educational evolution.

In C. MacArthur, S. Graham & J. Fitzgerald (Eds.), *Handbook of writing research* (pp. 96–114). The Guilford Press.

Bollen, K. A. & Curran, P. J. (2006). *Latent curve models: A structural equation perspective*. John Wiley & Sons.

Collins, A. & Gentner, D. G. (1980). A framework for a cognitive theory of writing. In L. W. Gregg & E. R. Steinberg (Eds.), *Cognitive processes in writing* (pp. 51–72). Lawrence Erlbaum Associates.

Costa, L. C. (2014). *The relations among the development of written language and executive functions in elementary aged students* [Doctoral dissertation, University of North Carolina at Chapel Hill]. Carolina Digital Repository. https://doi.org/10.17615/nsn0-rn93.

Curran, P. J., Lee, T., Howard, A. L., Lane, S. & MacCullum, R. (2012). Disaggregating within-person and between person effects in multilevel and structural equation growth models. In J. R. Harring & G. R. Hancock (Eds.), *Advances in longitudinal methods in the social and behavioral sciences* (pp. 217–253). Information Age Publishing.

Graham, S. (2018). A writer(s) within community model of writing. In C. Bazerman, V. Berninger, D. Brandt, S. Graham, J. Langer, S. Murphy, P. Matsuda, P. Rowe & M. Schleppegrell (Eds.), *The lifespan development of writing* (pp. 272–325). National Council of Teachers of English.

Graham, S. & Harris, K. R. (2005). Improving the writing performance of young struggling writers: Theoretical and programmatic research from the center on accelerating student learning. *The Journal of Special Education, 39*(1), 19–33.

Hancock, G. R. & Harring, J. R. & Lawrence, F. R. (2013). Using latent growth modeling to evaluate longitudinal change. In G. R. Hancock & R. O. Mueller (Eds.), *Structural equation modeling: A second course* (2nd ed.) (pp. 171–196). Information Age Publishing.

Hayes, J. & Flower, L. (1986). Writing research and the writer. *American Psychologist, 41*(10), 1106–1113.

Hooper, S., Costa, L. J., McBee, M., Anderson, K., Yerby, D., Knuth, S. & Childress, A. (2011). Concurrent and longitudinal neuropsychological contributors to written language expression in first and second grade students. *Reading and Writing, 24*(2), 221–252.

Hu, L. T. & Bentler, P. M. (1999). Cutoff criteria for fit indexes in covariance structure analysis: Conventional criteria versus new alternatives. *Structural Equation Modeling, 6*(1), 1–55. https://doi.org/10.1080/10705519909540118.

Kellogg, R. T. (1996). A model of working memory in writing. In M. C. Levy & S. E. Ransdell (Eds.), The science of writing: Theories, methods, individual differences and applications (pp. 57– 71). Laurence Erlbaum Associates.

Kim, Y-S. & Schatschneider, C. (2017). Expanding the developmental models of writing: A direct and indirect effects model of developmental writing (DIEW). *Journal of Educational Psychology, 109*(1), 35–50. https://doi.org/10.1037/edu0000129.

Kline, R. B. (2005). *Principals and practice of structural equation modeling* (2nd ed.). The Guilford Press.

Kolenikov, S. & Bollen, K. A. (2012). Testing negative error variances: Is a Heywood case a symptom of misspecification? *Sociological Methods and Research, 41*(1), 124–167.

McCutchen, D. (2006). Cognitive factors in the development of children's writing. In C. MacArthur, S. Graham & J. Fitzgerald (Eds.), *Handbook of writing research* (pp. 115–130). The Guilford Press.

Miyake, A., Friedman, N., Emerson, M., Witzki, A., Howerter, A. & Wager, T. (2000). The unity and diversity of executive functions and their contributions to complex 'frontal lobe' tasks: A latent variable analysis. *Cognitive Psychology, 41*(1), 49–100.

National Center for Education Statistics. (2012). *The nation's report card: Writing 2011.* Institute of Education Sciences, U.S. Department of Education (NCES 2012–470). https://nces.ed.gov/nationsreportcard/pdf/main2011/2012470.pdf.

Pennington, B. F., Bennetto, L., McAleer, O. & Roberts, R. J. (1996). Executive functions and working memory: Theoretical and measurement issues. In G. R. Lyon & N. A. Krasnegor (Eds.), *Attention, memory, and executive function* (pp. 327–348). Brookes.

Psychological Corporation. (1998). *Vigil Continuous Performance Test.* Harcourt Assessment.

Roberts, R. J. & Pennington, B. F. (1996) An interactive framework for examining prefrontal cognitive processes. *Developmental Neuropsychology, 12*(1), 105–126. https://doi.org/10.1080/87565649609540642.

U.S. Department of Education. (2003). National assessment of educational progress (NAEP), 2002 writing assessment. U.S. Department of Education, Institute of Education Sciences, National Center for Education Statistics.

Wechsler, D. (2002). *Wechsler individual achievement test-second edition.* Harcourt Assessment, Inc.

Wechsler, D., Kaplan, E., Fein, F., Kramer, J., Morris, R., Delis, D. & Maerlender, A. (2004). *Wechsler intelligence scales for children | Fourth edition integrated.* Harcourt Assessment, Inc.

Woodcock, R. W., McGrew, K. S. & Mather, N. (2001). *Woodcock-Johnson III tests of cognitive abilities.* Riverside Publishing.

Zelazo, P., Carter, A., Reznick, J. & Frye, D. (1997). Early development of executive function: A problem-solving framework. *Review of General Psychology, 1,* 198–226.

Zelazo, P., Muller, U., Frye, D. & Marcovitch, S. (2003). The development of executive function in early childhood. *Monographs of the Society for Research in Child Development, 68*(3), 1–137.

Zelazo, P. D., Qu, L. & Kesek, A. (2010). Hot executive function: Emotion and the development of cognitive control. In S. D. Calkins & M. A. Bell (Eds.), *Child development at the intersection of emotion and cognition* (pp. 97–111). American Psychological Association.

Zins, J. & Hooper, S. R. (2012). The integration of child development principles and the development of written language. In E. Grigerenko, E. Mambrino & D. Pleiss (Eds.), *Handbook of writing.* The Psychology Press.

CHAPTER 11.

INTERPRETING AND EXPLAINING DATA REPRESENTATIONS: A COMPARISON ACROSS GRADES 1–7

Diana J. Arya
Anthony Clairmont
Sarah Hirsch
University of California, Santa Barbara

"Writing as a knowledge-making activity isn't limited to understanding writing as a single mode of communication but as a multimodal, performative activity" (Ball & Charlton, 2016, p. 43). One of these modes is graphical data representation. Situated in the visual, data representations are a critical part of visual culture. That is, "the relationship between what we see and what we know is always shifting and is a product of changing cultural contexts, public understanding, and modes of human communication" (Propen, 2012, p. xiv). What is little understood is how such knowledge develops across the lifespan. The developmental path to fluency in interpreting and analyzing various visual representations is largely unknown, yet such textual forms are increasing in presence across various disciplinary and social media outlets (Aparicio & Costa, 2015). Therefore, the development of competence in understanding and working with data representations is a critical part of the lifespan development of writing.

When we look at writing as a knowledge-making activity, the word and the image contribute to one another in an activity of meaning-making. As art historian John Berger attests in his seminal work, *Ways of Seeing,* (1972), writing and seeing aren't mutually exclusive, in that what we see "establishes our place in the surrounding world; [and we] explain that world with words" (p. 7). The interplay between the word and the image "asks students . . . to explore their assumption about images" (Propen, 2012, p. 199). These assumptions are central to our interests in learning how children develop meaning-making skills and critically engage with visual culture. How do young readers begin to develop ways to understand and access visual entities such as informational graphics and data charts or tables? Are there particular features that are more accessible than others? Are there patterns that we can detect and apply in curricular devel-

DOI: https://doi.org/10.37514/PER-B.2020.1053.2.11

opment with regards to data representations? Such questions guide the inquiry of this present study.

In his book, *Beautiful Data*, historian Orit Halpern (2015) describes how early representations of reality for the purpose of knowledge building moved from literal recreations of local individual entities (e.g., intricate renderings of flora and fauna as viewed by the naked eye) to increasingly complex phenomena that encompasses large assemblages of information across time. Halpern's historical account highlights the natural human inclination to make visible the unknown, and to understand the intricacies of reality. Readers of his account are taken on a historical journey that centers on renowned mathematician Norbert Wiener, popularizer of the term cybernetics. Wiener led the way to more expansive attempts to understand reality. His algorithmic contributions allowed for the process of aggregating copious amounts of information in order to represent past, present and future potentials for various phenomena of human interest. Born out of the demands of knowing as much as possible about the enemies of World War II, Wiener's work sparked a new aesthetic science of representing reality. The rise of visual representations of aggregated data (i.e., charts, tables and figures that reduces large amounts of information into consumable knowledge) in the decades following the war "saw a radical reconfiguration of vision, observation, and cognition that continues to inform our contemporary ideas of interactivity and interface" (Halpern, 2014, p. 249).

Minimally mentioned by Halpern (2014) is the work of statistician Edward Tufte (1983), who described the ideal (and less so) characteristics of visual displays of quantitative information. His seminal work is a critique of various historical and current examples of such graphical creations, highlighting the best and worst practices for articulating phenomena to intended audiences. He explains through these examples what counts as meaningful information as opposed to "chartjunk" (1983, p. 107), which includes irrelevant and potentially distorting elements (e.g., decorative features or seemingly engaging images) that waters down the "data density" of such graphical displays (p. 168). Tufte's recommendation to "maximize the data-ink ratio, within reason" (1982, p. 96 served as a guiding principle for our current study of how elementary students (grades 1–7) make sense of and compose interpretive messages about data representations that vary according to information density and presence of non-relevant content (1983). New school standards emphasizing the goals of understanding and applying graphical information for a variety of educational purposes (Lee et al., 2013; Next Generation Science Standards Lead States, 2013, Appendix M) offer a warrant for a deeper exploration into ways in which children across grades interpret and communicate such forms of textual information. To date, there are no such explorations to the best of our knowledge.

Within the grand historical context of visual representations of aggregated data (referred herein as data representations, or DRs), we can place a similar progression in the history of school science standards in the US. The earliest version of such standards is the Committee of Ten (National Education Association, 1894), from which we can view what aspects of visual representation were deemed most important for science education (among other disciplines). The expressed consensus among committee members was that "no text-book should be used . . . the study should constantly be associated with the study of literature, language and drawing" (1894, p. 27). Such declarations echo the early days of observing and recording natural phenomena like the 1728 work of famous knowledge gatherer and publisher Ephrain Chamber (1728), exampled in Figure 11.1. The representation of scientific knowledge was considered an essential task for students, but one which, like much Eurocentric education of the eighteenth and nineteenth centuries, emphasized copying rather than interpretation and communication.

Copying or tracing artifacts found in nature was a common convention of knowledge building for biologists. Thus, the practice of engaging in representative drawings from nature was a key standard for demonstrating university readiness (National Education Association, 1894).

Modern academic institutions no longer emphasize the development of such discrete representations of nature. Rather, today's school standards highlight the importance of textual reasoning and explaining aggregated information about various natural phenomena. This shift in standards has emerged in parallel with global, interdisciplinary concerns about the rising "prominence of data as social, political and cultural form" (Selwyn, 2015, p. 64) and the increasing need for helping students across the grade span to critically navigate such forms. Hence, developing practices of interpreting and analyzing DRs support the expressed need for all students to become "critical consumers of scientific information" (National Research Council, 2012, p. 41). While these needs are assuredly urgent, concerns about the ways that graphical displays of information are taken up and used by students and their teachers were documented well before the social media explosion made possible via the internet.

Gillespie (1993), for example, points out in her review of studies that very few students (approximately 4 percent) demonstrated mastery level understanding of graphic information presented in a standardized test (see also Kamm et al., 1977; National Assessment of Educational Progress, 1985). Gillespie (1993) highlights the importance for teachers to have explicit conversations with students about DRs that include sequential (e.g., flow charts) or quantitative (bar graphs or pie charts) information, maps, diagrams (blueprints or drawings), and tables or charts that allow for comparing and contrasting information. While she mentions the limitations of DRs embedded in basal textbooks, the source of this issue is the lack of variety in purpose and format rather than on information density as Tufte (1983) described (see also Hunter et al., 1987). Clearly, emerging scholarship on data representations will need to address Gillespie's concern with variety and utility as well as the matter of quality taken up by Tufte.

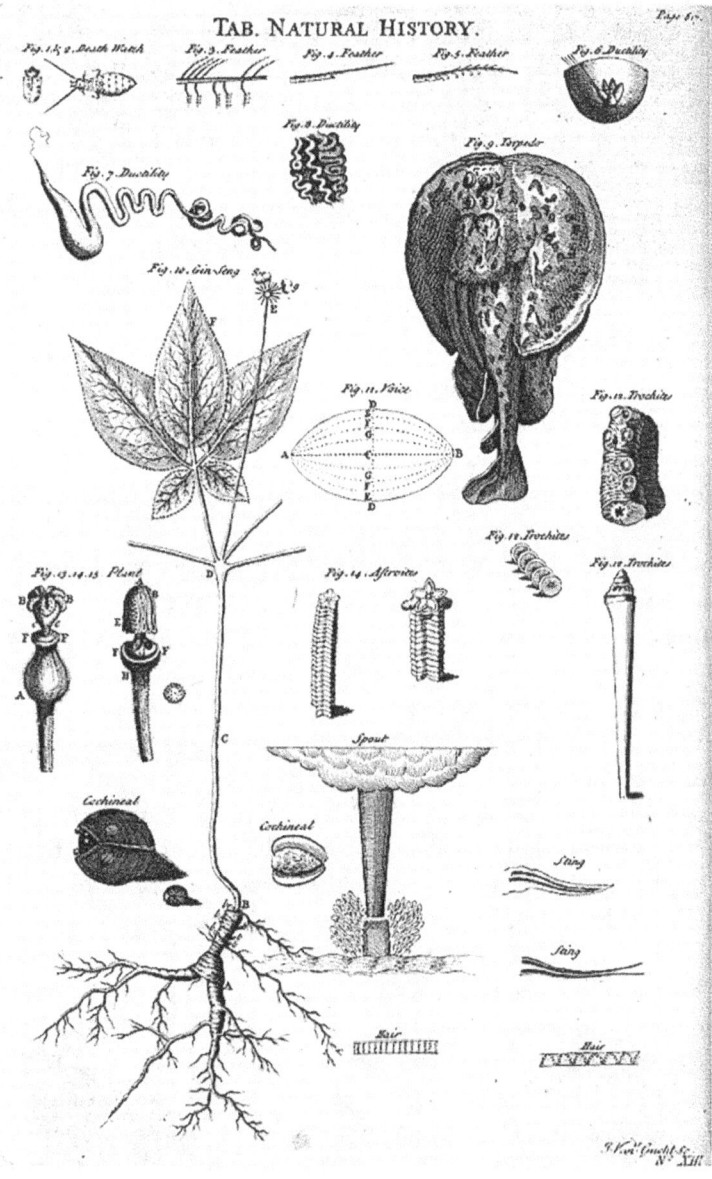

Figure 11.1. Drawings in Chamber's 1728 encyclopedia.

The need to foster student understanding of DRs has received greater attention in the most recent educational science standards, the Next Generation Science Standards (Next Generation Science Standards Lead States, 2013). The new standards provide rich descriptions about key scientific practices that students should begin learning in kindergarten, and that together comprise an idealized developmental sequence. One such practice is analyzing and interpreting data, which begins in the earliest grades (K–2) as making direct observations of phenomena to determine patterns (e.g., comparing the properties of various objects). Within this particular strand of practices, the notion of DRs is present in benchmark descriptions starting in the third grade; students in grades K-2 are expected to engage in analysis via exploration and experimentation of phenomena rather than graphical representations of such. Middle school students (grades 6–8), however, are expected to build on initial explorations of graphical displays to include pictorially captured data (e.g., photo images of microbial activity) and projections of activity across time. High school students are then expected to embark on the challenge of gathering and transforming information into visual representations and using them to support claims and explain phenomena. While no statement is provided to explain such a progression of standards or logic of development, readers can infer that (a) DRs are appropriate for children in grades 3–12, (b) DRs including future projections are more appropriate for students in grades 6–12, and (c) only high school students should be expected to create and transform data into DRs for making claims. However, these assumptions lack empirical support. Nor is there clarity about the variation of the purpose and complexity of DRs or guidance about whether certain forms with particular amounts of information should be introduced before others to form a developmentally appropriate sequence. There is also a lack of understanding about how teachers should introduce and support the exploration of DRs. Most concerning, there are no visual examples for teachers to understand the kinds of DRs that would be useful for particular grade bands. Research associated with "infographics" has thus far touted the importance and engaging nature of explicit discussions about DRs during classroom instruction (e.g., Kraus, 2012; Lamb et al., 2014; Martix & Hodson, 2014), yet like the new scientific standards, such research lacks a developmental view of such instruction across the K–12 spectrum.

This study traces our initial exploration of how 28 students across grades 1–7, who represent various sociocultural backgrounds, understand and compose interpretations of DRs in small-group, collaborative discussions. Using a communities of practice lens (Gee, 2005), we systematically explored video-recorded, focus group discussions about various selected data representations and all written explanations produced during these sessions. We view this initial exploration as a beginning point for building a testable theory about the developmental trajectory for interpreting and analyzing DRs. By including participants from different grade levels, we have the opportunity to compare and contrast how groups of students representing different stages of development respond to DRs, and such an approach has long been noted to be effective for revealing key aspects of knowledge and skill development (Bruner, 1990). Hence, we addressed the following lines of inquiry: What are the general patterns observed in recorded discussions and composed explanations about DRs among different grade-level groups? What do these patterns reveal about the development of and instructional support for fostering skills and abilities needed for sense making and communicating about DRs? Such questions support our overarching goal of this study, which explores how elementary students across grades 1 through 7 interpret and explain the phenomena DRs aim to communicate.

METHODOLOGY

Participants

A total of 28 children (nine identified as female and 19 male) ranging in ages 6 to 13 participated in one of 10 focus groups, each organized by grade level. Based on reported information from parents, participants represented a range of cultural backgrounds that included 14 (50%) White, 11 (39%) Latinx, and three (11%) Asian students. The majority of students (18 in total, 64%) reported English as their home language while seven (21%) reported Spanish as the main language used at home. Two participants (7%) reported Tagalog as their home language. The remaining student spoke Mandarin as the home language. Participants also represented a range of schooling experiences and associated activities. All participants attend public or private elementary and junior high schools within the same local community. Based on reported information from parents, 10 students received special education services during the regular school year.

Selection of DRs

A total of 11 DRs were selected for this study. A panel of five researchers (two graduate students, two junior faculty members and one senior faculty member) engaged in three planning sessions that involved gathering and reviewing potential DR candidates. Final selection was determined by topic relevance (e.g., ethnicities of movie characters) and by representing a wide range of aspects identified by Tufte (1983), including informational density and the presence of non-relevant information. Figure 11.2 represents the varied complexity of the selected DRs.

Interpreting and Explaining Data Representations

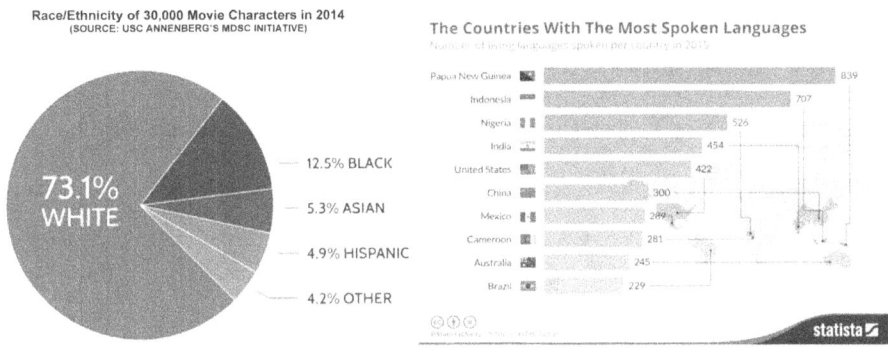

Figure 11.2. Images of two selected DRs.

A previous pilot study involving 25 fourth grade participants informed the final selection of and discussion guide for the DRs included in the present study.

CONTEXT AND DATA SOURCES

All participants attended a summer literacy camp during the time of this study (2018). The camp took place at a local research university that houses a center designed to provide intensive literacy support for students in grades K–8. The children's center supports students with a wide range of backgrounds and abilities during the school year; children enter the program either through family referral or through partnership programs with neighboring schools and after-school clubs. Summer camp takes place during the month of July and is available on a first come, first served basis. All summer camp attendees were organized by grade level and further divided into groups with no more than 6 members.

The present study took place over a two-day period during summer camp. All instructors received two training sessions on the use of the discussion protocol (a revised version from the previous pilot) and facilitating responses while avoiding additional prompting and scaffolding beyond the protocol prompts (e.g., please say more about that; what do others think?). Based on instructors' observations of interpersonal dynamics and personalities, some of the groups were further divided to ensure that all members would have the opportunity to contribute to group discussions about a small set (three in total) of DRs. Each group engaged in three distinct discussion events marked by the introduction of a DR and either wrote explanations of each individually or collectively via dictation. Table 11.1 presents information about recorded discussion events for each group.

Table 11.1. Overview of DR Discussion Groups

Group	Grade Level	Number of Students	Duration of Recorded Discussions	Number of Written Explanations Produced**
Group A	1	3	29:25	3
Group B	2	2	24:06	4
Group C	2	1*	22:35	1
Group D	2	2	35:09	3
Group E	3	2	39:49	3
Group F	4	2	1:01:48	3
Group G	4	3	39:12	5
Group H	5	5	1:49:58	6
Group I	6	5	50:11	6
Group J	7	3	14:20	2

* Based on particular instructional needs of this student who has autism, exchanges excluded other students.

**For all groups in grades 1–3, written explanations were expected to be collected via dictation.

DISCUSSION PROCESS

Instructors presented each of three different data representations (i.e., representations that varied in density of graphical elements and conceptual meaning) in separate succession, asking the group to respond to questions including the following: What do you see? What do you think the person who made this wanted to say? What does this make you wonder? Facilitating instructors followed up with clarifying questions (e.g., tell me more) and questions designed to elicit a critical assessment (What do you want to know more about? What advice do you have for the author?). Following discussion, all groups collectively composed interpretations of the first two DRs and selected one of these to collaboratively compose an explanation for a student in a younger grade. Groups in higher grades (fourth graders and older) were expected to compose their own individual interpretations of the third and final DR presented, while younger groups continued to collectively compose interpretations that instructors captured verbatim. However, participants in the sixth and seventh grade groups (Groups I & J) did not complete their written explanation of this third DR due to time constraints related with the summer program. Further, the seventh-grade participants expressed their interest in using the available whiteboard to compose explanations of the first two DRs and as such, one student served as scribe for the group.

All discussions were video recorded using an iPad. Instructors invited student participants to decide where the iPad should be placed within the room in order to capture their discussion. The sessions began with an explanation that scientists want to learn from children how to make their work easier to understand. As such, participants were positioned from the beginning as "cultural guides" (Green et al., 2007) to help the instructor learn what was meaningful, useful, confusing, or lacking about each of the presented DRs from the students' perspectives.

Families of participating children were first informed of the study and prior to the recorded sessions via the camp newsletter, which included the explanation of our goal to help students across the grades develop critical reasoning skills required for understanding and explaining the ever increasing number of tables and graphics in various school-related texts. English and Spanish versions of the newsletter were available to families. All participating children had signed consent from their parents to participate in the study.

ANALYTIC FRAMEWORK

Units of analysis were organized by discussion event (Bloome et al., 2004), which was bounded according to each DR presented to the group. All video recorded sessions were reviewed separately by two researchers who identified levels of collaboration and communicative moves during group discussions. Following Gee's (2005) Communities of Practice (COP) framework, analysis centered on the social space rather than on individuals. As such, we focused on instances of "mutual engagement" according to constructs of interest among members of the group (p. 592). We analyzed efforts in sense making and explaining through the constructs of "collaboration" and "communicative moves" as informed by prior research. Specifically, our construct map for gauging levels of collaboration during reading discussions was informed by theoretical frames from psychology (Vygotsky, 1980), sociology (Hutchins, 1991), discourse analysis (Gee, 2004), and the learning sciences (Hershowitz et al., 2001; Johnson & Johnson, 1990). Figure 11.3 features the construct map we developed with the guidance of the BEAR Assessment framework (Wilson, 2004) for analysis of video recorded discussions. Thus, this framework takes a "building block" approach for educational assessment practices; construct maps serve as the first step in gauging development.

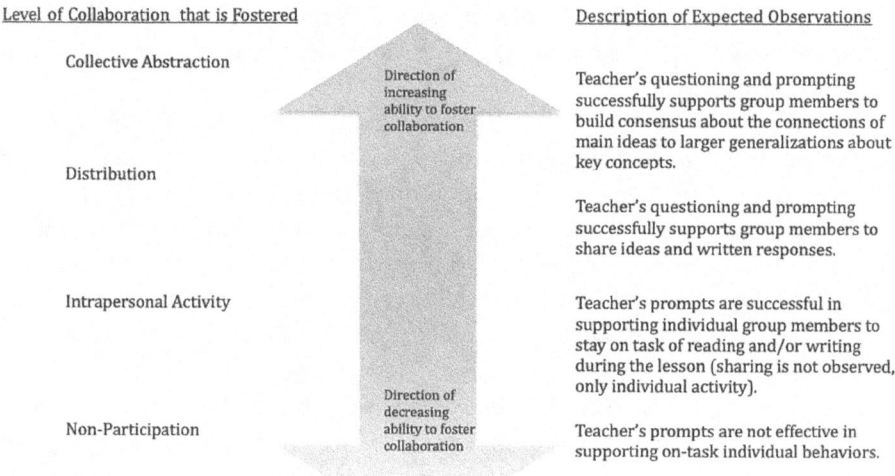

Figure 11.3. Construct map for levels of collaboration.

We further investigated the particular communicative moves demonstrated during instances of collaboration (distribution, building, and collective abstraction). Based on our research of potential communicative moves for comprehending and explaining phenomena and previous findings from our pilot study, we selected the following four codes for our analysis: narrative, or narrativizing (Bruner, 1990), focusing illusion (Kahneman et al., 2006) or the attention to familiar yet not necessarily salient ideas (Gillespie, 1993; Groes, 2016), connecting with prior knowledge and experiences and use of multimodal resources (Cole, 1998). Any inconsistencies between analyses of a common discussion were deliberated as a team and resolved with little difficulty. While there were a few disagreements in perceived levels of collaboration, there were no inconsistencies with identified communicative codes. Transcriptions of video-recorded interactions followed micro-ethnographic devices by Bloome et al. (2004) that focus on how the assertions were uttered, which follow the general structure of message units. Phatic displays were captured in bold text and indications of questioning were marked with an upwardly directed arrow ("↑") in order to further contextualize transcribed commentary.

FINDINGS

General Lack of Exposure and Practice

Preliminary findings from analysis of video-recorded discussions suggest that students in earlier grades (i.e., third grade and younger) have varied levels of exposure to data representations in school as part of a lesson or activity. For example, a third-grade student from one school had no experience with such representations (I've never seen anything like this) while another third grader from a different school had moderate exposure (this line means growth). Those familiar with the basic formats presented (e.g., pie charts) generally reported learning about them outside of school via popular media or news. Basic interpretational tasks were highly laborious or out of reach for most of the students in our study. This finding was consistent in our previous pilot study, which also included data representations along a wide continuum of difficulty and a variety of topics.

Student Collaboration

Our theory of development involved three collaborative levels: Distribution (students sharing without connecting to each other's comments); Building (students adding to or evaluating comments from others); and Collective Abstraction (students collectively working together towards larger generalizations). Of these three levels, the most common was Distribution. Among the young students especially, there was a lot of sharing and working through ideas but rarely were students responding to each other's comments. While we observed instances of thinking aloud, this form of thinking was rarely realized collectively. The next level observed was Building, as some groups did show instances in which students were working off one another's comments in their attempt to identify the DR message(s). The instances of Building were mostly attributed to the older students in grades 4–7. There were very few demonstrations of Collective Abstraction; such instances involved two students who took the lead in explaining the DR to others who were either confused or disengaged.

Requesting Textual Explanations for DRs

When soliciting feedback from students about what might be improved about each graphic, more textual description was the most common substantive request. Paradoxically, during the actual process of interpreting data representations, students delayed reading the text that was available. This neglected text, such as titles and legends, included information essential to the intended messages of the data representation. In some cases, students worked to interpret data representations for periods exceeding ten minutes without mentioning, or apparently noticing, key text. This pattern was more prevalent among younger students, particularly those in grades 1–4. Sixth graders, however, read the titles first and moved quickly to accurate interpretations of the graphics.

THE FOCUSING ILLUSION

Creating narratives about the content of data representations is a task that seemed somewhat easier for children in older grades. A successful account of the messages communicated by data representations necessarily involved narration, but not all potential narratives were plausible. We found that students sought to narrativize aspects of the DRs even before registering the presence and meaning of all available information. For example, second- and third-grade students became so focused on the fact that the DR contained a map of the US that they did not mention any other element of the graphic in their subsequent narratives, all of which centered on geography or the map's color scheme. Borrowing a term from heuristics research in behavioral economics, we call this phenomenon a focusing illusion (Kahneman et al., 2006). The illusion occurs when people implicitly give too much importance to small features of a larger whole, effectively ignoring or downplaying information outside the temporary locus of attention (Kahneman, 2011).

FROM INTERPRETATION TO WRITING

The findings described above were informative of the written products from students. Expectedly, patterns identified in written expressions produced during DR discussions echo the communicative moves identified during verbal interactions. For example, Figure 11.4 shows a stylized pie chart that was presented to groups representing grades 1–5. This DR elicited a focusing illusion (apples) from the first and second graders while the interpretation of the third-grade students captured the key point (spending habits of children). The following exchange between a first-grade student ("S") and the instructor ("I") demonstrates this focusing illusion:

I: what do you think that this picture means↑

S: food

I: food

why do you think it means food↑

S: because it's an apple

and an apple is a food

The first-grade student goes on to explain that the apple is "organic" and that is grown from a tree, and that more apples can be grown using apple seeds. However, the shape of the pie chart is a superficial element of the data representation. The students' focus on this detail (what we identified as a focusing illusion) spawns a narrative that derails the interpretative process. Likewise tripped by

Interpreting and Explaining Data Representations

chartjunk, the second graders have a similar conversation, fixing their attention on both the apple shape and the colors. The third-grade students, by contrast, are able to discern that the shape of the pie chart is a superficial element ("It's shaped like an apple. They try to make it interesting for kids."). While the apple shape is the also the first element noted by the third-grade students, they quickly move away from this observation, as shown in the following exchange:

> I: Tell me what you see
>
> and how would you explain it
>
> to someone who is younger
>
> S: Uhhh
>
> pie chart↑
>
> I: say there's a younger student
>
> what's the first thing you would tell them↑
>
> S: this is how kids use money↑

The students' prior familiarity with at least one format of data representation—the pie chart—as well as his early attention paid to the title, grounds a plausible interpretation of the data representation.

The two examples featured above were typical of the patterns of discourse that preceded writing about DRs across grade groups. Figure 11.4 includes the most representative explanations produced either through dictation or individual writing by each of the grade-level groups; original spelling and grammatical structure for handwritten accounts from students in grades four and five were maintained.

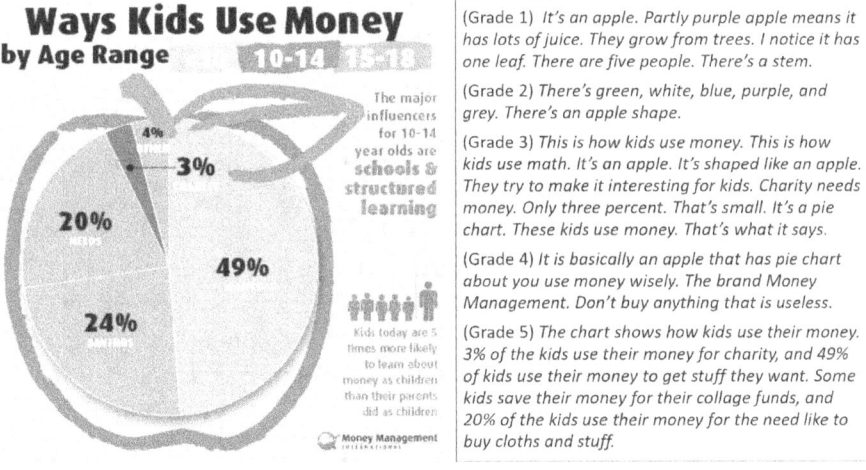

Figure 11.4. Third DR presented to groups with associated written explanations.

The progression of communicative moves observed across such composed explanations highlight a general movement in constructing narratives anchored by a focusing illusion (grade 1) towards narratives focused on key textual ideas (grade 5). The various observed communicative moves from participants, such as narrativizing and making connections utilizing prior knowledge, were not prompted by the instructors, nor was there any indication that students were drawing on any specific techniques previously taught in school.

DISCUSSION

Findings from our present study suggest that the developmental lifespan for understanding and explaining data representations (or infographics) begins in early grades with an over-emphasized eye on familiar objects or concepts (e.g., an apple), from which less textually relevant narratives are constructed. Students in older grades tend to use more (but sparingly) textual information to anchor understandings about the DR. While there seems to be a developmental shift across grades (as represented in Figure 11.4), we observed a general struggle in understanding key information presented in charts, graphs, maps, tables, diagrams and drawings. Further, there is evidence of variability in exposure to DRs for children within the same grade. Such observed variability within a local community context suggests that young students may not have consistent opportunities to explore data representations. This finding runs contrary to current educational standards, which emphasize the importance of teaching such scientific practices beginning in kindergarten, hence making resources and activities "accessible to younger students but ... broad enough to sustain continued investigation over years" (NRC, 2012, p. 31). Findings from analysis of group discussion suggests that the following practices develop across the represented grades:

- Collaborative thinking and knowledge building (moving from disconnected sharing toward abstraction),
- Narrative explanations (moving from focusing illusions toward graphically anchored connections), and
- Critical synthesis of presented elements (moving from discrete explanations toward critical analysis).
- Such observed differences between student groups organized by grade level suggests that across the lifespan, one's communicative understanding of DRs grows along with collaborative skills and multiple exposure to various textual sources.

We found that graphical information generally constitutes a mode of communication that many students find difficult to interpret. This finding highlights the need for explicit instruction for supporting development of such critical reading skills. This need is particularly important in light of the general increase in the number of DRs that children are encountering both in their textbooks and in the media that surrounds them (Lamb et al., 2014). As noted, participants who recognized aspects of the DRs mentioned that they had seen something like the graphic in math class, on the news, or even in a movie. Therefore, we can conclude that students are encountering DRs regularly among a variety of different formats and environments, even if they don't identify them as such. However, mere recognition is insufficient given the inherent complexities of DRs, coupled with the pedagogical exigencies of current educational standards.

As mentioned in the findings, many of the students desired more textual information to help with explanation of graphical displays, yet most groups (particularly those of younger grades) seem to avoid using the text already available to them in titles and embedded text. In future research, we hope to better understand this disjuncture between stated desires and performance. By modeling different techniques with which to approach data representations in the classroom, much like how a math formula is explained or complete sentence composition is demonstrated, teachers could demonstrate potential approaches for students while attempting to interpret DRs. Such instruction may help students gain greater understanding about aggregate data by regularly incorporating such modalities into classroom practices. Further, students in early grades may become more comfortable with engaging in such a modality, hence curtailing focusing illusions and non-relevant narrativization.

We suspect that the low levels of engagement and collaboration shown by some students is a side effect of confusion. DRs represent a wide range of relevance and accessibility and as such, students would benefit from activities that would enable ample practice in engaging with such complex academic texts. If the student has had little to no prior exposure to a particular type of graphic (e.g., regression line across time), but has received explicit instruction about the general nature and purpose of DRs, the tasks of understanding and articulating may become more engaging and even enjoyable, hence positioning the activity as an opportunity to discover something new about the world. The ubiquitous nature of DRs has elevated this need to support such readerly opportunities for discovery.

The recorded group discussions described in this study provided a way of seeing how students develop sense making and interpreting DRs across the gradespan. From this initial phase of exploration, we have the foundations for a theory of development that may inform how teachers can support students' communicative proficiency with DRs. For example, findings presented here may inform the selection of particular graphics for particular grade bands for class activities (e.g., pie charts and bar graphs with minimal seductive elements for earlier grades). We have found that such grade-appropriate variation will indeed involve a closer examination of informational density and conceptual relevance. With collaborative levels and communicative moves identified, next empirical stages will include iterative, large-scale investigations. Specifically, we aim to create systematically varied DRs to test emerging theories about the effects of informational density and conceptual relevance on sense making and explanation from students across grades 1–7.

REFERENCES

Aparicio, M. & Costa, C. J. (2015). Data visualization. *Communication Design Quarterly Review*, *3*(1), 7–11.

Ball, C. E. & Charlton, C. (2016). All writing is multimodal. In L. Adler-Kassner & E. Wardle (Eds.), *Naming what we know: Threshold concepts of writing studies*. (classroom ed., pp. 42–43). Utah State University Press.

Berger, J. (1972). *Ways of seeing*. BBC and Penguin.

Bloome, D., Carter, S. P., Christian, B. M., Otto, S. & Shuart-Faris, N. (2004). *Discourse analysis and the study of classroom language and literacy events: A microethnographic perspective*. Routledge.

Bruner, J. (1990). Culture and human development: A new look. *Human Development*, *33*(6), 344–355.

Cole, M. (1998). Can cultural psychology help us think about diversity?. *Mind, Culture, and Activity*, *5*(4), 291–304.

Gee, J. P. (2004). *An introduction to discourse analysis: Theory and method*. Routledge.

Gee, J. P. (2005). Meaning making, communities of practice, and analytical toolkits. *Journal of Sociolinguistics*, *9*(4), 590–594.

Gillespie, C. S. (1993). Reading graphic displays: What teachers should know. *Journal of Reading*, *36*(5), 350–354.

Green, J., Skukauskaite, A., Dixon, C. & Córdova, R. (2007). Epistemological issues in the analysis of video records: Interactional ethnography as a logic of inquiry. In R. Goldman, R. Pea, B. Barron, & S. J. Derry (Eds.), *Video Research in the Learning Sciences* (pp. 115–132). Lawrence Erlbaum.

Groes, S. (2016). Against nostalgia: Climate change art and memory. In S. Groes (Ed.), *Memory in the twenty-first century* (pp. 175–187). Palgrave Macmillan.

Halpern, O. (2015). *Beautiful data: A history of vision and reason since 1945*. Duke University Press.

Hershkowitz, R., Schwarz, B. B. & Dreyfus, T. (2001). Abstraction in context: Epistemic actions. *Journal for Research in Mathematics Education*, 195–222.

Hunter, B., Crismore, A. & Pearson, P. (1987). Visual displays in basal readers and social studies textbooks. In D. Willows & H. Houghton (Eds.), *The psychology of illustration* (Vol. 1, pp. 116–135). Springer-Verlag.

Johnson, D. W. & Johnson, R. T. (1990). *Cooperative learning and achievement*. In S. Sharan (Ed.), *Cooperative learning: Theory and research* (p. 23–37). Praeger Publishers.

Kahneman, D. (2011). *Thinking, fast and slow*. Farrar, Straus and Giroux.

Kahneman, D., Krueger, A. B., Schkade, D., Schwarz, N. & Stone, A. A. (2006). Would you be happier if you were richer? A focusing illusion. *Science, 312*(5782), 1908–1910.

Kamm, K., Askov, E. & Klumb, R. (1977). Study skills mastery among middle and high school students. ERIC Document Reproduction Service No. ED 141 780.

Lamb, G. R., Polman, J. L., Newman, A. & Smith, C. G. (2014). Science news infographics: Teaching students to gather, interpret, and present information graphically. *The Science Teacher, 81*(3), 25.

Lee, O., Quinn, H. & Valdés, G. (2013). Science and language for English language learners in relation to Next Generation Science Standards and with implications for Common Core State Standards for English language arts and mathematics. *Educational Researcher, 42*(4), 223–233.

Martix, S. & Hodson, J. (2014). Teaching with infographics: Practising new digital competencies and visual literacies. *Journal of Pedagogic Development, 3*(2), 17–27.

National Assessment of Educational Progress (NAEP). (1985). National assessment of education progress, reading in America: A perspective on two assessments (Report 06-R-01). United States GPO.

National Education Association. (1894). *The report of the committee of ten*. American Book Company.

National Research Council. (2012). *A framework for K–12 science education: Practices, crosscutting concepts, and core ideas*. The National Academies Press.

Next Generation Science Standards (NGSS) Lead States. (2013). *Next generation science standards: For states, by states*. The National Academies Press.

Propen, A. D. (2012). *Locating visual-material rhetorics: The map, the mill & the GPS*. Parlor Press.

Selwyn, N. (2015). Data entry: towards the critical study of digital data and education. *Learning, Media and Technology, 40*(1), 64–82.

Tufte, E. R. (1983). *The visual display of quantitative information*. Graphics Press.

Vygotsky, L. S. (1980). *Mind in society: The development of higher psychological processes*. Harvard University Press.

Wilson, M. (2004). *Constructing measures: An item response modeling approach*. Routledge.

CHAPTER 12.

INFORMING INQUIRY INTO WRITING ACROSS THE LIFESPAN FROM PERSPECTIVES ON STUDENTS WITH LEARNING DISABILITIES OR AUTISM SPECTRUM DISORDER

Apryl L. Poch
Duquesne University

Matthew C. Zajic
Teachers College, Columbia University

Steve Graham
Arizona State University

The value of writing is not limited to single points of time in our lives but serves many different purposes across the lifespan (Bazerman et al., 2018). For instance, young children begin to experiment with writing as early as two years of age, using it as a vehicle for play, communication, and self-expression (Rowe, 2008). With the advent of school, the purposes for writing expand greatly to include writing to inform, persuade, describe, summarize, learn, and narrate to identify just some of the ways children, adolescents, and young adults learn to write and use writing as part of their education. During adulthood, writing is a staple of life at both work and home. White and blue collar workers commonly use writing to perform their jobs (Light, 2001), and adults frequently use writing throughout the day to initiate and maintain personal connections, as they tweet, text, email, and connect with each other using a variety of social networks and media (Freedman et al., 2016).

Over 85 percent of the world's population now writes (Roser & Ortiz-Ospina, 2018). People who do not know how to write or find writing challenging enough that they limit its use are at a disadvantage socially, educationally, and occupationally. Persons with a disability are at special risk for experiencing difficulties learning to write. For example, the most recent National Assessment of Educational Progress in the United States (National Center for Educational Statistics, 2012; an updated report is due in mid-2020) revealed that 95 percent of eighth and twelfth-grade students with a disability scored at or below the basic level of writing competence, denoting only partial mastery of grade-level writing skills. While not every person with a disability experiences problems learning to write or continues to experience difficulty with writing as they move into adulthood, writing problems are so pronounced that persons with disabilities score lower than peers without disabilities on every measure of writing in almost every study conducted to date with school-aged children (Albertini & Schley, 2011; Graham et al., 2016, 2017, 2020; Mayes & Calhoun, 2003; Myklebust, 1965; Savaiano & Hebert, in press). Even so, we know virtually nothing about the writing of individuals with disabilities across the lifespan. This chapter addresses this issue by considering perspectives on writing development in individuals with two different types of disabilities: learning disabilities (LD) and autism spectrum disorder (ASD). LD is a neurological disorder and accounts for 33 percent of students who receive special education services in schools across the United States, whereas ASD is a neurodevelopmental disorder and accounts for 11 percent of students who receive special education services in the United States (Hussar et al., 2020; Kauffman et al., 2017). The prevalence and increasing awareness of LD and ASD makes these two areas of disability good focal points for considering writing and disabilities across the lifespan.

For both LD and ASD, we examine evidence describing how the characteristics of the disability impact writing. This includes the strengths that persons with LD and ASD bring to writing and learning to write as well as the challenges they face. This analysis is informed by a lifespan perspective that recognizes that the development of writing is complex and variable, involves the reconfiguration of cognitive and social capabilities that evolved separately from it, is shaped and shapes other forms of language and learning development, requires learning how to use language resources flexibly and intentionally, and occurs in multiple contexts (including school) that are influenced by changing social needs, opportunities, resources, and technologies (Bazerman et al., 2018).

It is important to realize that the systematic study of writing with persons with disabilities has been mostly limited to the first 22 years of life. Research on the writing of persons with disabilities beyond college is virtually non-existent. While there is some longitudinal research with students with disabilities that examines the writing capabilities of the same students across more than a single school year (e.g., Nauclér & Magnusson, 2002), this is limited to the study of a small set of writing skills, as was done by Maeland and Karlsdottir (1991) with the handwriting and spelling of students with LD. In fact, almost all of what we know about the writing of persons with LD or ASD is based on cross-sectional research comparing their writing to the writing of peers without a disability in one or more grades (see Finnegan & Accardo, 2018; Graham et al., 2017) or research that involves one or more manipulations to determine how specific factors such as executive control impact their writing (Graham, 1997; Zajic & Wilson, 2020). While such studies can provide valuable insights, they are not a replacement for longitudinal research conducted both in and out of school at different points of development in the life of persons with LD or ASD. As a result, it is essential to view the writing of persons with disabilities through a lifespan lens.

WRITERS WITH LD

According to the Individuals with Disabilities Education Act (IDEA), an LD refers to "a disorder in one or more of the basic psychological processes involved in understanding or in using language, spoken or written, which disorder may manifest itself in the imperfect ability to listen, think, speak, read, write, spell, or to do mathematical calculations" (Title 1, Part A, § 602(30), 2004). Although individuals with LD exhibit average to above average intellectual functioning, their unexpected underachievement is largely unexplained. LD has consistently been one of the largest disability categories through which students receive special education supports, with 33 percent of students receiving special education services for an LD during the 2018–2019 academic year in the United States (Hussar et al., 2020). Though receipt of special education services is contingent on the qualification of possessing an LD in consonance with the IDEA definition, other definitions of LD, such as the definition of the National Joint Committee on Learning Disabilities (LD Online, 2015), emphasize the potential of the occurrence of LD across the lifespan.

Students with LD experience strained foundational writing and cognitive skills which impact their ability to develop more advanced writing skills. In K–12 school settings, the writing challenges often demonstrated by students with LD have been grouped into two categories: approach to writing and knowledge of writing (Graham & Harris, 2012). The approach that students with LD tend to adopt—knowledge-telling—relies on the telling and recalling of content that is already known about a given topic. This approach is typically adopted in an effort to cope with the demands of writing (Graham & Harris, 2012). The writing of students with LD is less organized, contains fewer details, and is less likely to stick to the intended topic of focus compared to their peers (Gillespie & Graham, 2014). They also spend less time planning, translating, and reviewing. When reviewing, changes largely focus on surface level details and oftentimes the changes they make to their writing make no significant contribution or detract from the quality of their written response. The challenges that students with LD experience in regard to knowledge of writing—when compared with typically achieving peers—reflect a lack of knowledge surrounding different genres of writing (e.g., narrative and expository), as well as how writing works (Gillespie & Graham, 2014). They also struggle with grapho-motor skills and writing mechanics, and their writing is often choppy and may contain incomplete sentences.

Difficulties with approach and knowledge of writing exist alongside cognitive demands, as a lack of fluency with writing tasks drains necessary cognitive resources for developing writing. As McCutchen (2011) noted, fluent language processes allow writers—especially beginning writers—to manage the working memory constraints induced by writing, whereas writing knowledge helps writers manage the constraints of short-term memory.

One of the most recent meta-analyses examining the writing characteristics of students with LD when compared to their typically developing peers is reported by Graham et al. (2017). Of the studies reviewed, they found that students with LD obtained lower scores on several writing outcomes compared to their peers, including writing quality, organization, vocabulary, sentence fluency, conventions (i.e., spelling, handwriting, and grammar), genre elements, output, as well as motivation. These differences were both statistically significant and clinically significant. Their results suggest that writing is exceptionally challenging for students with LD and that deficits across these outcomes are pervasive over time as these variables were present in studies examining children in grades 1–12. Thus, students with LD do not just struggle with certain writing skills at one point in time (e.g., spelling and handwriting in elementary school); their writing challenges are persistent across time.

LD AND WRITING: A LIFESPAN PERSPECTIVE

Though more research abounds at the elementary level, relatively little is known about the youngest writers with LD, particularly around the pre-K and kindergarten grade levels. This could be because young students have not yet been identified as having an LD. While disabilities can develop and be identified at different times, LD is typically diagnosed around third grade (this is the same time there is a shift in academic instruction from teaching students how to write to how to use writing to learn new content). In one study (Boudreau & Hedberg, 1999), preschool children with specific language impairments performed lower than matched peers on measures of language, processing, and print-related skills. Though this study included students with language impairments rather than LD, it is important to note the role that early language skills play in writing development (Graham et al., 2020).

Much of what is known about elementary writing begins in or after first grade and expands in late elementary (e.g., grades 3–5). Although research in elementary grades has focused on aspects of writing quality and the developmental process of writing ideas, there is a larger focus with students with LD at these grade levels on transcription skills and the mechanics of composing, including spelling, handwriting, grammar, and syntax. This literature regularly demonstrates that students with LD experience much greater difficulty with these transcription skills when compared to their typically developing peers (Berninger, 1999).

At the secondary level, from middle through high school, much less is known about the components of writing that are essential or critical for learners with LD (Poch & Lembke, 2017). While there is continued interest in transcription-level skills, these skills are generally assumed to be established by the early secondary grades, despite evidence that transcription-level challenges continue to develop across this time and continue to be constraining for adolescents with disabilities (McCutchen, 2011). With the increasing need for secondary students to use writing to demonstrate content expertise, elements of text generation—such as structure, idea development, and clarity of communication—tend to gain prominence over transcription-level skills. However, secondary students who experience difficulty learning to write often continue to struggle with transcription skills (e.g., Graham & Santangelo, 2014).

At the post-secondary level, very little research has explored the writing of individuals with LD. In a literature synthesis from 1990 to 2000, Li and Hamel (2003) identified seven studies that explored characteristics and error patterns in the writing of college students with LD and writing difficulties, with many of these studies comparing students with LD to students without LD. Li and Hamel (2003) suggested that the studies generally focused on mechanical errors (e.g., spelling, punctuation, and capitalization) and content problems (e.g., planning, organization, and coherence), both of which are consistent with those discussed earlier in the section above. No updated studies appear to be available, leaving a gap in this research over nearly the last two decades.

WRITERS WITH ASD

In addition to LDs, writing development can be affected by a wide array of other neurological differences, like those identified in ASD. Though ASD is diagnosed from a medical framework, a growing community push for self-advocacy and autistic identity exists embedded within a neurodiversity framework (Kapp et al., 2013). As these two perspectives differ, it is useful to consider the core characteristics of ASD from both the medical perspective from the Diagnostic and Statistical Manual of Mental Disorders (5th Edition; DSM-5; American Psychiatric Association, 2013) and the self-advocacy perspective from the Autistic Self Advocacy Network (ASAN; ASAN, n.d.).

The DSM-5 describes ASD as a neurodevelopmental disorder characterized by difficulties with social communication and by the presence of restricted interests or repetitive behavioral patterns (American Psychiatric Association, 2013). Additionally, clinicians are required to make two further judgments when diagnosing ASD: the severity of required support (specified as low, medium, or high); and the presence of additional co-occurring conditions (i.e., intellectual disability or language impairment), associations with either biological or environmental factors, or associations with other neurodevelopmental disorders. The ASAN (n.d.) offers a similar yet different definition of ASD described via seven commonly exhibited characteristics. These seven characteristics include (a) different sensory experiences; (b) atypical approaches to learning and problem solving; (c) extreme passion or deeply focused thinking about specific subjects or topics; (d) atypical and repetitive movements; (e) desire for consistency, routine, and order, as disruptions can result in increased anxiety and frustration; (f) difficulties with understanding and expressing typically used verbal and non-verbal language; and (g) difficulties in understanding and engaging in social interactions.

Current prevalence estimates suggest that the number of eight-year-old children in the United States diagnosed with ASD is one in 54, with boys four times as likely as girls to be identified (Maenner et al., 2020). In educational contexts, approximately 11 percent of children diagnosed with ASD are served under the IDEA (Hussar et al., 2020). A growing body of research suggests that children with ASD commonly present a heterogeneous range of educational strengths and challenges (Bauminger-Zviely, 2013; Keen et al., 2016). Research on the writing development of children with ASD has been generally limited to writing done for academic purposes where evidence has suggested a similar wide array of strengths and challenges (Zajic & Asaro-Saddler, 2019; Zajic & Wilson, 2020). Relatively few studies have focused specifically on issues of writing development for individuals with ASD, with no longitudinal studies currently available. A recent meta-analysis analyzed 13 available studies to find that individuals with ASD demonstrate lower overall performance compared to their typically developing peers across standardized measures of handwriting, spelling, and text generation (Finnegan & Accardo, 2018). A thorough review of all available research is beyond the scope of this chapter (see Zajic & Wilson, 2020), but the following provides a brief overview of available research describing the range of transcription and text generation research done across the school-age and postsecondary years. Given the current body of literature, it is important to acknowledge that broad claims about the writing development of individuals with ASD—particularly across the lifespan—

are difficult at this time, and the following noted characteristics should be seen as preliminary points of consideration requiring further empirical investigation.

WRITING DEVELOPMENT IN INDIVIDUALS WITH ASD

Children with ASD commonly demonstrate transcription difficulties across the school-age years. Kushki et al. (2011) identified seven studies that demonstrated difficulties seemingly related to fine motor and visual-motor integration difficulties with challenges noted for overall handwriting legibility and letter formation. Additional studies have further explored these challenges (Johnson, Papadopoulos et al., 2013) or additional challenges with grip strength (Alaniz et al., 2015) and letter form or spacing (Johnson, Phillips et al., 2015). Cross-sectional research has found that children with ASD show these handwriting difficulties across the school-age years (Mayes et al., 2019). Spelling difficulties were noted in relation to typically developing peers (Finnegan & Accardo, 2018), but other studies have noted minimal spelling difficulties (Mayes & Calhoun, 2006).

Difficulties with text generation have also appeared to be quite common for students with ASD across a variety of studies. Most commonly, studies report these children perform lower than typically developing peers on standardized expository (Mayes & Calhoun, 2003, 2006, 2008), persuasive (Brown et al., 2014), and narrative writing measures (Myles et al., 2003). Few studies have focused on distinct subpopulations—like individuals who no longer met an ASD diagnosis (Troyb et al., 2014) or who qualified as gifted and talented (Assouline et al., 2012; Foley-Nicpon et al., 2012)—or on specific predictors of written language challenges, including social communication (Brown et al., 2014), oral language (Dockrell et al., 2014), and attention (Zajic et al., 2018). Studies have typically not focused on specific age ranges and have commonly included children in elementary through secondary school contexts (Zajic & Wilson, 2020). Some of the writing challenges experienced by school-age children with ASD appear distinct from those demonstrated by children with LD, even when children with either disability may demonstrate similar learning profiles (Zajic et al., 2019).

Beyond the school-age years, little empirical work has examined ASD and writing in postsecondary education and adulthood. Jurecic (2007) took an analytical perspective to one college student with ASD, though this work has been critiqued for offering a medical rather than neurodiverse perspective (Lewiecki-Wilson et al., 2008). Gerstle and Walsh (2011) offered accommodation and pedagogy practices for college students with ASD, but they offered limited theoretical takeaways (Pacton, 2013). Similarly, Cherney (2017) explored writing center tutoring practices for college students with ASD but offered pedagogical implementation strategies rather than empirically derived findings. Gillespie-Lynch et al. (2020) adopted a participatory research approach that examined strengths and challenges of autistic college students, finding autistic college students may face challenges overcoming perfectionistic writing tendencies. Tomlinson and Newman (2017) adopted a neurodiversity approach and surveyed autistic writers online about their own life writing, arguing for approaches from universal design for learning to support postsecondary writing development. Two additional empirical studies echo difficulties observed in the school-age population. Beversdorf et al. (2001) reported preliminary evidence of handwriting difficulties in adults with ASD compared to typically developing peers. Brown and Klein (2011) compared short writing samples (narrative and expository) of adults with ASD to typically developing peers to find that adults with ASD wrote lower quality narrative and expository texts and shorter narrative texts. They also found a positive association between theory of mind and writing quality and length for both text types.

ADVANCING LIFESPAN RESEARCH ON INDIVIDUALS WITH LD OR ASD

Current research leaves much to be understood about the development of writing abilities and writing practices across the lifespan for individuals with disabilities like LD or ASD. Three areas of further research predominantly absent from the above syntheses are discussed next that may help to further unpack the lifespan writing development of individuals with LD or ASD. However, it should be noted that perhaps the greatest limitation that has the potential to significantly hamper the growth of a lifespan understanding of the writing development of individuals with disabilities is the field's understanding and definition of terms like LD and ASD, which can unintentionally skew the participants who qualify for future research studies. As definitions change or are updated, it makes it difficult to know whether comparable subgroups of participants are truly similar and have been reliably identified with a disability across contexts. Compounding this challenge through adulthood is the need to account for how individuals with disabilities have learned to manage their disability and make adaptations to their writing in terms of both the changing cognitive demands of writing and the social contexts surrounding their lives.

Early Writing Development Precursors

Much of the above-mentioned research has involved children in elementary or secondary grades with relatively no research focusing on the development of early and emergent writing abilities in children with LD or ASD. Writing development begins long before early elementary school, as emergent literacy practices (Rowe, 2018) and early linguistic and cognitive development (Berninger, 2015) serve as important precursors to later writing development. Investigation into these abilities may help specify early characteristics of LD or ASD that may guide long-term writing development inquiries.

For individuals with ASD, in addition to oral language, exploring the impact of early social development on early writing skills may offer new insights into written language development. As oral language and written language share an interrelated developmental trajectory (e.g., Berninger, 2015), further research into these areas may help explain difficulties with transcription and text generation experienced across the lifespan (Graham et al., 2020).

For individuals with ASD, in addition to oral language, additional focus to the role of early social development may offer new insights into written language development. The development of social communication abilities is a noted ongoing challenge for individuals with ASD impacted by an array of abilities throughout development (American Psychiatric Association, 2013). Looking to the development of joint attention abilities, one of the earliest developmental abilities related to social cognition (Mundy, 2016), may be important in the context of lifelong writing development.

Joint attention refers to the ability to coordinate attention with other people to fluidly adopt a common point of reference (or point of view) and assists with learning in structured and unstructured environments (Mundy, 1995, 2016; Mundy & Newell, 2007). For example, an adult may point to and label a specific object of reference (i.e., a toy or an animal), and the infant makes a behavioral move (i.e., attending to the item) to form an underlying connection (i.e., the name of that item) through a social communicative framework. Though this example relies on the overt use of behavior, the early social cognitive foundations remain throughout development while the process becomes more fluid and more covert (see Mundy et al., 2017). Joint attention typically begins in early infancy and becomes increasingly complex within the first two years of life (Bakeman & Adamson, 1984). It contributes to early lexical, vocabulary, and language development (Baldwin, 1995; Mundy, Sigman et al., 1990; Tomasello, 1988) and develops into a core underlying process involved in human social engagement (Mundy, 2016; Mundy et al., 2017). Early and ongoing challenges with the development of joint attention are a hallmark feature of ASD (Mundy, 2016; Mundy et al., 2017), and investigating the relationship between joint attention (and later social cognition) and writing development across the lifespan may help to fill specific gaps in early and later writing development. Specifically, better understanding this relationship may support the social cognitive abilities required for writing practices and underlying writing knowledge. However, understanding these areas further may only be a component of broader writing development concerns, as Tomlinson and Newman (2017) noted that not all writing challenges experienced by adults with ASD should be attributed to such underlying difficulties.

PERSPECTIVES FROM INDIVIDUALS WITH LD OR ASD

Much of the available research has focused on the writing done by individuals with LD or ASD rather than incorporating the perspectives and beliefs of these individuals into the research design. For individuals with LD, the role of knowledge in writing development remains relatively unstudied, with specific attention needed at the adolescent and young adult levels (Lin et al., 2007; Saddler & Graham, 2007). For individuals with ASD, research must echo the ongoing need to adopt flexible research designs that straddle medical and neurodiversity perspectives to include insights from autistic individuals across the lifespan (Kapp et al., 2013). Some research at the postsecondary level has argued that hearing from autistic individuals can inform writing instruction based off their demonstrated needs as opposed to diagnostic recommendations that often leave writing too narrowly conceptualized and fail to properly account for autistic individuals' own writing strengths and challenges (Gillespie-Lynch et al., 2020; Tomlinson & Newman, 2017; Walters, 2015). However, it is also important to note that while postsecondary attendance rates for individuals with ASD are increasing, attention should fall outside of educational contexts as well, including the need to look at prolific writers with ASD (Van Goidsenhoven, 2017). Further research is needed that incorporates perspectives that highlight strengths and challenges with producing writing across different writing genres for different purposes and that elucidate perspectives from the writers themselves as to their own processes and composing strategies. Incorporating further perspectives may help add to the understanding of what might be assumed incorrectly about writing development in individuals with LD or ASD by providing further insights into the complexity of skills involved with writing and how those skills change across the lifespan.

FOCUS ON STRENGTHS AND ON DEVELOPMENT BEYOND SCHOOL-BASED GENRES

Predominantly through the school-age years and somewhat into postsecondary contexts, available empirical work has narrowly focused on in-school writing development, neglecting other contexts where writing development occurs throughout the lifespan. From the writer(s)-within-community framework (Graham, 2018), available research on writing development in LD or ASD has focused on cognitive mechanisms without much attention to the socially embedded contexts. Ongoing research needs to consider both the psychological processes and the social contexts that may impact writing development in individuals with LD or ASD across the lifespan. As not all individuals with LD or ASD experience difficulties with writing (or experience writing challenges to the same extent), further research is needed that is guided by both researchers and informed community stakeholders on helping to identify sources of interindividual and intraindividual strengths and challenges with writing development that draw from different methodological perspectives (e.g., Zajic & Poch, this volume). Accounting for the various lifespan trajectories requires balancing social and psychological factors that affect development across the lifespan to understand the highly varied writing profiles of individuals with LD or ASD, to capture how these individuals navigate their writing experiences, and to combine approaches from researchers and community members to identify the challenges and to support the strengths that emerge for individuals with LD or ASD across the lifespan beyond school contexts.

ACKNOWLEDGMENTS

Matthew C. Zajic received support during the drafting of this chapter from a Postdoctoral Research Fellow Training Program Grant in Education and Autism Spectrum Disorders from the National Center for Special Education Research at the Institute of Education Sciences (R324B180034) awarded to the University of Virginia.

REFERENCES

Alaniz, M. L., Galit, E., Necesito, C. I. & Rosario, E. R. (2015). Hand strength, handwriting, and functional skills in children with autism. *The American Journal of Occupational Therapy, 69*(4), 1–9. https://doi.org/10.5014/ajot.2015.016022.

Albertini, J. & Schley, S. (2011). Writing: Characteristics, instruction and assessment. In M. Marschark & P. E. Spencer (Eds.), *The Oxford handbook of deaf studies, language and education* (Vol. I, 2nd ed., pp. 130–143). Oxford University Press.

American Psychiatric Association. (2013). *Diagnostic and statistical manual of mental disorders: DSM-5*. American Psychiatric Association.

Assouline, S. G., Foley Nicpon, M. & Dockery, L. (2012). Predicting the academic achievement of gifted students with autism spectrum disorder. *Journal of Autism and Developmental Disorders, 42*(9), 1781–1789. https://doi.org/10.1007/s10803-011-1403-x.

Autism Self Advocacy Network. (n.d.). About autism. https://autisticadvocacy.org/about-asan/about-autism/.

Bakeman, R. & Adamson, L. B. (1984). Coordinating attention to people and objects in mother-infant and peer-infant interaction. *Child Development, 55*(4), 1278–1289. https://doi.org/10.2307/1129997.

Baldwin, D. A. (1995). Understanding the link between joint attention and language. In C. Moore & P. J. Dunham (Eds.), *Joint attention: Its origins and role in development* (pp. 131–158). Lawrence Erlbaum Associates.

Bauminger-Zviely, N. (2013). *Social and academic abilities in children with high-functioning autism spectrum disorders*. The Guilford Press.

Bazerman, C., Applebee, A. N., Berninger, V. W., Brandt, D., Graham, S., Jeffery, J. V., Matsuda, P. K., Murphy, S., Rowe, D. W., Schleppegrell, M. & Wilcox, K. C. (Eds.). (2018). *The lifespan development of writing*. National Council of Teachers of English.

Berninger, V. (1999). Coordinating transcription and text generation in working memory during composing: Automatic and constructive processes. *Learning Disability Quarterly, 22*, 99–112. https://doi.org/10.2307/1511269.

Berninger, V. W. (2015). *Interdisciplinary frameworks for schools: Best professional practices for serving the needs of all students*. American Psychological Association.

Beversdorf, D. Q., Anderson, J. M., Manning, S. E., Anderson, S. L., Nordgren, R. E., Felopulos, G. J. & Bauman, M. L. (2001). Brief report: Macrographia in high-functioning adults with autism spectrum disorder. *Journal of Autism and Developmental Disorders, 31*(1), 97–101. https://doi.org/10.1023/A:1005622031943.

Boudreau, D. M. & Hedberg, N. L. (1999). A comparison of early literacy skills in children with specific language impairment and their typically developing peers. *American Journal of Speech-Language Pathology, 8*(3), 249–260. https://doi.org/10.1044/1058-0360.0803.249.

Brown, H. M. & Klein, P. D. (2011). Writing, Asperger syndrome and theory of mind. *Journal of Autism and Developmental Disorders, 41*(11), 1464–1474. https://doi.org/10.1007/s10803-010-1168-7.

Brown, H. M., Johnson, A. M., Smyth, R. E. & Oram Cardy, J. (2014). Exploring the persuasive writing skills of students with high-functioning autism spectrum disorder. *Research in Autism Spectrum Disorders, 8*(11), 1482–1499. https://doi.org/10.1016/j.rasd.2014.07.017.

Cherney, K. (2017). Inclusion for the "isolated": An exploration of writing tutoring strategies for students with ASD. *Praxis: A Writing Center Journal, 14*(3), 49–55.

Dockrell, J. E., Ricketts, J., Charman, T. & Lindsay, G. (2014). Exploring writing products in students with language impairments and autism spectrum disorders. *Learning and Instruction, 32*, 81–90. https://doi.org/10.1016/j.learninstruc.2014.01.008.

Finnegan, E. & Accardo, A. L. (2018). Written expression in individuals with autism spectrum disorder: A meta-analysis. *Journal of Autism and Developmental Disorders, 48*(3), 868–882. https://doi.org/10.1007/s10803-017-3385-9.

Foley-Nicpon, M., Assouline, S. G. & Stinson, R. D. (2012). Cognitive and academic distinctions between gifted students with autism and Asperger syndrome. *Gifted Child Quarterly, 56*(2), 77–89. https://doi.org/10.1177%2F0016986211433199.

Freedman, S. W., Hull, G. A., Higgs, J. M. & Booten, K. P. (2016). Teaching writing in a digital and global age: Toward access, learning, and development for all. In D. H. Gitomer & C. A. Bell (Eds.), *Handbook of research on teaching* (5th ed., pp. 1389–1450). American Educational Research Association.

Gerstle, V. & Walsh, L. (2011). *Autism spectrum disorders in the college composition classroom: Making writing instruction more accessible for all students.* Marquette University Press.

Gillespie, A. & Graham, S. (2014). A meta-analysis of writing interventions for students with learning disabilities. *Exceptional Children, 80*(4), 454–473. https://doi.org/10.1177%2F0014402914527238.

Gillespie-Lynch, K., Hotez, E., Zajic, M., Riccio, A., DeNigris, D., Kofner, B., Bublitz, D., Gaggi, N. & Kavi, L. (2020). Comparing the writing skills of autistic and nonautistic university students: A collaboration with autistic university students. *Autism: The International Journal of Research and Practice.* Advance Online Publication. https://doi.org/10.1177/1362361320929453.

Graham, S. (1997). Executive control in the revising of students with learning and writing difficulties. *Journal of Educational Psychology, 89*, 223–234. https://psycnet.apa.org/doi/10.1037/0022-0663.89.2.223.

Graham, S. (2018). A writer(s) within community model of writing. In C. Bazerman, A. N. Applebee, V. W. Berninger, D. Brandt, S. Graham, J. V. Jeffery, P. K. Matsuda, S. Murphy, D. W. Rowe, M. Schleppegrell & K. C. Wilcox (Eds.), *The lifespan development of writing* (pp. 272–325). National Council of Teachers of English.

Graham, S., Collins, A. & Rigby-Wills, H. (2017). A meta-analysis examining the writing characteristics of students with learning disabilities and normally achieving peers. *Exceptional Children, 83*, 199–218. https://doi.org/10.1177/0014402916664070.

Graham, S., Fishman, E., Reid, R., Hebert, M. (2016). Writing characteristics of students with ADHD and their normally achieving peers. *Learning Disabilities Research & Practice, 31*, 75–89. https://doi.org/10.1111/ldrp.12099.

Graham, S. & Harris, K. R. (2012). *Writing better: Effective strategies for teaching students learning difficulties.* Paul H. Brookes Publishing.

Graham, S. & Santangelo, T. (2014). Does spelling instruction make students better spellers, readers, and writers? A meta-analytic review. *Reading & Writing: An Interdisciplinary Journal, 27*, 1703–1743. https://doi.org/10.1007/s11145-014-9517-0.

Graham, S., Hebert, M., Fishman, E., Ray, A. & Rouse, A. (2020). Do children classified with specific language impairment have a learning disability in writing: A meta-analysis. *Journal of Learning Disabilities, 53*, 293–310. https://doi.org/10.1177/0022219420917338.

Hussar, B., Zhang, J., Hein, S., Wang, K., Roberts, A., Cui, J., Smith, M., Bullock Mann, F., Barmer, A., and Dilig, R. (2020). *The Condition of Education 2020* (NCES 2020–144). U.S. Department of Education. National Center for Education Statistics. https://nces.ed.gov/pubsearch/pubsinfo.asp?pubid=2020144.

Individuals with Disabilities Education Improvement Act of 2004, 20 U.S.C. § 1400 *et seq.* (2004). https://uscode.house.gov/view.xhtml?req=(title:20%20section:1401%20edition:prelim).

Johnson, B. P., Papadopoulos, N., Fielding, J., Tonge, B., Phillips, J. G. & Rinehart, N. J. (2013). A quantitative comparison of handwriting in children with high-functioning autism and attention deficit hyperactivity disorder. *Research in Autism Spectrum Disorders, 7*(12), 1638–1646. https://doi.org/10.1016/j.rasd.2013.09.008.

Johnson, B. P., Phillips, J. G., Papadopoulos, N., Fielding, J., Tonge, B. & Rinehart, N. J. (2015). Do children with autism and Asperger's disorder have difficulty controlling handwriting size? A kinematic evaluation. *Research in Autism Spectrum Disorders, 11*, 20–26. https://doi.org/10.1016/j.rasd.2014.11.001.

Jurecic, A. (2007). Neurodiversity. *College English, 69*(5), 421–442.

Kapp, S. K., Gillespie-Lynch, K., Sherman, L. E. & Hutman, T. (2013). Deficit, difference, or both? Autism and neurodiversity. *Developmental Psychology, 49*(1), 59–71. https://psycnet.apa.org/doi/10.1037/a0028353.

Kauffman, J., Hallahan, D. & Pullen, P. (2017). *Handbook of special education* (2nd ed.). Routledge.

Keen, D., Webster, A. & Ridley, G. (2016). How well are children with autism spectrum disorder doing academically at school? An overview of the literature. *Autism: The International Journal of Research and Practice, 20*(3), 276–294. https://doi.org/10.1177/1362361315580962.

Kushki, A., Chau, T. & Anagnostou, E. (2011). Handwriting difficulties in children with autism spectrum disorders: A scoping review. *Journal of Autism and Developmental Disorders, 41*(12), 1706–1716. https://doi.org/10.1007/s10803-011-1206-0.

LD Online. (2015). *National joint committee on learning disabilities.* http://www.ldonline.org/.

Lewiecki-Wilson, C., Dolmage, J., Heilker, P. & Jurecic, A. (2008). Two comments on "neurodiversity." *College English, 70*(3), 314–325.

Li, H. & Hamel, C. M. (2003). Writing issues in college students with learning disabilities: A synthesis of the literature from 1990 to 2000. *Learning Disability Quarterly, 26*, 29–46. https://doi.org/10.2307/1593683.

Light, R. (2001). *Making the most of college.* Harvard University Press.

Lin, S-J. C., Monroe, B. W. & Troia, G. A. (2007). Development of writing knowledge in grades 2–8: A comparison of typically developing writers and their struggling peers. *Reading & Writing Quarterly, 23*(3), 207–230. https://doi.org/10.1080/10573560701277542.

Maeland, A. & Karlsdottir, R. (1991). Development of reading, spelling, and writing skills from third to sixth grade in normal and dysgraphic school children. In J. Wann, A. Wing & N. Sovik (Eds.), *Development of graphic skills* (pp. 179–189). Academic Press.

Maenner, M. J., Shaw, K. A., Baio, J., et al. (2020). Prevalence of autism spectrum disorder among children aged 8 years—Autism and Developmental Disabilities Monitoring Network, 11 Sites, United States, 2016. *Morbidity and Mortality Weekly Report Surveillance Summaries, 69*(4), 1–12. https://doi.org/10.15585/mmwr.ss6904a1.

Mayes, S. D., Breaux, R. P., Calhoun, S. L. & Frye, S. S. (2019). High prevalence of dysgraphia in elementary through high school students with ADHD and autism. *Journal of Attention Disorders, 23*(8), 787–796. https://doi.org/10.1177/1087054717720721.

Mayes, S. D. & Calhoun, S. L. (2003). Analysis of WISC-III, Stanford-Binet:IV, and academic achievement test scores in children with autism. *Journal of Autism and Developmental Disorders, 33*(3), 329–341. https://doi.org/10.1023/A:1024462719081.

Mayes, S. D. & Calhoun, S. L. (2006). Frequency of reading, math, and writing disabilities in children with clinical disorders. *Learning and Individual Differences, 16*(2), 145–157. https://doi.org/10.1016/j.lindif.2005.07.004.

Mayes, S. D. & Calhoun, S. L. (2008). WISC-IV and WIAT-II profiles in children with high-functioning autism. *Journal of Autism and Developmental Disorders, 38*(3), 428–439. https://doi.org/10.1007/s10803-007-0410-4.

McCutchen, D. (2011). From novice to expert: Implications of language skills and writing-relevant knowledge for memory during the development of writing skill. *Journal of Writing Research, 3*(1), 51–68.

Mundy, P. (1995). Joint attention and social-emotional approach behavior in children with autism. *Development and Psychopathology, 7*(1), 63–82. https://doi.org/10.1017/S0954579400006349.

Mundy, P. (2016). *Autism and joint attention: Development, neuroscience, and clinical fundamentals.* The Guilford Press.

Mundy, P. & Newell, L. (2007). Attention, joint attention, and social cognition. *Current Directions in Psychological Science, 16*(5), 269–274. https://doi.org/10.1111/j.1467-8721.2007.00518.x.

Mundy, P., Novotny, S., Swain-Lerro, L., McIntyre, N., Zajic, M. & Oswald, T. (2017). Joint-attention and the social phenotype of school-aged children with ASD. *Journal of Autism and Developmental Disorders, 47*(5), 1423–1435. https://doi.org/10.1007/s10803-017-3061-0.

Mundy, P., Sigman, M. & Kasari, C. (1990). A longitudinal study of joint attention and language development in autistic children. *Journal of Autism and Developmental Disorders, 20*(1), 115–128. https://doi.org/10.1007/BF02206861.

Myklebust, H. R. (1965). *Development and disorders of written language* (Vol. 1). Grune & Stratton.

Myles, B. S., Huggins, A., Rome-Lake, M., Hagiwara, T., Barnhill, G. P. & Griswold, D. E. (2003). Written language profile of children and youth with Asperger syndrome: From research to practice. *Education and Training in Developmental Disabilities, 38*(4), 362–369.

National Center for Educational Statistics. (2012). The nation's report card: Writing 2011 (NCES 2012–470). Institute of Educational Sciences, U.S. Department of Education.

Nauclér, K. & Magnusson, E. (2002). How do preschool language problems affect language abilities in adolescents. In F. Windsor & M. Kelly (Eds.), *Investigations in clinical phonetics and linguistics* (pp. 99–114). Lawrence Erlbaum Associates.

Pacton, A. M. (2013). Autism spectrum disorders in the college composition classroom: Making writing instruction more accessible for all students. *Composition Studies, 41*(1), 149–152.

Poch, A. L. & Lembke, E. S. (2017). A not-so-simple view of adolescent writing. *International Journal for Research in Learning Disabilities, 3*(2), 27–44. https://doi.org/10.28987/ijrld.3.2.27.

Roser, M. & Ortiz-Ospina, E. (2018). Literacy. *Our World In Data*. University of Oxford. http://www.iarld.com/wp-content/uploads/2018/02/IJRLD-Volume-3-Issue-2.pdf.

Rowe, D. (2008). The social construction of intentionality: Two-year-olds' and adults' participation at a preschool writing center. *Research in the Teaching of English, 42,* 387–434.

Rowe, D. W. (2018). Writing development in early childhood. In C. Bazerman, A. N. Applebee, V. W. Berninger, D. Brandt, S. Graham, J. V. Jeffery, P. K. Matsuda, S. Murphy, D. W. Rowe, M. Schleppegrell & K. C. Wilcox (Ed.), *The lifespan development of writing* (pp. 55–110). National Council of Teachers of English.

Saddler, B. & Graham, S. (2007). The relationship between writing knowledge and writing performance among more and less skilled writers. *Reading & Writing Quarterly, 23*(3), 231–247. https://doi.org/10.1080/10573560701277575.

Savaiano, M. & Hebert, M. (in press). A cross-sectional examination of the writing of students with visual impairments. *Journal of Visual Impairment and Blindness*.

Tomasello, M. (1988). The role of joint attentional processes in early language development. *Language Sciences, 10*(1), 69–88. https://doi.org/10.1016/0388-0001(88)90006-X.

Tomlinson, E. & Newman, S. (2017). Valuing writers from a neurodiversity perspective: Integrating new research on autism spectrum disorder into composition pedagogy. *Composition Studies, 45*(2), 91–112, 273.

Troyb, E., Orinstein, A., Tyson, K., Helt, M., Eigsti, I.-M., Stevens, M. & Fein, D. (2014). Academic abilities in children and adolescents with a history of autism spectrum disorders who have achieved optimal outcomes. *Autism: The International Journal of Research and Practice, 18*(3), 233–243. https://doi.org/10.1177/1362361312473519.

Van Goidsenhoven, L. (2017). How to think about "autie-biographies"? Life writing genres and strategies from an autistic perspective. *Language, Literature and Culture, 64*(2), 1–17.

Walters, S. (2015). Toward a critical ASD pedagogy of insight: Teaching, researching, and valuing the social literacies of neurodiverse students. *Research in the Teaching of English, 49*(4), 340–360.

Zajic, M. C. & Asaro-Saddler, K. (2019). Issue editor foreword: Supporting writers across the autism spectrum. *Topics in Language Disorders, 39*(2), 123–127. https://doi.org/10.1097/TLD.0000000000000182.

Zajic, M. C., Dunn, M. & Berninger, V. W. (2019). Case studies comparing learning profiles and response to instruction in autism spectrum disorder and oral and written language learning disability at transition to high school. *Topics in Language Disorders, 39*(2), 128–154. https://doi.org/10.1097/TLD.0000000000000180.

Zajic, M. C., McIntyre, N., Swain-Lerro, L., Novotny, S., Oswald, T. & Mundy, P. (2018). Attention and written expression in school-age, high-functioning children with autism spectrum disorders. *Autism: The International Journal of Research and Practice, 22*(3), 245–258. https://doi.org/10.1177/1362361316675121.

Zajic, M. C. & Wilson, S. E. (2020). Writing research involving children with autism spectrum disorder without a co-occurring intellectual disability: A systematic review using a language domains and mediational systems framework. *Research in Autism Spectrum Disorders, 70*. Advance Online Publication. https://doi.org/10.1016/j.rasd.2019.101471.

CHAPTER 13.

VISUALIZING WRITING DEVELOPMENT: MAPPING WRITERS' CONCEPTIONS OF WRITING THROUGH THE LIFESPAN

Erin Workman
DePaul University

> We all travel through our lives acquiring different experiences, trying new things, and meeting different people, and each of these events in our lives contributes to our personal voice that we then express as words on a paper.
>
> – Hudson, First-Year College Student

> Because different individuals bring such variety to the task of learning to write, they may have very different trajectories of development across their lifespans.
>
> – Bazerman et al., 2018, p. 43

In their recent collection *The Lifespan Development of Writing*, Bazerman et al. (2018) call for a "description of writing development that is realistic and rich," one that "recognize[s] the roles of both early and continuing life experiences and of individual variation" (p. 20). Within the *Lifespan* collection, Berninger et al. (2018) take up writers' individual variation, reporting on two studies that asked early developing writers "to explain what writing is" as a way of "gaining insight into the perspectives that developing writers *themselves* bring to the task of learning to write" (p. 155; emphasis added). Berninger et al. (2018) found that writers' explanations of writing "appeared to reflect a continuum of metacognition," ranging from writers who articulated no definition of writing to those who defined writing according to function to those who described multiple forms of writing (p. 164). Taking a similar approach, I conducted a nine-month study of 18-year-old writers, focusing on whether, how, and why these writers' conceptions of writing changed as they moved "*through* and *across* space-times, modalities, genres, [and] communities" (Smith, this volume) as they completed their first year of college. In addition to defining writing, participants in my study mapped their definitions of writing by identifying key concepts and visually depicting connections among them, creating *visual maps* that served as documentation of their definitions at discrete moments in time. In this chapter, I draw from my research to outline *visual mapping*—an adaptation of concept mapping—and to demonstrate its promise as a method for lifespan writing research.

Researching conceptions of writing is methodologically challenging, in part because of the "tacit nature of writing-related knowledge" (Roozen, 2016, p. 152) and in part due to the inaccessibility of cognitive structures (Ifenthaler et al., 2011). While North American writing studies (NAWS) researchers have approached the first challenge using stimulated recall techniques to prompt a writer's articulation of tacit knowledge—including retrospective accounts (e.g., Greene & Higgins, 1994), document-based interviews, and reflective interviews (Roozen, 2016)—researchers in education and educational psychology have responded to the second challenge using concept mapping to elicit a learner's conceptual knowledge within a particular domain (e.g., Kinchin, 2014; Novak, 2010; Schroeder et al., 2018). Although education researchers have used concept mapping since the early 1970s (Novak, 2010), NAWS researchers are only beginning to take up this method. Wette (2017), for example, uses mind mapping[1] to study graduate student writers' "conceptual knowledge development in a genre-based ESP writing course" (p. 59), and similarly, Rounsaville (2017) uses concept mapping to study writers' "genre repertoires from below" (p. 319). Like Wette, I use visual maps to study writers' conceptual knowledge over time, and like Rounsaville (2018) and Berninger et al. (2018), I use visual maps to study writers' perspectives on their conceptual writing knowledge and their perceptions of whether, how, and why that knowledge changes along lifelong and life-wide dimensions.

This chapter outlines the utility of visual mapping for lifespan writing research. First, I review concept mapping research to demonstrate its efficacy for studying changes in learners' conceptual knowledge. Second, I distinguish visual mapping from concept mapping by identifying key differences between the methods and describing the procedures for using visual mapping as a research method. Third, with these definitions established, I provide a brief case study of one writer to illustrate how this method works and what it can contribute to our understanding of individual writers' conceptions of writing through the lifespan. In concluding the chapter, I address the limitations of my study and propose promising directions for using visual mapping in future lifespan writing research.

---

1 Although some researchers use the terms "mind maps" and "concept maps" interchangeably, those working in the Novakian tradition (e.g., Hay & Kinchin 2006; Novak, 2010) distinguish concept maps from mind maps by emphasizing the importance of linking words between concepts that can be read as propositional phrases.

CONCEPT MAPPING: A METHOD FOR ELICITING A LEARNER'S CONCEPTUAL KNOWLEDGE

Used in many disciplinary and professional domains for both pedagogic and research purposes, concept maps are "graphical tools for organizing and representing knowledge" that "include concepts, usually enclosed in circles or boxes of some type, and relationships between concepts indicated by a connecting line linking two concepts" (Novak & Cañas, 2006). A typical concept map uses lines and short phrases to connect concepts into a proposition, or "meaningful statement" (Novak & Cañas, 2006). Often organized hierarchically, concept maps represent a response to a "focus question." Figure 13.1 shows an example concept map. In response to the focus question, "What is a concept map," the concept map indicates several interconnected propositions, including: "concept maps represent organized knowledge useful for effective learning/teaching," "concept maps include propositions, concepts, and linking words," "propositions are units of meaning," etc.

Though most often associated with the classroom, concept mapping was first developed as a research method. Many researchers (e.g., Hay & Kinchin, 2006; Kandiko et al., 2012; Kinchin et al., 2000; McNeil, 2015; Miller et al., 2009) attribute the development of this method to Joseph Novak, a botanist and education researcher who, in 1972, began a twelve-year longitudinal study on elementary science students' emerging knowledge (Novak, 2010). Through the course of the project, Novak's research team recognized the need for a tool that would facilitate easier identification of patterns in the lengthy and complex transcriptions of interviews with students; thus, concept mapping was developed as an effective means for seeing these patterns and tracing changes in subjects' propositional knowledge of science (Novak, 2010; Vanhear & Reid, 2014).

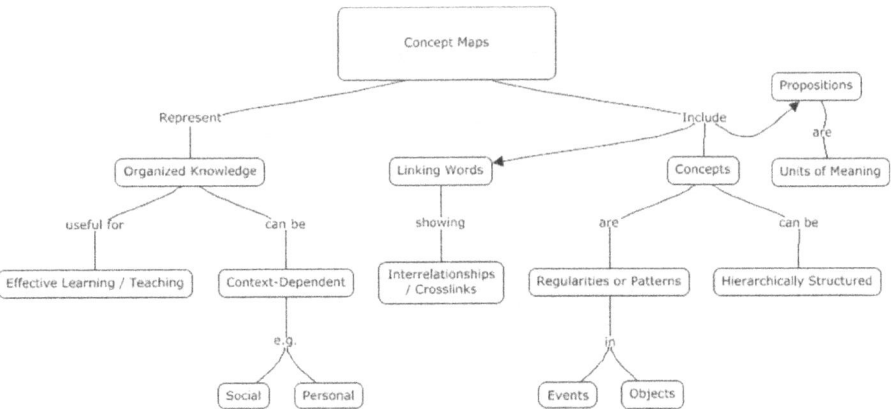

Figure 13.1. Example of a concept map. This figure illustrates how concepts are linked via propositional phrases into a knowledge structure.

Concept mapping offers learners a means to "express [their] mental models" (McNeil, 2015, p. 77) making it a valuable tool for researchers interested in learning because, as Ifenthaler and colleagues (2011) point out, "it is not possible to measure cognitive structures directly [so] individuals have to elicit or externalize them before researchers can analyze and interpret them" (p. 44). Education researchers have documented the utility of this method for "capturing changes in students' conceptions over time" (Ritchhart et al., 2009, p. 5) and "facilitat[ing] the empirical measurement of learning" (Kinchin, 2014, p. 235). Ritchhart et al. (2009) elucidate the process, explaining, "[w]hen a student maps the same topic in the course of their study, then a comparison of two or more such 'snapshots' enables measurement of learning quality" (p. 5). Wette's (2017) research on second-language writers' developing genre knowledge used concept mapping to this end, demonstrating its efficacy for studying writers' changing conceptual knowledge as evidenced through multiple maps in as little as two weeks. That Wette identified changes in writers' maps within such a short time period is encouraging for researchers interested in observing changes that might occur over a much more extended time period, such as the nine-month span of my study or the complete span of a writer's life.

VISUAL MAPPING: A METHOD FOR STUDYING A WRITER'S CONCEPTION(S) OF WRITING

Given the efficacy of concept mapping for studying learners' conceptual knowledge at discrete moments in time, I adapted concept mapping for use in researching writers' *conceptions of writing*, calling it visual mapping for two reasons: (1) to distinguish it from other common forms of mapping (e.g., mind mapping, concept mapping, topic mapping), and (2) to foreground its use for *seeing* a writer's conception of writing, a property allowing for quick identification of change from one map to the next. Because concept mapping was developed as a research and pedagogical tool for investigating and facilitating learning in K–12 contexts, education researchers have argued that this method must be revised for use in post-secondary contexts: "For the purpose of using concept mapping at the university level, what is important is being able to include [a] *wider range of representational forms*, not just because this allows more to be said, but also because, otherwise, concept-mapping cannot be a means of learning from the whole of narrative" (Kandiko & Hay, 2010, p. 250; emphasis added). McNeil (2015), a teacher-scholar of a multimedia design and development course, echoes this concern, suggesting that "expressing mental models through a *drawing process* rather than a preset format [like concept mapping] may provide individuals with a higher degree of freedom to express concepts in ways that they may have otherwise been unable to do" (p. 77; emphasis added).[2] Likewise, Miller et al. (2009) advocate for a more open-ended approach to concept mapping that "does not provide restrictions on how the map may be drawn" because "[t]his enables creators to construct the concept map in accordance with their personal semantic understanding of knowledge of a concept" (p. 366).

It is just this kind of open-ended approach to knowledge representation that visual mapping was designed to facilitate. While both methods ask participants to identify concepts crucial for understanding a particular domain and to represent connections that link those concepts into a knowledge structure, visual mapping offers participants a wider range of semiotic resources—including word, image, color, layout, proximity, and symbols—for depicting and connecting concepts in personally meaningful ways. This open-ended approach also makes visual mapping a more fitting tool for qualitative research, as Wheeldon and Faubert (2009) explain: "A broader definition of maps, allowing for data collection based on a participant's generated visual expression of meaning, is more in line with the theoretical starting place generally associated with qualitative research" (pp. 71–72). In keeping with Wheeldon and Faubert's argument, visual maps function as a "participant-centric means to ground theory within data" (2009, p. 68) because, "[i]nstead of looking to the researcher to search for codes, concepts, and categories within the data, maps allow for the identification of concepts and connections based on how the participant frames their experience" (pp. 72–73). Oriented to an individual's perspective, visual mapping grants the researcher an emic view of a writer's conception of writing, making it well-suited to the study of writing in the lifespan.

To illustrate the affordances of visual mapping for lifespan writing research, I offer an example of one writer drawn from a nine-month study that used visual mapping to document and trace changes in writers' conceptions of writing during their first year as college students at a large research university in the southeast. Participants were recruited from a 2000-level transfer-focused writing course that engaged students in developing theories of writing informed by rhetorical concepts (e.g., rhetorical situation, genre, audience) and composed iteratively through sustained reflective activities.[3] During the first week of the course, participants were asked to create their first visual map by completing a sequence of tasks: first, to define writing; second, to identify five to eight key

---

2   Although McNeil expresses a similar concern about the representational affordances and constraints of the traditional concept mapping approach, she does not engage the considerable body of research on university-level concept mapping by Ian M. Kinchin, David Hay, Camille Kandiko, and various colleagues.

3   This writing course design was adapted from the Teaching for Transfer model outlined by Yancey et al. (2014).

terms important for defining writing; and third, to map the definition by depicting connections among the key terms. Participants created four additional maps throughout the study: two while they were still enrolled in the course, and two the following semester—in January and April—as part of document-based interviews. Participants also completed two surveys, one after the writing course ended, and another midway through the following semester. Thus, my data set for each participant included: (1) five visual maps with accompanying written descriptions for the first three, (2) three document-based interviews, (3) two surveys, and (4) participant-selected samples of writing.

Initially, my analysis focused exclusively on the key terms that participants retained, added, and deleted to their visual maps over the study. This approach enabled easy identification of the concepts that endured for participants over time as well as those added during the course of the study. However, this exclusive attention to key terms provided a partial view of participants' writing development. Tracking changes in key terms yielded limited insight into why participants had chosen these terms, what these terms meant to participants, and how terms came to hold these meanings. Returning to the data sets, I noticed and began to identify texts that participants described writing, people that participants connected to those texts, locations in which participants produced texts, and key concepts that participants associated with those texts. Tracing these networks of texts, people, locations, and concepts became challenging, so, like Novak's research team, I began mapping each mention of these as a way of visualizing connections among them. After several iterations of this process, I developed a lifespan map (see Figure 13.5), charting lifelong development along the y-axis and life-wide development along the x-axis. As I illustrate in the next section, these lifespan maps offer insight into a writer's development as they move through lifeworlds.

AN ILLUSTRATION OF VISUAL MAPPING IN ACTION: HUDSON'S WRITING DEVELOPMENT

To illustrate the affordances of visual mapping, I offer a brief case study of one writer, focusing first on the writer's visual maps and then on my lifespan map of this writer. At the beginning of the study, Hudson self-identified as an 18-year-old white man and "a first-generation college student" from a working-class family. He began his undergraduate career majoring in music composition with the goal of "one day becoming a successful composer." Looking to Hudson's visual maps, his identification as a musician did not appear to influence his conception of writing, though the lifespan map of Hudson's writing development uncovered the deep connections Hudson made between writing and composing. For instance, when Hudson created his first visual map (see Figure 13.2), he identified four key concepts linked via 1:1 connections in a linear sequence, as indicated by the three large arrows connecting *write* to *express*, *express* to *experience*, and *experience* to *interaction*. Hudson further explained these terms with "sub-bubbles" that included five additional key terms—*personal, ethos, questions, perspective*, and *application*. Read together, these nine concepts depict writing as a process with three stages: a writer's expression of content, a writer's projection of the reader's experience of text, and a reader's interaction with the text. Hudson described his map by explaining, "writing should include an interaction of ethos, emotions, feeling, and should provide more questions than answers. I believe that is the only way writing can assist us into the future of fresh ideas and revolution."

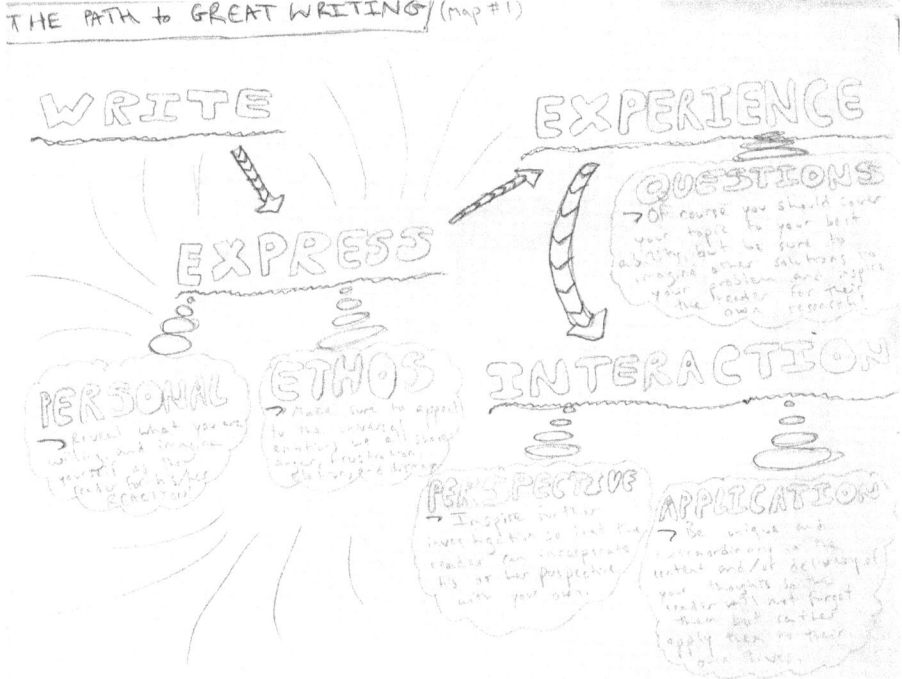

Figure 13.2. Hudson's first visual map created 8/2015.

Four months later, Hudson created a third visual map (Figure 13.3), which he described as "simpler" than his previous maps because it "generalizes all of the key terms [for defining writing] that were mentioned in the previous maps into five terms: *purpose, express, audience, context*, and *genre*." Unlike map one, these key terms are multiply connected with double-headed arrows, indicating a shift away from a linear, process-based understanding of writing toward a more dynamic rhetorical conception of writing. Hudson attributed this changed conception to the content of the transfer-focused writing course, explaining, "Whenever I am writing, I remember to consciously remind myself of what my *purpose, audience*, and *genre* is so that I can create the most effective piece of writing possible. This is something that was not as present in my initial [visual map] and has therefore been significantly developed over this course." Reading map three alongside map one, then, indicates a changed conception of writing, but these maps alone do not provide insight into why Hudson's conception of writing changed and whether that change extended beyond the writing class.

Created approximately four months after his third map (Figure 13.3), Hudson's final visual map (see Figure 13.4) retains four key terms—*audience, purpose, genre,* and *personal expression*—and adds two new terms—*delivery* and *material*. In his verbal remarks about the map, Hudson explained that the double line between audience and purpose symbolizes the importance of that connection, while the dotted lines between *delivery, material,* and *personal expression* indicate variations in a writer's agency in choosing the material of their text, the audience for whom they write, and the method(s) through which they deliver this text, such as in school settings where these choices are often constrained by an assignment. As with previous maps, map five reveals changes to Hudson's conception of writing, but the map provides no indication as to Hudson's choice to add *delivery* and *material* to his writing definition.

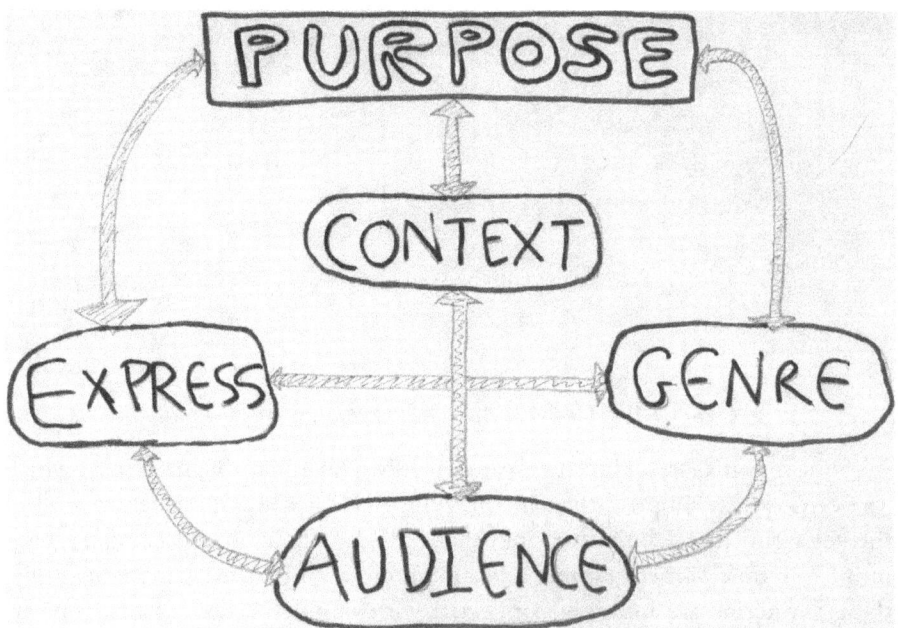

Figure 13.3. Hudson's third visual map created 12/2015.

Visualizing Writing Development

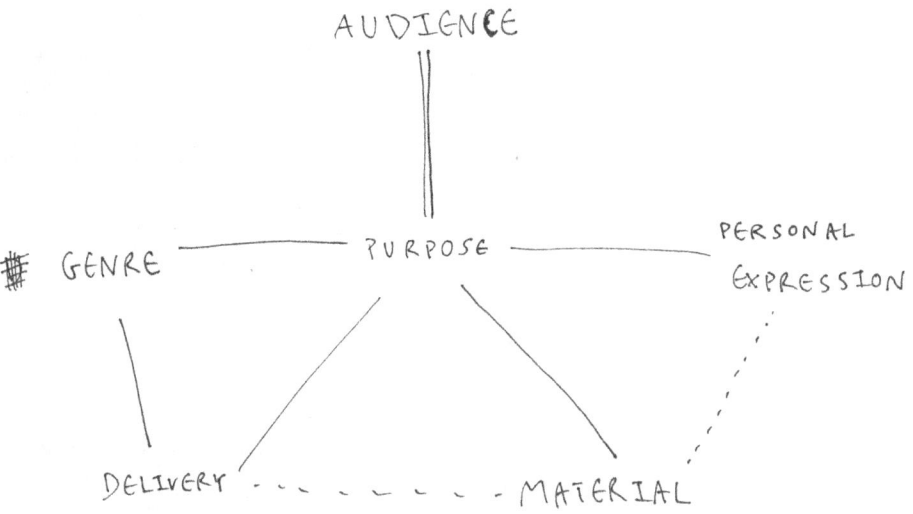

Figure 13.4. Hudson's fifth visual map created 4/2016.

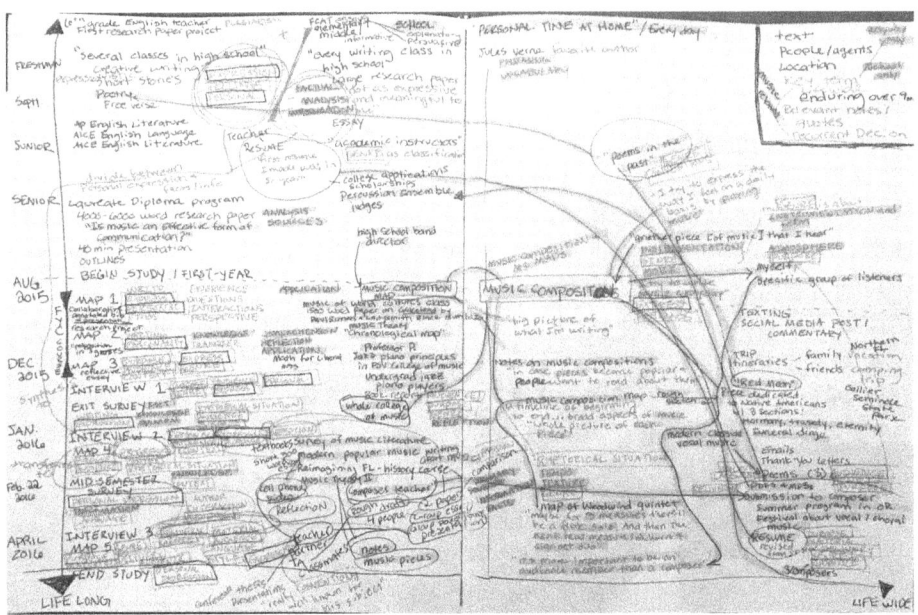

Figure 13.5. Lifespan map of Hudson's writing development.

The lifespan map of Hudson's writing—developed by tracing Hudson's references to texts he had written, and the people, locations, and concepts connected to those texts—provided a fuller, if still incomplete, portrait of his writing development. And, because Hudson described some of his writing experiences in middle and high school, I was able to plot those on the lifespan map (see Figure 13.5), using the y-axis to indicate lifelong writing and the x-axis to chart life-wide writing. The lifespan map covers the time period beginning with the earliest writing experience Hudson described—his "first research paper project" assigned by a sixth grade English teacher—and ending with the study's conclusion. The black dotted line along the middle indicates the beginning of the study, which coincides with Hudson's first year in college. The division between school writing on the left-hand side of the page and everyday writing on the right reflects Hudson's distinction between these lifeworlds in his first definition of writing. The key in the top right corner indicates color coding for text, people, location, and key terms, which are further coded by (1) endurance over nine months, (2) recurrence after the writing course, and (3) presence across lifeworlds. Highlighting references to everyday, school, life-wide, and music-related writing revealed interesting patterns in Hudson's writing development that were not visible in analysis of Hudson's visual maps.

Hudson's identification as musician and composer does not seem to influence the definition of writing depicted in his visual maps. As indicated by the location and prevalence of orange highlighting in the lifespan map, however, "music compositions" and "music composition maps" are texts that Hudson reported composing frequently both in school and during his "personal time at home." For instance, as a high school student, Hudson completed a research project on music as an effective form of communication and composed a piece entitled "Red Moon" for his percussion ensemble to perform for an "adjudication." After starting college, Hudson began creating "music composition maps," a method for composing music that Hudson attributed to his high school band director. Although Hudson learned about music maps in high school, it was not until he began creating visual maps in his writing class that he started composing music maps in his personal time. When he made the connection between visual maps of writing and music maps, that connection was transformative for both his writing and composing development. As Hudson explained in his final interview:

> Sometimes when I compose—this was a problem I was running into—I would sit down at the piano and start improvising on ideas and I would be like "oh that was cool" and I would write it down, but I was never thinking about the whole thing. So what the [music] map helped me to do was *think about the entire picture of the piece*. And it helped me to like make *a solid unit of a musical piece* versus just like a lot of ideas strewn together. (emphasis added)

Likewise, Hudson described thinking of "the big picture of writing," that is, the "overall picture of what you're trying to do versus just like specifically trying to do a piece of writing just to accomplish whatever you're required to do [in a writing assignment]." Hudson's development as a writer (re)shaped and was (re)shaped by his development as a composer, both driven by his discovery of a "big picture" approach to writing and composing.

The lifespan map also provides insight into the endurance of specific concepts, including variations of *personal expression* stemming from Hudson's experiences with creative writing in high school, as well as *genre, purpose, audience,* and *rhetorical situation/context* (synonymous terms for Hudson), terms Hudson began including on his visual maps at the conclusion of the writing class. Hudson consistently uses these concepts to describe both school and everyday writing, suggesting that they endure because of their relevance for Hudson's life-wide writing. His addition of *delivery* and *material* to the final visual map provides further evidence for the connection between enduring concepts and life-wide writing. Hudson attributed his use of these concepts to a group presentation in a history course:

> What we were required to do was bring a lot of new *material* to our *audience*, and even our teacher—he doesn't know everything about everything. . . . so I knew some things he would know, but I also wanted to bring some new *material* to what he saw in our presentation. So I thought of *delivery* because I think it kind of entails the *genre* [of the scholarly presentation] and also I've noticed like even in scholastic research papers it's not always—the language and the style are not always the same. Like it can be very professional and very formal, but it also can be kind of casual. But it depends on *how you're delivering the material*—or *the material that you are delivering.* That's a lot of the time what people care about. (emphasis added)

Just as Hudson discussed *delivery* and *material* in relation to the *genre* of his history class presentation, he used these three terms to describe texts composed for everyday life: an application to a summer program on vocal music written for a committee of three professional composers; poems modeled on published poetry that could serve as text for vocal music compositions; and music composition maps that "help [him] think about the entire picture of the piece." As Hudson talked through his visual maps, explaining each key term and articulating his rationale for choosing it, he revealed traces of a chronology of writing development unfolding through a network of artifacts, people, practices, and concepts. These traces can be marked and tracked on a lifespan map (see Figure 13.5), affording the researcher a way of "look[ing] forward, backward, and across in time . . . to understand the causes, triggers, and impacts on writing development in an individual's life" (Dippre & Phillips, this volume).

A WAY FORWARD: MAPPING LIFESPAN WRITING DEVELOPMENT

While this study was limited by a nine-month time span, it reveals the potential of visual mapping as a method for studying writing in the lifespan. As Hudson's case study illustrates, a visual map captures a writer's conception of writing at one moment in time, and when used as a repeated measure, a visual map *shows* change—or stability—in a writer's conception of writing as they move through and across lifeworlds. As documents, visual maps focus a writer's attention on their conceptual knowledge and, when used in document-based interviews, can help to reveal traces of a complex network of texts, people, locations, and concepts spanning time and space. When plotted on a lifespan map, this network provides a "perspective on [an individual writer's] learning pathways that no other individual has" (Smith, this volume). Read alongside each other, Hudson's visual maps show *that* his conception of writing has changed and *how* it has changed as he retains concepts like *personal expression*, adds concepts like *genre* and *delivery*, and deletes concepts like *application*. Used for document-based interviews, Hudson's visual maps serve as touchstones for elaborating his conception of writing, with each concept indexing a hidden network of texts, people, and locations. In other words, Hudson's talk about his visual maps begins to reveal *why* his conception of writing changed, and when plotted on a lifespan map, changes to this conception can be understood in relation to Hudson's "becom[ing] across contexts" (Smith, this volume).

Given the promise of visual mapping for studying developing writers' conceptions of writing, lifespan writing researchers can take up this method to further refine our understanding of individual trajectories of writing development. Though this study was limited to a nine-month timespan, it still uncovered changes in writers' conceptions of writing; what might we learn by extending the timespan to nine years? To nine decades? What further insights might be gained by sharing a researcher's lifespan map with the writer? By asking a writer to compose their own lifespan map? And what might a collection and comparison of individual writers' lifespan maps reveal about patterns in writers' developmental trajectories? There's much more to explore, and I invite you to join me in mapping writing through the lifespan.

REFERENCES

Bazerman, C., Applebee, A. N., Berninger, V. W., Brandt, D., Graham, S., Jeffery, J. V., Matsuda, P. K., Murphy, S., Rowe, D. W., Schleppegrell, M. & Wilcox, K. C. (Eds.). (2018). *The Lifespan development of writing*. National Council of Teachers of English.

Berninger, V. W., Geselowitz, K. & Wallis, P. (2018). Multiple perspectives on the nature of writing: Typically developing writers in grades 1, 3, 5, and 7 and students with writing disabilities in grades 4 to 9. In C. Bazerman, A. N. Applebee, V. W. Berninger, D. Brandt, S. Graham, J. V. Jeffrey, P. K. Matsuda, S. Murphy, D. W. Rowe, M. Schleppegrell & K. C. Wilcox (Eds.), *The lifespan development of writing* (pp. 151–180). National Council of Teachers of English.

Greene, S. & Higgins, L. (1994). Once upon a time: The use of retrospective accounts in building theory in composition. In P. Smagorinsky (Ed.), *Speaking about writing: Reflections on research methodology* (pp. 115–140). Sage.

Hay, D. B. & Kinchin, I. M. (2006). Using concept maps to reveal conceptual typologies. *Education + Training, 48*(2/3), 127–142.

Ifenthaler, D., Masduki, I. & Seel, N. M. (2011). The mystery of cognitive structure and how we can detect it: Tracking the development of cognitive structures over time. *Instructional Science, 39*, 41–61.

Kandiko, C. & Hay, D. B. (2010). Exploring the limits of concept mapping: When language takes over. In J. Sánchez, A. J. Cañas & J. D. Novak (Eds.), *Concept maps: Making learning meaningful. Proceedings of Fourth International Conference on Concept Mapping* (Vol. 1, pp. 248–256). Florida Institute for Human and Machine Cognition.

Kandiko, C., Hay, D. B. & Weller, S. (2012). Concept mapping in the humanities to facilitate reflection: Externalizing the relationship between public and personal learning. *Arts & Humanities in Higher Education, 12*(1), 70–87.

Kinchin, I. M. (2014). Concept mapping as a learning tool in higher education: A critical analysis of recent reviews. *The Journal of Continuing Higher Education, 62*(1), 39–49.

Kinchin, I. M, Hay, D B. & Adams, A. (2000). How a qualitative approach to concept map analysis can be used to aid learning by illustrating patterns of conceptual development. *Educational Research, 42*(1), 43–57.

McNeil, S. (2015). Visualizing mental models: Understanding cognitive change to support teaching and learning of multimedia design and development. *Education Technology Research Development, 63*, 73–96.

Miller, K. J, Koury, K. A., Fitzgerald, G. E., Hollingsead, C., Mitchem, K. J., Tsai, H. H. & Park, M. K. (2009). Concept mapping as a research tool to evaluate conceptual change related to instructional methods. *Teacher Education and Special Education, 32*(4), 365–378.

Novak, J. D. (2010). *Learning, creating and using knowledge: Concept maps as facilitative tools in schools and corporations* (2nd ed.). Routledge.

Novak, J. D. & Cañas, A. J. (2006). The theory underlying concept maps and how to construct and use them. https://cmap.ihmc.us/docs/theory-of-concept-maps.

Ritchhart, R., Turner, T. & Hadar, L. (2009). Uncovering students' thinking about thinking: Using concept maps. *Metacognition Learning, 4*(2), 2–30.

Roozen, K. (2016). Reflective interviewing: Methodological moves for tracing tacit knowledge and challenging chronotopic representations. In K. B. Yancey (Ed.), *Rhetoric of Reflection* (pp. 250–269). Utah State University Press.

Rounsaville, A. (2017). Genre repertoires from below: How one writer built and moved a writing life across generations, borders, and communities. *Research in the Teaching of English, 51*(3), 317–340.

Schroeder, N. L., Nesbit, J. C., Anguiano, C. J. & Adesope, O. O. (2018). Studying and constructing concept maps: A meta-analysis. *Educational Psychology Review, 30*, 431–455.

Vanhear, J. & Reid, A. A. (2014). Concept mapping and universal design for learning: Meeting the needs of learner variability in educational environments. In Paulo R. M. Correia, M. E. I. Malachias, A. J. Cañas & J. D. Novak (Eds.), *Concept mapping and learning to innovate: Proceedings of Sixth International Conference on Concept Mapping in Santos, Brazil*. Institute for Human and Machine Cognition.

Wette, R. (2017). Using mind maps to reveal and develop genre knowledge in a graduate writing course. *Journal of Second Language Writing, 38*, 58–71.

Wheeldon, J. & Faubert, J. (2009). Framing experience: Concept maps, mind maps, and data collection in qualitative research. *International Journal of Qualitative Methods, 8*(3), 68–83.

Yancey, K. B., Robertson, L. & Taczak, K. (2014). *Writing across contexts: Transfer, composition, and sites of writing*. Utah State University Press.

CHAPTER 14.

ADDRESSING THE FUTURITY OF LITERATE ACTION: TRACING THE ENDURING CONSEQUENCES OF ACTING WITH INSCRIPTIONS THROUGHOUT THE LIFEWORLD

Kevin Roozen
University of Central Florida

In articulating a model of writing development that adequately addresses the rich variety of textual engagements people encounter throughout the length and expanse of their lives, the Lifespan Development Writing Group (Bazerman et al., 2018) calls for theoretical and methodological perspectives that trace writers' becoming across multiple settings. Noting that the biographical sequence of literate activities shaping people's experiences of their hobbies, religious worship, schooling, government bureaucracy, and employment function as "pathways for engaging with and practicing new genres, for confronting different kinds of cognitive, linguistic, motivational, and social demands, and for developing new forms of communicative relationships" (Bazerman et al., 2018, p. 23), the LDWG asserts that as persons' "adolescent and adult social worlds expand into new professional, commercial, civic, and other affiliational contexts, so do the possibilities and exigencies for their writing development" (p. 23). This chapter offers one response to the call for increased attention to the textual trajectories of meaning-making that people build, and build continually from, throughout their lifespans and across their lifeworlds. Based on data collected for an IRB-approved multi-year longitudinal case study of one writer throughout his college years, but that also reaches back to his early childhood, this chapter traces his use of a variety of everyday inscriptions in ways that extend across and weave together his engagements with disciplinary science and religious worship.

As an undergraduate microbiology major, Samuel's (a pseudonym) science coursework found him navigating a dense network of "inscriptions," a term for material documents that "covers everything that is used to refer to some thing or phenomenon in the material world, including photographs, naturalistic drawings, diagrams, graphs, tables, lists, and equations" (Johri et al., 2013, p. 8). His organic chemistry class, for example, immersed Samuel in drawing a series of diagrams (see, for example, Figure 14.1) that graphically represent the structure of common organic molecules.

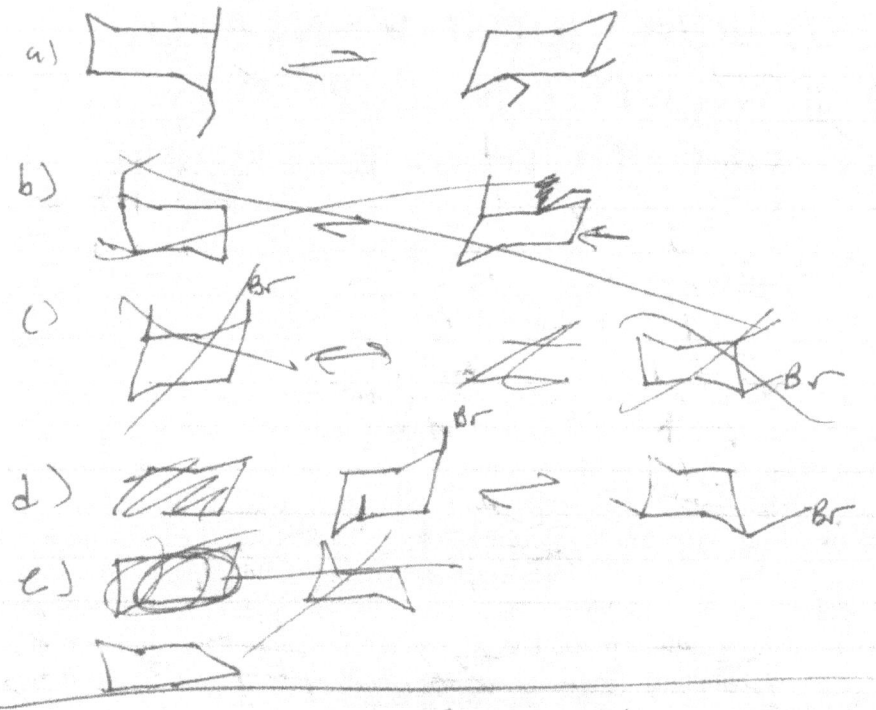

Figure 14.1. An excerpt from a page of Samuel's organic chemistry notebook showing his efforts to graphically represent organic molecules.

Working from the diagrams he copied from the whiteboard during class lectures and the ones displayed on the pages of his textbook, Samuel painstakingly drew and redrew different versions of these diagrams until they adequately made visible the molecules' key features, shapes, and arrangements, properties which cannot be seen with the naked eye or even with advanced imaging technologies.

Noting the mundane nature of inscriptions, Latour (1990) writes that they are "so practical, so modest, so pervasive, so close to the hands and the eyes that they escape attention" (p. 21), and yet, he acknowledges their vital importance to scientific ways of knowing. Articulating the centrality of inscriptions as the locus of the scientific enterprise, Latour (1990) asserts that, "Scientists start seeing something once they stop looking at nature and look exclusively and obsessively at prints and flat inscriptions" (p. 39). What might seem like errant doodles or a simplistic shorthand are, as Latour (1990) states, "innovations in graphism" (p. 29). In learning how to see, draw, and act with these inscriptions, Samuel is acquiring what Latour (1990) describes as "the precise practice and craftsmanship of knowing" (p. 21) for chemistry. Developing a facility with producing and using these inscriptions, then, is a key part of Samuel's rhetorical education toward becoming a scientist.

Samuel's acting with these diagrams situates him firmly in the densely textual landscape of chemistry. And yet, as I have come to realize throughout my case study of Samuel's literate activities (Prior, 1998; Prior & Shipka, 2003), his encounters with these diagrams is also deeply entangled with his extensive history of engagement with religious worship. In contrast with dominant mappings of writing development within specialized communities, my analysis of Samuel's becoming as a scientist-in-the-making illuminates the ways people's disciplinary becoming emerges across the assumed boundaries of everyday, academic, and professional activities rather than from engagements within any single social world. Ultimately, this chapter argues for increased attention to what Gries (2015) refers to as "futurity" of literate action as a way of making visible the complexly historical and heterogeneous character of writing, learning, and becoming.

TRACING TRAJECTORIES OF BECOMING

In keeping with what Beaufort (2007) described as writing studies' dominant metaphor of writing development, "one of writers moving from outsider to insider status in particular discourse communities or activity systems" (p. 24), the dominant stories about disciplinary development that have emerged from writing studies' scholarship locate writers and their writing tightly within a particular disciplinary world (Carroll, 2002; Dias et al., 1999; Geisler, 1994; Haas, 1994; Poe, Lerner & Craig, 2010; Winsor, 1996). These accounts configure histories of development in terms of newcomers entering an unfamiliar disciplinary territory and moving from the periphery toward some more central location, mostly through increasingly deeper, fuller participation with a set of core ways of writing, representing, knowing, and being shared by all full members. Viewed from this vantage point, development is depicted as a fairly straightforward process of taking up the already-established genres and identities available within the well-policed borders of an already-made social world.

These tightly situated accounts of literate development within the assumed borders of disciplinary worlds seem fairly commonplace, but only if we focus on people's participation in this single social world. Consider, though, how such mappings sever the historical trajectories people trace as their lives play out across expansive lifeworlds, lives textured with multiple engagements that extend across multiple timescales. Studies that have attended to the trajectories people chart across their lifeworlds have illuminated the ways disciplinarity is deeply entangled with those histories (Artemeva, 2009; Chiseri-Strater, 1991; Durst, 2019; Medway, 2002; Prior, 1998, 2018; Prior & Shipka, 2003; Roozen & Erickson, 2017). All told, these perspectives suggest that when our models of development fix writers and their writing solely on what happens within the presumed borders of a particular disciplinary world and solely on people's encounters with its privileged forms of writing and knowing, we risk an overdetermined, incomplete, and ultimately very confusing account of the pathways for disciplinary development.

To sharpen our view of those dynamic processes across temporalities and spaces, I have turned to a body of theoretical approaches that addresses the complex heterogeneity and heterochronicity of human mediated action and the prominent role such heterogeneity plays in the co-development of artifacts, practices, and persons across times, places, and activities (Engeström, 1993; Latour, 2005; Scollon, 2001; Vygotsky, 1978; Wertsch, 1991, 1998). Rejecting the notion of activity as unified, Engeström (1993) writes that, "An activity system is not a homogeneous entity. To the contrary, it is composed of a multitude of disparate elements, voices, and viewpoints. This multiplicity can be understood in terms of historical layers. An activity system always contains sediments of earlier historical modes, as well as buds and shoots of its possible futures" (p. 68). The profound heterogeneity of activity means that moments of mediated action function as points of emergent, dynamic blending.

In addition to shaping action in the emergent here and now of a present moment, the interplay of heterogeneous elements also serves as the basic semiotic mechanism of development, as words, artifacts, practices, identities, and social worlds are slowly and incrementally transformed through being selectively reaccentuated and interwoven. Such transformations are vital in shaping the ways that elements might, and might not, be taken up in later activities in the near and distant future. Invested in understanding the continual becoming of semiotic resources, Gries (2015) argues for perspectives focused not on a specific element's use in any single social interaction, but rather on how an element is re-used across a historical sequence of interactions. She offers a conceptual and methodological framework for tracing the pathways of how a particular element circulates through a series of encounters, the continual re-shaping that occurs as an element is assembled with others, and the implications such re-shaping holds for an element's potential uses in the future. For Gries (2015) it is through the dynamic, ongoing process of "rhetorical transformation" that any particular element "becomes rhetorical in divergent ways as it circulates with time, enters into new associations, transforms, and generates a multiplicity of consequences" (p. 14). In other words, elements "become rhetorical as they crystallize, circulate, enter into relations, and generate material consequences, whether those consequences unfold in conceptual or physical realms" (p. 11). What emerges from such heterogeneous associations are artifacts laminated with multiple histories heading into unknown and unpredictable futures.

In terms of understanding how people and artifacts come to be in the world, attention to the complexly laminated heterogeneity of situated action makes visible the ways artifacts, practices, and people are flexibly transformed through being entangled into heterogeneous associations as well as the long-term implications such transformations hold for their continual becoming. In this sense, the associations people build in a present moment of situated action provide the very resources people then build from as they take up newly transformed elements into later moments of action in their near and distant futures. Methodologically, attention to lamination suggests that analysis of practice should begin with people's activity in particular sites of engagement, but should also address the extensive historical trajectories that flow into and emanate from such sites. According to Gries (2015), it is only by close attention to what she refers to as "futurity," "the strands of time beyond the initial moment of production and delivery when rhetorical consequences unfold, often unpredictably, as things circulate and transform across space, form, genre, and function" (p. 14), that such histories can be disclosed and opened for examination. For Gries (2015) it is "[o]nly with an eye toward futurity" that researchers can "actually account for how things circulate, take on a life of their own, and help constitute and reconstitute collective existence" (p. 8) along a history that is "always unfolding into an unknown future" (p. 27).

DATA COLLECTION

Samuel is a Black (his chosen term) microbiology major at a large public university in the southeast. He had just started his second year of college when our study began. According to Samuel, his intense interest in science began with the inquisitive nature he displayed as a child. As he described it, "growing up I always had a love for animals and I was always the thinker, always asked a bunch of questions." He noted, though, that "growing up in the area I grew up in, it wasn't cool to really pursue that, so like in my science classes, I really wasn't that interested in that." Through his volunteer work with a pet care center and his experiences in labs for his high school science classes, Samuel grew increasingly interested in "just finding out how something works at the atomic level and molecular level and cellular and the tissue, organs, developing into the organism and how all of that works." By the middle of high school, Samuel indicated that he "just fell in love with biology. I was able to immerse myself in it. And I'm like, 'I'm really good at this.'" His engagements with animals eventually drew him toward college in pursuit of a career in veterinary medicine.

Like much qualitative inquiry, the research design emerged as the study progressed. I first got to know Samuel as a student in a class I was teaching. Over the course of that semester, Samuel indicated that he was a microbiology major engaged in a wealth of literate activity for his science coursework. The following semester, I invited him to participate in a research study to understand the textual practices for his science coursework. As the research moved forward, Samuel took up the role of "co-researcher" (Ivanic, 1998, p. 110) in the sense that, understanding the goals of the study, he brought new data in to interviews, suggested we might want to talk about this or that practice, offered his own insights, and responded constructively and critically to my emerging understandings. Initially, I collected sample texts from and conducted text-based interviews regarding his engagements with science. During our early interviews, Samuel frequently mentioned his religious faith (e.g., his knowledge of the Bible, his parents' roles in the church they attended) and his activities associated with religious worship (e.g., attending church services, studying and memorizing religious texts). Because I sensed that his faith and these activities related to his faith were important to him, and because attending church figured prominently in my own history, they became something we talked about during our interviews.

Subsequent interviews on both Samuel's activities led to more focused interviews about those textual engagements, and included collection of sample texts in whatever representational media were appropriate (e.g., hard copy and digital inscriptions). Sample texts were crucial for text-based interviews that focused on Samuel acting with specific texts and textual activities rather than on his involvement with literate activities more generally. Such interviews were often process- and practice-based in order to make visible Samuel's efforts toward creating and acting with various texts. Process-based portions of interviews involved having Samuel create retrospective accounts (often supported by texts and other artifacts) of the processes involved in the invention, production, and circulation of a particular text (e.g., the current draft of one of Samuel's chemistry lab reports), and key elements (e.g., other people or texts, inscriptional tools and technologies) involved in those processes. Practice-based portions of interviews aimed at understanding why and how such elements were employed.

I paid particular attention to moments when Samuel mentioned instances of difficulty or of learning something new. A key principle of sociohistoric research (Latour, 2005; Prior, 2008; Vygotsky, 1978, 1997; Wertsch, 1991) is that persons become much more consciously aware of action and practice during moments of genesis—when they are in the process of participating in or learning practices that are somewhat new or unfamiliar to them—and in moments of disruption—when their usual practices are disrupted. During such instances, when participation in practice slows down and persons become much more consciously aware of what they are doing, it is much easier to get a sense, from the participants' perspective, of action in-the-making (Latour, 1987).

In all, we conducted eight formal interviews, which resulted in just over 14 hours of video- and audiotape data. I supplemented the formal interviews with dozens of follow-up questions developed while I examined the interview recordings, my notes, and texts that Samuel had brought to the interviews or had emailed me. I emailed these follow-up questions to Samuel after the formal interviews and he either emailed his responses, brought them up during later formal interviews, or mentioned them during informal conversations when he stopped by my office or during chance meetings on campus.

This ongoing series of interviews provided opportunities for the kinds of "longer conversations" and "cyclical dialogue around texts over a period of time" that Lillis (2008, p. 362) identified as crucial for understanding literate practice within the context of a participant's history. They also allowed for what Stornaiuolo et al. (2017) describe as "the unprecedented, surprising, and meaningful to emerge in observations of human activity without predetermined and text-centric endpoints of explanations" (p. 78). One insight that slowly emerged from the series of interviews was Samuel's frequent use of diagrams and other inscriptions and their prominent importance in his science coursework as well as his other textual engagements. In terms of his science coursework, for example, I noticed how fully he was immersed in an extensive cascade of inscriptions for his biology and chemistry classes and labs. I also noticed how frequently talk about diagrams and other inscriptions related to his various science courses became a focal topic of our interviews. In terms of some of his other literate activities we explored, I noticed how he used inscriptions in those activities (e.g., using diagrams as a way of prompting discussion during Bible study meetings, copying Bible passages on notecards to aid in memorization). I also noticed how frequently during our interviews he would draw out the diagrams he mentioned and how quickly he generated them.

Another insight that emerged slowly during the early stages of the study was the tension Samuel felt between his deep engagement in science and his faith.

As I would eventually come to realize, the one thing that gave Samuel serious pause about pursuing a career in science was the impact it might have on his deep engagement with the church, a vital part of his upbringing and family life. Members of Samuel's family are active in the Black Presbyterian church they have attended for generations. Both of his parents hold positions in the church leadership, and Samuel and his brother have been involved with church activities since their early childhood. Recalling the tension he felt about maintaining his faith and presence in the church as his interest in science grew, Samuel stated,

> When I first started really pursuing science, I had trouble trying to see science and God in the same vein because of the way our culture works. We see them as two polarized, very opposite entities, that you can't pursue knowledge of the world or try to understand creation and God himself. . . . All of the people that I would talk to would be like either, "Yes! Science is the answer, science is the way, science gives me all of the answers that I could ever possibly need to know." And then others were like, "No, science is not this. You can't believe that all of this makes sense."

Faced with the dichotomy offered by this powerful cultural narrative, Samuel considered forsaking his interest in science for what he described as a "steady job" that would allow him to stay actively involved in his church. At the point Samuel started college, he had shifted toward a different stance, reconciling himself to pursuing a career as a veterinarian while keeping his religious engagement fairly private.

DATA ANALYSIS

In order to focus on Samuel's engagement with diagrams, analysis of the data was oriented toward understanding the histories of Samuel's use of inscriptions and inscriptional practices across multiple times, spaces, and representational media. To develop a sense of Samuel's histories with inscriptions, I analyzed these data interpretively and holistically (Durst, 2019; Miller et al., 2003). I first arranged data representations (i.e., sample texts, sections of interview transcripts, interpretive notes, copies of images, printed versions of still images captured from video, drawings Samuel had created during interviews, etc.) chronologically in the order in which Samuel engaged with them. Those data representations were examined for instances where I sensed that, or Samuel indicated that, he was acting with particular inscriptions or employing particular inscriptional practices.

This analysis of the data generated a large number of histories reaching across seemingly different literate activities. Based on those analyses, I constructed brief initial narratives of Samuel's histories with practice across multiple engagements. Those initial narratives were reviewed and modified by checking and re-checking those constructions against the data representations (to ensure accuracy and seek counter instances) and by submitting them to Samuel for his examination. At these times I often requested additional texts from Samuel, and frequently he volunteered to provide additional materials and insights that he thought might be useful in further elaborating and extending the narratives I generated. It was frequently the case that my understanding of the use of practices for these different literate activities needed significant modification as a result of closer inspection of the data, identification of additional relevant data, or discussions with Samuel during interviews or via email. Accounts of these interactions were modified according to Samuel's feedback. Finally, Samuel was invited to member check final versions of the narratives in order to determine if they seemed valid from his perspective.

To represent Samuel's histories of acting with diagrams along trajectories that flow into and emanate from his engagement with his science coursework, and also to make my own analytic practices more visible, I present the results of the analysis as a documented narrative (Prior, 1998), or what Gries (2015) refers to as a "risky account" (p. 8) rather than as a structuralist analysis. Doing so allows me to present the history of Samuel's acting with diagrams in a coherent fashion without flattening out the richness, complexity, and dynamics of their continually emergent becoming across multiple engagements.

In the sections that follow, I first examine the way Samuel's actings with the diagrams he encounters for his scientific coursework come to be deeply textured by his engagement with religion. Next, I explore how Samuel's laminated engagement with diagrams shapes his use of them for later moments of action, first for a Bible study he leads later during the semester, and then two years later as he writes his senior thesis.

MAKING PRESENT ABSENT THINGS

From the very beginning of Samuel's organic chemistry course, diagrams played an especially important role. Much of the activity centered around acting with a variety of molecular diagrams, bare-bones depictions that make readily visible a molecule's key relevant features and its spatial arrangement and allow them to be closely examined, like the ones shown on the page from Samuel's organic chemistry notebook offered in Figure 14.2.

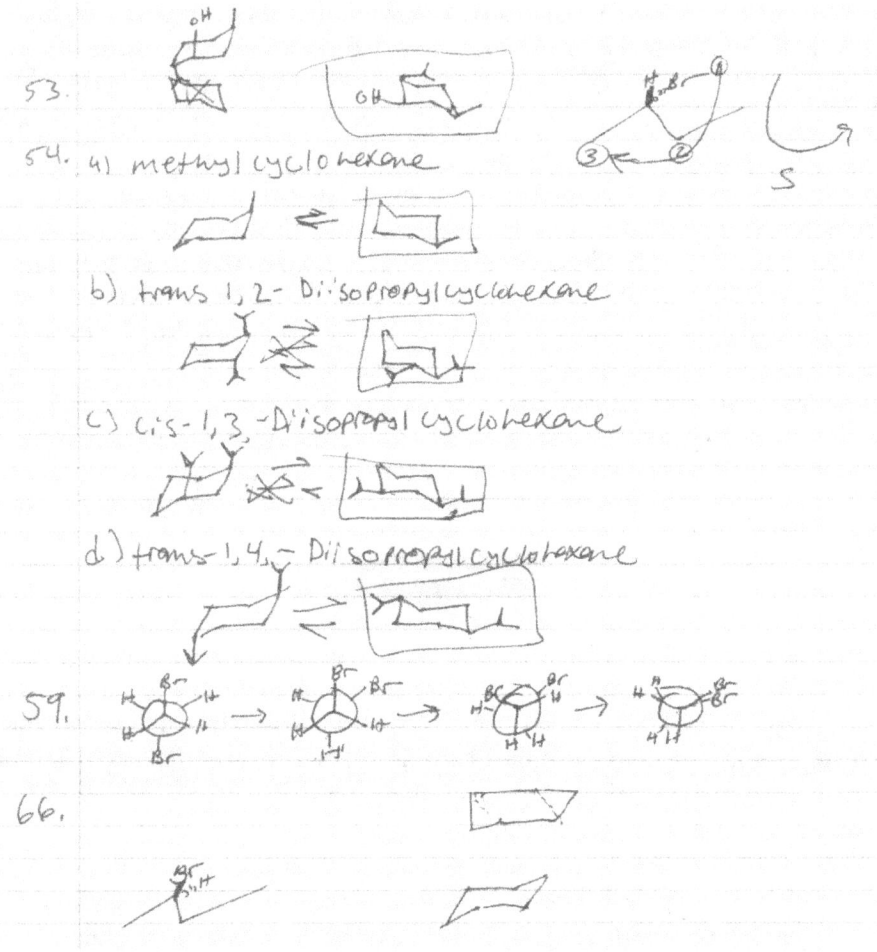

Figure 14.2. A page from Samuel's notes for his organic chemistry class.

Describing a typical class lecture, for example, Samuel indicated that his professor "doesn't write too, too much on the board unless it's drawing a structure. . . . Like a Newman projection, she'll draw that on the board. Like an organic structure she may draw on the board and then talk about chirality of a compound. 2-bromobutane is one of her favorites. At least for showing stereoisomers." Pointing to a diagram at the top right of the page from his notebook (see Figure 14.2) we were looking at, Samuel stated "This is 2-bromobutane. We were talking about chirality and how to figure out what the chirality is." Samuel indicated that he was somewhat surprised at the emphasis placed on students being able to draw the diagrams themselves. I include below a brief excerpt from one of our interviews during which Samuel describes his organic chemistry professor's emphasis on knowing how to draw chair conformation diagrams:

> **Samuel:** I don't write very neatly and I don't draw very well. So the fact that I had to draw these chair confirmations [the diagrams in Figure 14.2 with the boxes drawn around them] in pen is just weird. Plus, like, one example of drawing them, like learning how do it . . . She taught us to set up each of these. [Samuel picks up a pen and draws the top of the two chair conformation diagrams at the very bottom right-hand side of the page shown in Figure 14.2.] Draw 2 parallel lines, set them each apart, and then draw an equilateral triangle. Well, whenever I would do it like that, my chair confirmations would come out looking like this [laughing, and pointing to the top conformation diagram he drew at the bottom of the page]. And I'm like, I don't understand!
>
> **Kevin:** I see. So you're trying to get it to look like this [pointing to one of the chair conformation diagrams in the middle of the page].
>
> **Samuel:** So I learned, ok if I do this and draw this up and draw this down, just do dramatic everything then it comes out looking like a chair conformation [drawing the chair conformation diagram at the very bottom right-hand side of the page].

In this portion from the interview, Samuel describes and illustrates two different techniques he has encountered for drawing chair conformation diagrams. The first strategy, shown to him by his professor, involves drawing two slightly offset parallel lines and connecting them with two equilateral triangles. His comments regarding the second strategy suggest that it is a version of the first technique, but involves drawing sharper, more "dramatic" triangles.

Despite their mundane and practical nature, these inscriptions allow chemists to re-represent molecules that can't be seen with the naked eye, and that are too messy and complex to make out even when made visible by cutting edge imaging technologies. Employing a few short line segments, simple geometric shapes (circles, rectangles, wedges, and arrows), and letters, these diagrams depict a neatly and precisely arranged structure. The precise ordering is what allows chemists to see features like the positioning of particular atoms and the angles of the various bonds between them. These features, in turn, afford chemists a way of understanding how bonds are likely to change in response to interactions with other molecules, or how easily bonds might be formed or broken.

While scientific diagrams certainly allowed Samuel to see the key features and arrangements of molecules, they also presented to his eye a great deal more. For Samuel, whose life history includes a deep and sustained engagement with religious worship, his ability to see, use, and construe scientific diagrams was deeply laminated with, and thus shaped by, his engagement with his faith. Over multiple interviews, Samuel routinely mentioned how these renderings illuminated God's handiwork to him. His laminated seeing of chemical inscriptions surfaced quite unexpectedly, for example, during one of our interviews while discussing some of the Bible passages he was working to memorize. I include below an excerpt from that interview where we were discussing a passage from Colossians:

> **Samuel:** So Colossians 1:17, [reading from an index card with the verse from Colossians 1:17 written on it] "He is before all things and in him all things hold together." . . . There's nothing apart from him, literally nothing apart from him because everything, institutions, atoms, subatomic particles, everything holds together in Christ.
>
> **Kevin:** I can see why you chose that one.
>
> **Samuel:** And then when people ask me why I believe what I believe or why I think the way I think I say, "Hey, well, here's what the Bible tells me" and it actually makes a lot of sense when you study like chemistry, we learn how the trend for the universe is randomness but the very nature of matter, even at the most seemingly insignificant of levels, the microscopic levels, there's organization. There's organization that we can actually notice plus there's still things that we don't understand about the organization and the structure of an atom, of the nucleus, of orbitals or electrons. We can't tell with any true 100 percent certainty where an electron is around an atom in orbit. And that becomes increasingly difficult when we talk about hybridization and the bonding that occurs between an SP3 orbital and an SP3 orbital like in ethane.

After reading the verse, Samuel elaborates the phrase "all things hold together" by emphasizing that "all things" encompasses "institutions, atoms, and subatomic particles." Following my brief comment about his decision to choose Colossians 1:17, Samuel then indicates that everything being held together by a divine maker is consistent with what the study of chemistry has illuminated regarding the ordered design of even the smallest levels of organization for the physical world. As examples, he evokes the structure of the atom and its constituents and the bonds between the carbon atoms in a molecule of ethane, structures typically represented in the diagrams he would have encountered during lectures for his science courses, on the pages of his course textbook, and those he accessed online. For Samuel, the organization and order "at the microscopic levels" made visible by diagrams depicting the sp3 bonding in ethane, for example, evidence God's ability to "hold all things together."

To echo Latour (1990), science is not all that Samuel is seeing, or doing, when he starts looking exclusively and obsessively at the inscriptions animating his science coursework. Samuel's seeing of the ethane molecule is heterogeneously situated across and complexly mediated by his engagements with science and religious worship. In addition to Samuel's seeing with the diagrams being informed by his engagement with science, it is also deeply, densely laminated with his long history of religious worship and the texts that it involves. In Gries's (2015) terms, the diagrams have become "dynamic, complex entanglements that often change right before our very eyes as they experience new associations" (p. 13). It is through this lamination that for Samuel, these scientific diagrams take on what Gries (2015) refers to as their rhetorical "life," their "complex and intense vitality" (p. 8). One important consequence of this lamination for Samuel is that it occasions the opportunity for him to draw his faith together with his science and his science together with his faith.

As I elaborate in the two sections that follow, Samuel's laminations of science and religion do not just lead brief, fleeting half-lives in the flow of Samuel's history. Rather, these interweavings have long-term consequences for his becoming. In the next section, I examine how Samuel's laminated seeing of chemical diagrams is employed in a Bible study meeting he led midway through the semester.

"WE WERE TALKING ABOUT GOD AND WE WERE TALKING ABOUT CHEMISTRY"

During his sophomore year of college, the same semester he was enrolled in organic chemistry, Samuel and some of his friends organized a Bible study in his residence hall, and Samuel's co-organizers "volunteered" him to lead the group's meetings. While Samuel was excited, he was also "exceedingly nervous" because he hadn't had much experience leading small groups of people he knew fairly well, and because he couldn't come up some productive activities for the group's first session. He considered a fairly typical move of examining some passages of scripture, but decided against it because he didn't want to dive into verses that participants would not have had time to read and think about beforehand. He was, as he described it to me, "freaking out." One of his co-organizers with some experience leading small Bible studies suggested that Samuel could prompt some discussion by showing participants a fairly simple diagram of a wheel representing key components of the Christian walk. Based on Samuel's account of that initial meeting, his use of this inscription worked to stimulate conversation fairly well. For leading the group's later meetings throughout the semester, Samuel typically relied upon some type of diagram (e.g., a flowchart showing the progression of Christian growth) or representation (e.g., a brief outline of the chronology of the book of John) and some selected Bible passages group members agreed to read and study beforehand.

In addition to the more immediately recognizable religious-themed inscriptions, one of the diagrams from Samuel's organic chemistry course would also find its way into the Bible study meetings he led. In the interview excerpt I've included below, Samuel starts to describe one of the group's recent meetings, one held just the day before our interview.

> **Samuel:** In the Bible study in my dorm yesterday, we were talking about God and we were talking about chemistry, this was before the study started. We were talking about order and how the smallest level that we can now possibly know of, to some relative amount, that there is order. Scientists will say that there are shell levels within the nucleus, quarks, the different types of sub-nuclear constituents, they all are organized. There's order in the nucleus. And then there's order in the electron shells. There's order in the way the molecules arrange. And so, we're talking enantiomers. [Picking up a pen and looking for a piece of paper].
>
> **Kevin:** What's an enantiomer? [Getting paper out for Samuel].
>
> **Samuel:** [While drawing the diagram in Figure 14.3]. An enantiomer is a stereoisomer, or stereoisomers that are mirror images of each other. So, I have 2-bromobutane. And then this will be my mirror plane. I have the same thing, basically. But the thing about enantiomers are that even though they're mirror images they're not superimposable. You can't put one on top of the other and have it match up. You see that we have this and this [pointing to the top and bottom diagrams on the left-hand side of Figure 14.3]. They're two different conformations.

Addressing the Futurity of Literate Action

Figure 14.3. Samuel's drawing of skeletal structures of 2-bromobutane, created during our interview, that he used at his Bible study.

Samuel mentions that he and members of the Bible study were "talking about God" and "talking about chemistry" prior to the start of the meeting as part of a discussion regarding the ordered character of the universe, from the smallest nuclear and sub-nuclear particles to the molecular level, and adds that the discussion turned to enantiomers. In response to my query about what enantiomers are, Samuel explains that enantiomers are stereoisomers, molecules that have the same composition but with a slightly different arrangement, drawing two different conformations of 2-bromobutane, his professor's favorite example of a stereoisomer, as he does so. He uses the diagrams to show me that the top and bottom versions of 2-bromobutane, while seeming almost identical, differ in terms of which way the bromine (Br) and hydrogen (H) atoms are arrayed in space (depicted by his use of the wedge-dash in Figure 14.3 to indicate that the Br and H atoms are extending out of the back and front of the plane of the page). This small detail has important consequences for how the two versions react with light and with other molecules. In his very precise, meticulous fashion, over the next ten minutes of the interview Samuel offered a lengthy and detailed explanation of why this one tiny detail meant that the two versions were not superimposable, and why that made such a pronounced difference.

Curious about how he saw the 2-bromobutane connecting to the Bible study meeting he had mentioned, when Samuel ended his explanation I circled back to the topic of the Bible study meeting, inviting Samuel to say more about how it came to pass that the members of a Bible study were discussing chemistry. In the excerpt from that interview I've included below, Samuel explains how 2-bromobutane came to be entangled with the discourse of the Bible study:

> **Kevin:** You mentioned that you were talking about some of this before your Bible study started. What prompted that? Are there people in your Bible study that are chem[istry] majors or?

> **Samuel:** Chem[ical] E[ngineering]. One of them was a Chem E major and I was talking to him about it. We were just talking about order and disorder and I was like "ok, here's what I think about it. 2-bromobutane."
>
> **Kevin:** And he knew what you were talking about?
>
> **Samuel:** I mean, I just drew it out for him. I explained to him what an organic structure looked like and what all these things were, that is was a three-dimensional thing, non-super imposable, ok what are the implications of that? And then it was like ok, so, why is it that there are implications for order in design? Not just in with life, but even at the most basic of levels. The way in which inorganic, or organic in this case, materials react with things like light. The way that they polarize it or don't polarize it because this rotates polarized light at the D line of sodium. So like, 589 nanometers. It rotates it clockwise. This one does. So it does so in a negative direction. The angle of incidence from 0 is -23.1. And it's the opposite for the counterclockwise direction. So these 2 enantiomers rotate the angle of incidence at the same magnitude but where the light goes is implied based on the structure. The 3-dimensional structure.

In response to my question about how the topic of chemistry came up, Samuel indicates that one of the study members was a Chemical Engineering major. He then indicates that the discussion the two of them were having about the ordered nature of the physical world was grounded in a hastily-sketched diagram of 2-bromobutane—his organic chemistry professor's favorite molecule to draw and thus one Samuel had encountered many times in organic chemistry lectures and homework—that Samuel had quickly generated in the midst of their conversation.

When I asked Samuel how he thought the discussion between himself and the Chem E guy went, he responded by saying that:

> He was following me. I didn't add this stuff [pointing to the -23.1 and +23.1 on the diagram] in, I didn't start thinking about that until I was writing in my [chemistry] book, writing the notes and I was just like, man, even the way that these molecules, which are already structured and organized, react with light, there's a distinction and it's constant under these circumstances. It just amazes me. The fact that they are equal and opposite. He's [the Chem E guy] like, "Well it makes a

lot of sense because of the structure" and "I'm like, ok, but it's order. At a very basic level."

From Samuel's perspective, the Chem E guy was able to understand the complex points he was working to make about the tiny differences between the two versions of the molecule Samuel had drawn and the consequences of those differences.

Based on what Samuel describes in the interview, then, he and the Chem E guy, and perhaps other participants as well, were using Samuel's quick sketch of these two versions of 2-bromobutane to "talk about God and talk about chemistry," focusing on the tiny difference between the two versions of the molecule made visible by the wedge dash projection in the diagram to talk about the order and design apparent at some of the smallest scales imaginable as a mark of God's handiwork and creativity. Samuel's comments that the numerical figures ("-23.1" and "+23.1") on the diagram are ones he added at some point after the Bible study meeting when he was writing in his chemistry notebook and engaging with his chemistry notes suggest that the discussion of 2-bromobutane during the Bible study prompted him to examine the molecule's features and properties even more carefully later that evening when he was studying his organic chemistry materials.

Having encountered scientific diagrams as a means of making visible God's handiwork in the physical arrangement of molecules to himself, Samuel deploys his quickly drawn diagram of 2-bromobutane in the space of his Bible study meeting to make God's character visible to one of the participants, a Chemical Engineering major who likely had encountered that diagram throughout his own studies. In doing so, Samuel's organic chemistry professor's favorite example to draw to illuminate differences between stereoisomers becomes a means of making God's character visible to others. Gries (2015) notes that as a visual artifact "circulates with time" and "enters into new associations," it "generates a multiplicity of consequences" (p. 14). Samuel's reuse of the 2-bromobutane diagram certainly generates a number of consequences. First, in incorporating the diagram into the discourse of the meeting, the 2-bromobutane diagram functions as an inscriptional space into which Samuel can draw religion and science together in his life. Another consequence of deploying the diagram into the space of the meeting is that it offers Samuel a means of fashioning a possibility for selfhood that he might not otherwise have had available. As the result of acting with the diagram, Samuel has the possibility of becoming a person who is more comfortable leading a Bible study for people he knows fairly well, something that he mentioned was a source of anxiety for him as he prepared to lead the meetings at the start of the semester. Finally, by sharing the diagram with the Chem E guy, Samuel is able to enjoin someone else in weaving together science and religion into their life. In these ways, Samuel's acting with the

2-bromobutane diagram affords what Gries (2015) refers to as "the ability to reassemble collective existence" (p. 13).

In the next section, I examine the enduring consequences of Samuel's laminated encounters with scientific diagrams on his becoming as a scientist-in-the-making as they are described in the undergraduate honors thesis he wrote throughout his final undergraduate year.

EXPLORING "THE RELATIONSHIP BETWEEN SCIENCE AND FAITH"

To fulfil the capstone requirements for his undergraduate honors program, Samuel was required to write a senior thesis on a topic of his choosing related to his major in microbiology. For his thesis topic, Samuel opted to examine the relationship between science and religion. The initial portions of Samuel's forty-page, multi-chapter thesis explore how historical figures including Galileo and Jonathan Edwards navigated the seeming disjunctures between science and faith, but throughout the latter sections Samuel's discussion offers readers some glimpses into his own experiences navigating this relationship over his college years. In contrast to the dominant cultural narrative that understands science and faith as "mutually exclusive or at the very least thought to operate in vastly different spheres such that one ought not to influence the other," as he described it in his thesis, Samuel stated that by his senior year of college he had come to be entangled in his life to view science and faith as existing in a productive synergy. Articulating his central argument in the abstract of his thesis, Samuel writes, "the relationship between science and faith seems to be a synergistic one: the two enhance one another. As individuals study both the book of nature and the book of scripture, their love of God and enthusiasm for science are both enhanced."

In the opening portion of his thesis, Samuel indicates that he arrived at his conclusion based on his observations that science and faith had come together in a number of ways in his life as an undergraduate. Reflecting on the past four years in his introductory chapter, Samuel writes:

> As I began to grow in my knowledge of God and the Scriptures, I was also growing in my knowledge of biology and chemistry. . . . As I studied science more deeply, He seemed more fascinating, more brilliant, and more beautiful than I'd first realized. This, in turn, made me want to study science even more so that I could see more of the awesomeness of God.

Over the next thirty-nine pages of his thesis, Samuel points to a number of particular instances in which science and faith had come to be entangled in his life, reaching back to his initial years as an undergraduate. Each of the instances Samuel describes involved his close encounters with inscriptions.

For example, in a passage from his brief concluding chapter, reflecting back over the full arc of his trajectory across the undergraduate curriculum, Samuel wrote,

> As I have studied science, from biology to biochemistry, I have become more fascinated by the God I had come to know through the scriptures. Studying His character and seeing some of His characteristics reflected through the ways in which the elegant molecular systems that allow all of life to function at times overwhelms me with elation. Many times I can barely contain my joy and awestruck wonder as more and more of the power, genius, and creativity of God become apparent through the study of the book of nature. It drives me to love and follow Him more fervently with my heart, mind, and soul, while simultaneously making me more eager to study the science through which these attributes emanate.

Here, Samuel indicates that it was through examining "the elegant molecular systems that allow life to function" made readily visible through the inscriptions he encountered in courses "from biology to biochemistry" that he became "fascinated by the God I had come to know through the scriptures." For Samuel, the "elegant systems" made visible by the inscriptions reflected "the power, genius, and creativity of God." This increased insight into the character of the Creator also motivated Samuel to engage more deeply with "the science through which these attributed emanate."

Latour (1990) notes that the mundane nature of inscriptions means that they often escape attention, but they certainly did not escape Samuel's. His seemingly mundane encounters with inscriptions held some enduring consequences for Samuel's becoming as a scientist-in-the-making. Samuel's thesis, written during his final year as an undergraduate, illuminates how his engagements with scientific diagrams have been consequential to the pace and path of his emerging disciplinary trajectory. For Samuel, multiple encounters with these inscriptions across multiple courses brought science and religion together for him. Based on what he describes throughout his thesis, the interweaving of science and religion is not just something he did initially in his early science courses and that eventually subsided as he progressed through the curriculum, and not something that faded as his knowledge of science deepened. Rather, it increasingly intensified. Over his undergraduate years, Samuel's laminated seeing of diagrams increasingly deepened and enriched not just his knowledge of science, but his enthusiasm for knowing more about science. In turn, that enriched view of science also deepened his enthusiasm for knowing more about God's character. To echo Engeström (1993), Samuel's laminated encounters with those mundane inscriptions in his science classes, and in the Bible study meeting as well, were the "buds and shoots" (p. 68) of his becoming as a scientist of faith.

DISCUSSION AND IMPLICATIONS

This tracing of Samuel's history of acting with scientific diagrams across multiple engagements helps illuminate the ways in which people, texts, and artifacts circulate, and, more importantly, are agentively circulated by particular actors throughout the expansive lifeworlds they navigate. As Dippre and Smith (this volume) point out, such circulations can be viewed productively as acts of contextualization, the continually emergent work of making and re-making social worlds. This analysis of Samuel's actings with inscriptions suggests that rather than focusing so intently on fixing textual action within a particular, already-made context, researchers might productively attend to people's acts of contextualization through continually tying, untying, and retying together histories of action in the emergent here and now through the ongoing repurposing of discourses, practices, and identities that have seen use across other thens and theres. In Samuel's case, consider how vitally important the continual weaving together of science and religion has been. In examining futurity in acts of meaning-making, Gries (2015) asserts the importance of addressing "what happens not only to an image but also to the people and other entities an image encounters when they all enter into complex relations" (p. 14). Over the course of this documented narrative, Samuel has shifted from a person who "had trouble trying to see science and God in the same vein" and who had opted to background his faith while pursuing a career in science to a scientist of faith. The lamination of science and faith also continued as Samuel navigated four years of veterinary school. During that time, Samuel led a large weekly Bible study for members of his cohort, and also co-facilitated a smaller Bible study as his schedule allowed. In addition, he was also deeply involved with some of the Christian veterinary organizations on his campus. Samuel graduated from veterinary school in Spring 2018 and has recently started work as a veterinarian in a large city in the same region as his hometown. He has also joined and become an active member of one of the nearby churches, and, as his busy schedule permits, he is hoping to continue his participation with the religiously affiliated veterinary medicine organizations at his alma mater.

In their discussion of the protean nature of context, Dippre and Smith (this volume) point out that addressing how writing can develop across the lifespan as part of changing contexts, the first principle of a model of writing development articulated in Bazerman et al.'s (2018) *The Lifespan Development of Writing*, demands an approach capable of illuminating "how literate actors move, in their work of producing writing, from one moment to the next, and how they keep the work of context going in the process of that work" (p. 33–34). Attention to the futurity of acts of inscription, to their emergent circulation toward unpredictable futures, can certainly help writing researchers account for and make more fully visible the ways in which what might seem like a series of discrete, autonomous textual moments come to be entangled together across our pasts, presents, and potential futures, to compose a richly literate life.

REFERENCES

Artemeva, N. (2009). Stories of becoming: A study of novice engineers learning genres of their professions. In C. Bazerman, A. Bonini & D. Figueiredo (Eds.), *Genre in a changing world* (pp. 158–178). The WAC Clearinghouse; Parlor Press. https://wac.colostate.edu/books/perspectives/genre/.

Bazerman, C., Applebee, A., Berninger, V., Brandt, D., Graham, S., Jeffrey, J., Matsuda, P., Murphy, S., Rowe, D. W., Schleppegrell, M. & Wilcox, K. (2018). *The lifespan development of writing*. National Council of Teachers of English.

Beaufort, A. (2007). *College writing and beyond*. Utah State University Press.

Carroll, L. A. (2002). *Rehearsing new roles: How college students develop as writers*. Southern Illinois University Press.

Dias, P., Freedman, A., Medway, P. & Paré, A. (1999). *Worlds apart: Acting and writing in academic and workplace contexts*. Lawrence Erlbaum Associates.

Durst, S. (2019). Disciplinarity and literate activity in civil and environmental engineering: A lifeworld perspective. *Written Communication, 36*(4), 471–502.

Chiseri-Strater, E. (1991). *Academic literacies: The public and private discourse of university students*. Heinemann.

Engeström, Y. (1993). Developmental studies of work as a testbench of activity theory: The case of primary care medical practice. In S. Chaiklin & J. Lave (Eds.), *Understanding practice: Perspectives on activity and context* (pp. 64–103). Cambridge University Press.

Geisler, C. (1994). *Academic literacy and the nature of expertise: Reading, writing, and knowing in academic philosophy*. Lawrence Erlbaum Associates.

Gries, L. (2015). *Still life with rhetoric: A new materialist approach to visual rhetoric*. Utah State University Press.

Haas, C. (1994). Learning to read biology: One student's rhetorical development in college. *Written Communication, 11*(1), 43–84.

Johri, A., Roth, W-M. & Olds, B. (2013). The role of representations in engineering practices: Taking a turn toward inscriptions. *Journal of Engineering Education, 102,* 2–19.

Latour, B. (1987). *Science in action: How to follow scientists and engineers through society*. Harvard University Press.

Latour, B. (1990). Drawing things together. In M. Lynch & S. Woolgar (Eds.), *Representation in scientific practice* (pp. 19–68). MIT Press.
Latour, B. (2005). *Reassembling the social*. Oxford University Press.
Lillis, T. (2008). Ethnography as method, methodology, and "deep-theorizing": Closing the gap between text and context in academic writing research. *Written Communication, 25*(3), 353–388.
Medway, P. (2002). Fuzzy genres and community identities: The case of architecture students' sketchbooks. In R. Coe, L. Lingard & T. Teslenko (Eds.), *The rhetoric and ideology of genre: Strategies for stability and change* (pp. 123–153). Hampton Press.
Miller, P., Hengst, J. & Wang, S. (2003). Ethnographic methods: Applications from developmental cultural psychology. In P. M. Camic, J. E. Rhodes & L. Yardley (Eds.), *Qualitative research in psychology: Expanding perspectives in methodology and design* (pp. 219–242). American Psychological Association.
Poe, M., Lerner, N. & Craig, J. (2010). *Learning to communicate in science and engineering: Case studies from MIT*. MIT Press.
Prior, P. (1998). *Writing/disciplinarity: A sociohistoric account of literate activity in the academy*. Lawrence Erlbaum Associates.
Prior, P. (2008, February 22–24). *Flat CHAT? Reassembling literate activity* [Paper presentation]. Third International Santa Barbara Conference on Writing Research; Writing Research Across Borders, Santa Barbara, CA, United States.
Prior, P. (2018). How do moments add up to lives: Trajectories of semiotic becoming vs. tales of school learning in four modes. In R. Wysocki & M. P. Sheridan (Eds.), *Making future matters*. Computers and Composition Digital Press/Utah State University Press. http://ccdigitalpress.org/makingfuturematters.
Prior, P. & Shipka, J. (2003). Chronotopic lamination: Tracing the contours of literate activity. In C. Bazerman & D. R. Russell (Eds.), *Writing selves, writing societies: Research from activity perspectives* (pp. 180–238). The WAC Clearinghouse; Mind, Culture, and Activity. https://wac.colostate.edu/books/perspectives/selves-societies/.
Roozen, K. & Erickson, J. (2017). *Expanding literate landscapes: Persons, practices, and sociohistoric perspectives of disciplinary development*. Computers & Composition Digital Press.
Scollon, R. (2001). *Mediated discourse: The nexus of practice*. Routledge.
Stornaiuolo, A., Smith, A. & Phillips, N. (2017). Developing a transliteracies framework for a connected world. *Journal of Literacy Research, 49,* 68–91.
Vygotsky, L. S. (1978). *Mind in society: The development of higher psychological processes*. Ed. M. Cole, V. John-Steiner, S. Scribner, and E. Souberman. Harvard University Press.
Vygotsky, L. S. (1997). *Problems of the theory and history of psychology* (R. van der Veer, Trans.). Plenum.
Wertsch, J. V. (1991). *Voices of the mind: A sociocultural approach to mediated action*. Harvard University Press.
Wertsch, J. V. (1998). *Mind as action*. Oxford University Press.
Winsor, D. (1996). *Writing like an engineer: A rhetorical education*. Lawrence Erlbaum Associates.

CONCLUSION AS PROLEGOMENA: FROM POINTS OF CONVERGENCE TO MURMURATIONS ACROSS SITES, RESEARCHERS, AND METHODS

Ryan J. Dippre
University of Maine

Talinn Phillips
Ohio University

The authors of this collection have shared a range of theoretical positions and empirical studies that uncover the complex literate lives of writers and point us towards more diverse and more robust paths to researching writing through the lifespan. We have looked at writing from grade school students (Arya et al., Chapter 11) to retirees (Bowen, Chapter 7), and from everyday inscriptions (Naftzinger, Chapter 5) to religious and school writings (Roozen, Chapter 14). We've examined concepts and methods as diverse as sociohistoric theory, autoethnography, and structural equation modeling, along with other theoretical and empirical approaches, and we've questioned everything from the role of context in the production of literate action (Dippre & Smith, Chapter 2) to the way that language as seemingly insignificant as prepositions shapes the ways that we think about lifespan writing and lifespan writing research (Smith, Chapter 1). We've explored innovative, even radical methodologies that push us out of our disciplinary comfort zones and examined how existing methodologies might be best leveraged to understand lifespan writing. Throughout these vibrant and diverse chapters, we have attempted to showcase the creative range and methodological flexibility needed to meet the challenges of understanding writing through the lifespan.

Yet a considerable challenge for lifespan writing research remains: how can we mobilize the various traditions, methods, and understandings of writing in these pages (and beyond) *together*, in ways that build on convergent themes, theories, methods, and stances but also take advantage of the divergences of each approach? How do we create unity from all this diversity? How, in other words, can we generate murmurations for a lifespan writing research agenda that includes the multiple approaches needed (including many more not represented in this text)? And how do we simultaneously orchestrate those approaches into harmonious, productive, and mutually enriching work? In our conclusion, we chart a path forward for a multidisciplinary, multi-site, multi-generational study of writing through the lifespan.

MOBILIZING CONVERGENCES TO EMBRACE RESONANCES

This collection suggests many moments of convergence: research that through methodological and epistemological stances, data sources, analytic choices, findings, or interests overlap and/or interact with one another in some way. Bowen's work on literacy tours, for instance, shares some significant theoretical assumptions with Roozen's work on semiosis and Dippre and Smith's work on context. The first "move" of our attempt to orchestrate our broad range of methods is to mobilize these *points of convergence*.

We do this by identifying, explicating, and elaborating upon the connections across the widely varying traditions that fall under the "big tent" of lifespan writing research. Much like Agar (1994) mobilizes a *frame clash* between ethnographic site and ethnographer into a *rich point* for research, we mobilize a *point of convergence* by (a) attending to the ways in which the intersecting traditions reached such a point, (b) uncovering the assumptions they bring with them, and (c) articulating the finer agreements and contradictions that emerge from such work.

Consider, for instance, the *point of convergence* that occurs between Roozen's and Naftzinger's chapters in this volume. Both Roozen and Naftzinger address ordinary, even mundane inscriptions. Roozen arrives at this point by following the work of Latour, trying to work out the ways in which everyday inscriptions shape and are shaped by the actions of his interviewee. Naftzinger comes to the concept of everyday writing by trying to get into the heads of the participants he is working with to see how they operationalize the concept of "everyday writing" for their own purposes. We can see two different but qualitative ways of envisioning what this "everyday writing" concept is all about.

So we have two studies, each of which has reached the concept of "everyday writing," but through different framings and with different intentions. Now, what might we have to say about the assumptions that these two chapters are bringing with them? How can we unpack that in ways that can help us go about the work of bringing these two together? A good starting point might be the agentive nature of inscriptions that Roozen's approach brings. By inviting in the work of Latour, we can see more clearly that inscriptions do things, much like other aspects of any given social situation. The inscriptions are *actants*, really, pulling on other actants, coordinating with other actants as meaning unfolds.

Naftzinger's text, on the other hand, does not attend to the agentive powers of the writing that he investigates. In fact, his work seems focused squarely on the understandings of the human beings in his study, and how they might come to understand this concept of everyday writing. So we have two different starting points for agency: Naftzinger's understanding, at least in this study, rests in the human being, whereas Roozen's rests in the interaction of elements, including the agentive power—that is, the ability to impact a situation—of inscriptions, even mundane ones. But is this an insurmountable difference? Might we find a third way forward to integrate these two or, at the very least, obviate on some occasions (i.e., in the pursuit of some kinds of study) a difference such as this?

Perhaps. An interesting aspect of the finer points of Roozen's uptake of Latour is in the distributed aspects of cognition that are caught up in Latour's thinking. This can be seen in Latour's (1996) response to Hutchins' *Cognition in the Wild*, which argues for understanding cognition as deeply situated, as occurring through the action and interaction of people and objects. This may be a particular way to understand Roozen and Naftzinger together and, by extension, move forward with lifespan-oriented research on writing.

Let us unpack this a bit more. Roozen envisions inscriptions as agentive in that they have bearing on the situation and help actors make sense of an unfolding scene of action. Naftzinger attends more closely to the individual understandings that unfold when writers reflect on the work of everyday writing. In both of these situations we can use Hutchins' work as a way of making sense of the material that we see—both Roozen's interview subject in bringing chemistry and religion together, and Naftzinger's subjects in identifying everyday writing. This work occurs amidst the coordinated efforts of people and objects, and it is through that that we can see both the blend of religion and chemistry and the acts of defining an everyday activity. So we can use distributed cognition as a divining rod, one that can be followed out in two ways: to treat everyday inscriptions as sense-making vehicles with their own agency, and to attend to acts of reflection by multiple interview subjects.

As the above example shows, mobilizing a point of convergence can bring more questions than answers, which is fine: through such articulations, we can identify further points of convergence, uncover connections to still more traditions, and thereby communicate across a range of theoretical, empirical, and disciplinary orientations. But such mapping, as we note above, is just the first "move" in the complex work of building a lifespan study of writing. At this point, as the name of the chapter suggests, we've merely *embraced resonance* by capitalizing on points of convergence that emerge from research that aims to understand writing through the lifespan. Though it's disappointing to tag such complex work with the word "merely," we have but only begun our work. In the next "move" of our process, we outline how we might move from the new insights that embracing resonances offers to then creating the coherence needed to move a multidisciplinary project forward.

EMBRACING RESONANCES TO CREATE COHERENCE

As readers will no doubt agree, the mark of a good research study is its integrity across its steps. While a research study should of course be on sound ethical ground, we focus here on a different definition of the word *integrity*: as *whole*, as *undiminished*. A study has *integrity* when its various parts are deeply interrelated. The research questions, theoretical assumptions, methods, and conclusions feed off of one another, each crying out for the choices made in the others, with those cries being answered effectively.

If such integrity is at the core of a strong research study, the aim of a coherent multidisciplinary research project should be to enable the pursuit of such projects. At this point the stakes are raised and points of convergence must be further mined so that a deeper understanding of each approach emerges, and with it a mutual orientation to the problem at hand. Building on the finer points of agreement provided in this next step, *creating coherence*, we can start to move forward in ways that inform future studies.

Much as we mobilized points of convergence in order to embrace resonances, we can use those resonances to create coherence through multiple steps. Our first step, *reciprocating*, brings our attention to the ways in which the disciplines we bring to the table can be used to support one another. Our second step, *motivating*, allows us to orient multi-disciplinary studies toward similar objects of interest. Drawing on two other studies from this collection—Bowen's (Chapter 7) literacy tours and Workman's (Chapter 13) cognitive mapping—we demonstrate these steps in use.

Bowen's and Workman's studies are miles apart in many ways: Bowen attends to the deeply material aspects of performing literate action, to the point of attending to the physical spaces within which writing happens, and Workman pays close attention to the cognitive constructs that her subjects carry around with them in their heads. Furthermore, Bowen works with an older writer in his 80s, while Workman interviews a college-aged student. On the surface, then, we can imagine that these two studies are essentially parallel lines, destined never to meet. Thankfully, our total disrespect for geometry allows us to identify places where we can see these parallel lines meeting.

Both of these authors have a basic interest in lifespan writing research and are orienting their studies in a lifespan direction. This gives us a starting point from which we might identify opportunities to *reciprocate*—that is, moments in theoretical framing, in data collection, and in analysis when each study might be used to support the other. This can be something as simple as using similar word choice in interview questions, or as complex as building up a set of connected, testable propositions that carry across from one research site to the next.

In the cases of Bowen and Workman, the two authors are paying close attention to sense-making practices, even if neither one uses the phrase directly. Workman is interested in a changing theory of writing over time and Bowen is interested in understanding the ways in which individuals organize themselves to engage in the act of writing. Both authors, in other words, attend to sense-making activity, albeit with different starting points and in different ways. This starting point or common frame can allow the two researchers to conduct future studies that can feed into their understandings of sense-making, while also collecting data that enriches each other's work. Workman, for instance, might offer an opportunity for participants to describe their writing environment as well as their theories. Bowen, on the other hand, may add some interview questions that allow her subjects to articulate the cognitive framework they use to think through writing.

Such reciprocity serves as a starting point: it gives each researcher some skin in the other's work, and by extension provides opportunities for further work together. From here, the researchers can take the next step, *motivating*, in which they begin to orient toward similar research objects.

This is not as easy as it sounds. After all, both Bowen and Workman are oriented toward writing, and in particular, writing through the lifespan. But, in their work with different theoretical frameworks, different methods, and different research questions, their studies are—with the exception of the sense-making focus addressed above—separate from one another. In the *motivating* step, we propose helping researchers identify and operationalize together the shared motivations that they have. Bowen's work, for instance, challenges a curriculum of aging as part of its lifespan-oriented agenda. Workman's study, on the other hand, complicates and challenges our notions of transfer and the complexity of the constructs we hold in our minds when going about the act of writing.

But there's an underlying connection at work, one that has sense-making as a component of it. Each of these researchers is attempting to understand a process that is at odds with contemporary accounts of related phenomena. Bowen sees older writers writing and develops a methodology of literacy tours to uncover some facts that push-back against the pervasive curriculum of aging. Workman, meanwhile, sees visual mapping as a way to uncover the complexity of writing across one's life, developing an account of that complexity that runs counter to simpler psychological accounts of writing and transfer.

Both of these authors, in other words, push back against contemporary accounts of writing and uncover persuasive supporting facts in the process. Because they are interested in challenging such notions of writing and writers, both Workman and Bowen attend carefully to the sense-making activity of their research participants. This careful attention pays dividends in developing persuasive cases that, with that sense-making activity at their center, productively disrupt commonplaces about writing. *It is the focus on sense-making that allows them to uncover persuasive facts.*

The connection between sense-making and push-back is the starting point for motivating these researchers to attend to similar phenomena in mutually productive ways. Bowen's challenge to a curriculum of aging could be further served by a raft of complex visual maps that trace out the richly literate lives of older writers, just as Workman's attempt to highlight the complexity of writing can be further enriched by attending to literacy tours. Thinking about the benefits of moving together toward shared goals—even goals as broad as countering contemporary accounts of writing—is the starting point for actually moving forward together. When we see how our research can benefit, we have motivation to move beyond simply embracing resonances to create the kind of coherence needed to generate murmurations.

CREATING COHERENCE TO GENERATE MURMURATIONS: DEVELOPING LINES OF INQUIRY ACROSS SITES, RESEARCHERS, AND METHODS

Our moves of mobilizing points of convergence to embrace resonance and then creating coherence give us a good starting point—a flexible framework that allows us to start from just about anywhere. In terms of having a useful, portable framework for multidisciplinary research, this is a good thing. In terms of establishing an ambitious, long-term research project at multiple sites around the world, though, it's inadequate. Once our metaphorical birds have taken flight together with some kind of coherence, we've got to be able to maintain that coherence while we're in flight. We will need to be able to define a goal and shift directions if we truly want to accommodate so many diverse disciplines, interests, and goals. Coherence gets our studies off the ground; murmurations keep them moving, together. Thus, our final move is to use the coherence we've created to develop *lines of inquiry*. These lines of inquiry give our murmurations enough structure that the flock stays together instead of splitting into multiple directions. We propose that lines of inquiry can allow us to prioritize the points of coherence, keep them linked, yet also allow their directions to shift over time as interests, exigencies, and, most important, the data dictate.

Elsewhere (Dippre & Phillips, in press), we define a line of inquiry as a rigorous investigation of a concept or set of concepts that can be traced through the lifespan and scaled from a case study to a large data set. Our work of developing a line of inquiry, then, begins with a concept or a phrase that has value to researchers throughout the Writing Through the Lifespan Collaboration. Consider, for instance, the focus of Dippre and Smith's chapter: *context*. Context is important for understanding how writing changes across time. Where people write, how they write, and the objects they use to write all impact their understandings of the limits and possibilities of writing, as well as their eventual uptakes. Dippre and Smith argue for a particular orientation to context, and although some chapters like Roozen's deliberately work within a similar framework, others like Zajic and Poch (Chapter 3) conceive of context as less "active," and instead operating as a steady backdrop that can allow for changes in writing to be brought into focus. This is a concept, then, that matters to multiple researchers and orientations, even if it matters in different ways.

After selecting a concept, then, we need to put it to work, using it to generate a question that is both intriguing enough to encourage researchers to join the work but broad enough for multiple disciplines to engage. Asking, for instance, "how does context impact writing development?" might indeed be a broad question, but too tightly bound to the orientation to context that Dippre and Smith develop, thereby excluding Zajic & Poch. The framing of such a question, then, is crucial to orienting researchers and beginning the work of creating coherence.

Perhaps a more useful framing of a question about context is "What is the relationship between context and writing through the lifespan?" Such a question, again, is too broad for a single research question, but can be pursued through a range of methods. Sociohistorical researchers, for instance, can examine the interactional work of contextual elements in order to develop a new understanding of the active role context plays in development, while psychometric researchers can begin treating certain elements of what they had previously considered to be inert contextual elements as active agents in understanding the results of their research studies.

Another example of a line of inquiry might be *agency*. Questions of how we foster participants' agency as researchers and how our research can highlight the agency of those participants are through-lines that intersect many chapters in this book. For instance, Bowen, Rosenberg (Chapter 6), and Zebroski (Chapter 9) each challenge researchers to consider the ways that agency manifests in older adults and argue that creating space for agency in our research designs is essential for capturing the complexity of lifespan writing; yet, they do so through very different theoretical and methodological orientations. Their collective interest in participants' agency forms linkages and accommodates a common focus and goals that can generate a murmuration even while their theoretical and methodological choices diverge. Moreover, agency-as-murmuration forms those linkages in a more substantive way than simply aligning along a shared demographic of older adults.

The final line of inquiry that we will suggest here is *semiosis*. Authors in these chapters explore multiple ways that their participants make meaning across the lifespan. Roozen and Naftzinger highlight the importance of everyday inscriptions for understanding the complexity of our writing lives while Arya et al. (Chapter 11) ask us to attend to data representations as an unexplored site for creating and assessing semiosis. Lee (Chapter 8) explores how her participants' literacies and thus semiosis have evolved and been shaped across multiple generations while Knappik (Chapter 4) argues for the unique value of the literacy narrative as a semiosis that reveals our sense-making of our literate lives. Again, this shared interest is able to unite work that is otherwise vastly divergent. Investigating how people make meaning, the tools they use, and how those tools shape meaning-making itself is essential to the lifespan research project and allows us to move forward, individually, but together.

CONCLUSION

We titled this chapter "Conclusion as Prolegomena" because we wanted to encourage our readers to see what we've developed throughout this text as the *starting point* for future multidisciplinary research, rather than as its end point. The frameworks, concepts, orientations, and understandings developed above are only meant to be initial scaffolding into the under-explored territory of lifespan writing research. Following writers from their first inscriptions to their last, from one generation to the next, is going to uncover information that we never realized we needed, suggest methods that our field has not yet considered, and lead to insights that we cannot predict. It would be foolhardy to close off such potential information, methods, and insights now, at the start of what we expect will be a century-long journey. We ask readers, then, to treat this concluding chapter as a starter pistol in what will no doubt be a long and sometimes grueling (but also incredibly rewarding) task of researching writing through the lifespan.

REFERENCES

Agar, M. (1994). *Language Shock: Understanding the culture of conversation*. William Morrow.

Dippre, R. J. & Phillips, T. (in press). Radically longitudinal, radically contextual: The lifespan as a focus for longitudinal writing research. In J. Fishman and A. K. Hea, (Eds.), *Telling stories: perspectives on longitudinal writing research*. Utah State University Press.

Latour, B. (1996). Review symposium: *Cognition in the wild* (Book). *Mind, Culture, and Activity, 3*(1), 46–63.

EPILOGUE

Deborah Brandt
University of Wisconsin-Madison

When Ryan Dippre and Talinn Phillips announced at the end of the 2016 Dartmouth Conference on Writing that they wanted to form an interdisciplinary, multilocational collaborative research group on writing development across the lifespan, the idea struck me as highly admirable and wildly improbable. Surely after the euphoria of the Dartmouth conference wore off, attendees would drift back to their separate locales and to the daily grind of campus life. Communications would sputter, and attrition would set in. Isn't coordinated research difficult enough with close colleagues? But across countries? Across fields? Across methodologies? Without a mega-grant? Really?

But in the months following the conference a working group did come together and stayed together. With the help of global technologies, the group talked, shared, reflected, and united in an inaugural conference that produced this volume. Within a scant three years, *Approaches to Lifespan Writing Research* took shape, solidifying a vibrant area for research. This volume challenges researchers to accept, indeed embrace, the conceptual and methodological demands of a difficult yet critical area of knowledge-making. By calling their effort a "murmuration," a wave of coordinated and buoyant energy produced by a flock of birds moving in the same direction, the authors clearly want lifespan writing research to take flight. But they also see that flight as necessarily collective, networked, and sensitive to changing conditions.

This volume focuses on some of the key perspectives and methods for generating understandings about writing across the lifespan. As the volume progresses, methods and perspectives proliferate. Some might find that frustrating, but it is the point. Look through multiple lenses. Start in different times and places and among different populations. Work forward. Work backward. Work across. Experiment. Be ready for confounding factors. Be inclusive before generalizing anything. Run qualitative hypotheses and findings through quantitative hypotheses and findings and vice versa. Look for convergence. But not too soon. Remember that writing development is embodied but not atomized. Individually driven but socially and historically contingent. Remember that learners' perspectives are indispensable to this endeavor because they put the life thread in lifespan development. Find partners—better yet, multidisciplinary partners—to design and undertake studies. *Persevere*.

WHAT IS AT STAKE?

What motivates lifespan writing research? Why should the larger community (of literacy educators, writing researchers, policy makers, assessment experts, parents, others) care about lifespan writing development? Who would be better off and what would be better off as a result of progress in this area? In what areas of teaching, learning, and society can this body of knowledge make a difference? What are the major problems facing writers and writing instructors today that a developmental perspective is best able to address? To engage wider audiences, these matters cannot be taken as self-evident.

WHAT ARE THE CORE QUESTIONS DRIVING RESEARCH IN LIFESPAN WRITING DEVELOPMENT (BEYOND HOW TO STUDY IT?)

This volume sensibly focuses on ontological, disciplinary and methodological matters. Before anyone goes to work in a serious way, perspectives need interrogation and the investigative toolkit must be assembled. This volume demonstrates how varied that toolkit can and must be. But what are the questions that lead researchers to their methods? Which questions tell us which tools to pick up? What kinds of questions does lifespan research best address? For what questions may it be less relevant? Identifying a common set of questions can focus collaborations and reveal similarities among the differences—both for researchers and for other constituencies in and out of academia. Now, if it is such that questions are not in common, that realization would be useful too.

WHAT DOES WRITING ITSELF DEVELOP?

For researchers in education and writing studies, the main interest is, of course, the development of writers. We see that focus in this volume. Among other things, chapters explore the contextual sources and stimulants for writing. Or they examine how a person grows as a writer or helps others to grow. Chapters explore how writers drive their own development, or how bodies and brains or prior experience contribute to or interfere with this pursuit. This focus will need to remain dominant given the needs for writing instruction around the globe. But there is an opposite end to this telescope. What do writers and writing contribute to the development of our worlds? The powerful force of writing as a technology is implicated in the production of wealth, knowledge, organization, art, religion, peace, and strife. People write not only toward their own development as writers but for other reasons. The working group that gave rise to this volume could serve as an example. Acts of writing sustained cohesion among members across time and space, served as a medium for developing and sharing understandings, and provided democratic access for consensus and disagreement. Out of these powers of writing, a fledgling field of inquiry is developing. Obviously, individual development of writing and societal development by way of writing are reciprocal processes with mutual impacts. But that is all the more reason to reverse the telescope and make the highly generative, globally relevant concept of *development* a key interest.

HOW MIGHT THE LIFESPAN WRITING DEVELOPMENT MOVEMENT FORM PARTNERSHIPS WITH OTHERS?

One of the most attractive features of the movement represented in these pages is the urge to think audaciously and follow what Charles Bazerman has called the impossible dream. Bazerman asks us not to dismiss the possibility of truly longitudinal studies, even as we recognize the logistical and conceptual difficulties. The gold standard in longitudinal studies would follow the same individuals from childhood across adulthood in a comprehensive way. This vision seems more possible after engaging with this volume. Seeing that a diverse set of researchers can work together across sites and methods makes the challenge less daunting and the burden seem lighter.

Another way to think about collaboration is to consider how developmental perspectives might be infused into traditional writing research and how the writing-development movement could form partnerships with more traditional writing researchers for mutual benefit.

One such potential partner is the National Assessment of Educational Progress which (rather lurchingly) is tracking writing achievement across childhood into adolescence. NAEP collects writing samples from fourth, eighth, and twelfth graders and sorts them by proficiency level. These studies do not follow the same students but rather give rise to a "report card" on the state of writing instruction by state in the United States. Interestingly the 2017 assessment is currently undergoing reanalysis because of what might be called a developmental oversight. In an effort to stay relevant to changing writing practices, NAEP had asked students to take the 2017 assessment on tablets, only to find out too late that many students lacked experience with tablets. That inexperience suppressed achievement scores. After such an expensive mistake, it would seem NAEP might be keenly interested in consulting with development-minded researchers going forward.

At the same time, NAEP findings provide big and tantalizing questions for those interested in writing development and especially those interested in finer grain approaches so admirably demonstrated in this volume. Here, in my view, are two big and tantalizing questions.

WHY IS PROFICIENCY IN WRITING (AS MEASURED BY NAEP) SO ELUSIVE?

According to the NAEP 2011 Writing Report Card, 24 percent of eighth and twelfth graders demonstrated proficiency when asked to plan, write, and compose essays in response to prompts. Only three per cent of the students achieved advanced proficiency. In a society where writing is increasingly connected to democratic and economic life, these results are discouraging. But what do they really mean?

What if NAEP could be convinced to add a developmental dimension to its studies? It could administer its assessment to a subset of the same individuals at grades 4, 8, and 12 and allow a development-minded team of researchers to do finer grained study of these individuals. For instance, from where does advanced proficiency arise at the fourth grade level? What changes and what does not change by the eighth grade? And the twelfth grade? Any and all of the methods and study designs introduced in this volume could be applied in such an undertaking. Such an inquiry could more fully address the questions to which NAEP seeks answers. What impact does instruction have on writing achievement? What factors in and out of school condition writing achievement? What do highly skilled writers share in common and how do they diverge? The same questions could be asked of writers achieving at the proficient, basic or below basic level, providing deep dives into similarities and differences within groups and across groups. For its part, the lifespan development movement would also stand to gain in such a partnership. It would have access to a national, representative population and, over the course of ten years, would have at least a partial longitudinal result among an age group of critical interest to educators. Fine-grained studies could get below apparent, broad correlations identified generally by NAEP (i.e., race, gender, socioeconomics, etc.) and explore the finer factors that drive writing development. Results would no doubt be surprising and useful. Many methodological and philosophical issues would need to be addressed to form such a collaboration but . . . nothing is impossible.

WHY DO GIRLS WRITE BETTER THAN BOYS (AS MEASURED BY NAEP)?

According to the 2011 Writing Report Card, girls as a group across race and socioeconomic background outperformed boys as a group in the NAEP writing assessment. Girls are overrepresented at the advanced proficiency level. To investigate such an interesting gap would be to investigate many of the factors that are of interest both to NAEP and to lifespan researchers. What gives rise to gender differences in NAEP results? Do those differences hold up in different contexts? How do gender identities and experiences condition achievement? How do these conditions matter over time? What are the implications? To do an exhaustive dive into just this one finding could begin to develop a template for investigating other findings and developmental factors. It could fill in the blanks for NAEP and developmentalists, not to mention teachers, parents, and policy makers.

So what I am suggesting is the potential of working with traditional writing research to find areas that can be enhanced by a developmental perspective. Convincing the larger research community to build developmental perspectives into any study of writing (not just longitudinal ones) could be a welcome outcome. In addition, such partnerships could build stronger political will for writing research, as writing continues to be neglected in comparison to reading in most national and international assessments of literacy.

As you can see, this is an afterword that only proliferates questions and possibilities. But I do hope that this response testifies to the provocative impact of this volume and to the contagious energy of murmuration.

REFERENCES

Bazerman, C. (2018). Lifespan longitudinal studies of writing development: A heuristic for an impossible dream. In Bazerman et al. (Eds.), *The lifespan development of writing* (pp. 326–365). National Council of Teachers of English.

National Center for Education Statistics. (2011). Writing 2011: National assessment of educational progress at grades 8 and 12. U.S. Department of Education. https://nces.ed.gov/nationsreportcard/pdf/main2011/2012470.pdf .

CONTRIBUTORS

Diana J. Arya is Associate Professor in the Department of Education at the University of California, Santa Barbara. Arya's research interests focus on community-based literacy practices and processes within K-12 and professional contexts. Through her investigations of text-based (data, simulations, co-constructions, etc.) and inquiry-based activities in third grade, middle school, high school, and professional contexts, she explores language in use and how disciplinary knowledge is constructed within the context of the discursive practices of scientists across disciplines.

Lauren Marshall Bowen is Assistant Professor of English at the University of Massachusetts Boston, where she teaches composition, rhetoric, and literacy courses and directs the first-year composition program. In addition to writing research across the lifespan, her research and scholarly interests include age studies and composition pedagogy. Her work has been published in *College Composition and Communication, College English, Literacy in Composition Studies*, and *Computers and Composition*, among others.

Anthony Clairmont is a doctoral candidate in the Department of Education at the University of California, Santa Barbara. His research explores the sociocultural conditions under which measurement is used and interpreted in educational contexts. Clairmont has been involved in the construction and validation of measures of reading skills and study behaviors.

Lara-Jeane C. Costa is a research project director for the University of North Carolina at Chapel Hill Department of Allied Health Sciences. She is an expert in both methodology and content (preK–12 writing), and draws from her former experience as a public school special education teacher. Her publications and research focus on intervention science, relationships among the development of writing skills and cognitive processes science, alignment of instruction and measurement, and improving education for children with learning disabilities. She holds a doctoral degree and master's degree in Educational Psychology, Measurement and Evaluation, both from the University of North Carolina at Chapel Hill.

Ryan J. Dippre is Assistant Professor of English and the Director of College Composition at the University of Maine. He earned his Ph.D. from University of California, Santa Barbara in 2015. He has published in *Literacy in Composition Studies* and *English Journal*, among other places. His book, *Talk, Tools, and Texts: A Logic-in-Use for Studying Lifespan Literate Action Development*, is available at the WAC Clearinghouse / University Press of Colorado. He serves as the co-chair of the Writing through the Lifespan Collaboration, a group of international scholars interested in developing a multi-site, multi-method, multi-generational study of writing through the lifespan. His research interests include lifespan writing research and writing program administration.

Steve Graham is Warner Professor of Education in the Division of Leadership and Innovation in the Mary Lou Fulton Teachers College at Arizona State University. For close to 40 years, he has studied how writing develops, how to teach it effectively, and how writing can be used to support reading and learning. In recent years, he has been involved in the development and testing of digital tools for supporting writing and reading. His research involves typically developing writers and students with special needs in both elementary and secondary schools, with much of it occurring in classrooms in urban schools. He is currently the editor of the *Journal of Educational Psychology*.

Jeffrey A. Greene is Professor in the Learning Sciences and Psychological Studies program at the University of North Carolina at Chapel Hill. He has published peer-reviewed articles, books, and book chapters on self-regulated learning, epistemic cognition, and online learning. He was the recipient of the 2016 American Psychological Association Division 15 Richard E. Snow Award for Early Contributions. He is co-editor of the *Handbook of Epistemic Cognition* and the *Handbook of Self-Regulation of Learning and Performance*. He holds a Ph.D. in educational psychology, as well as a master's degree in measurement, statistics, and evaluation, both from the University of Maryland.

Sarah Hirsch received her Ph.D. in English from UC Santa Barbara with an emphasis on American literature. She is a full time Continuing Lecturer for the UCSB Writing Program where she teaches journalism, magazine writing, writing for the visual arts, and writing for the humanities. Her work focuses on the visual and material rhetoric of New Orleans' iconography and culture. Through her research Sarah explores the interpretation of images and the reinterpretation and repurposing of them.

Stephen R. Hooper is Professor of Psychiatry, Pediatrics, Psychology & Neuroscience, and Education at the University of North Carolina at Chapel Hill. He also holds appointments in the Department of Psychiatry and Behavioral Sciences at Duke University Medical Center, and holds Fellow status at Frank Porter Graham Child Development Institute. Dr. Hooper also currently serves as the Associate Dean of Allied Health Sciences in the UNC-CH School of Medicine and is Chair of the Department of Allied Health Sciences. Dr. Hooper has published extensively in the fields of child psychiatry, psychology, and special education, with particular interests in child psychopathology, learning disabilities, intellectual and developmental disabilities, and intervention science. Current funding initiatives involve the study of written language in children, rare genetic disorders, 22q11.2 Deletion Syndrome, and pediatric chronic kidney disease. Dr. Hooper received his doctoral degree in school psychology from the University of Georgia, with clinical child psychology internship training at Vanderbilt School of Medicine and a postdoctoral fellowship in child neuropsychology at Brown University.

Magdalena Knappik received her Ph.D. at the University of Vienna, Austria. She currently works at the University of Wuppertal, Germany, in the School of Education, area: Multilingualities in Education. Her research interests include writing development research, academic literacies, linguistic ethnography, translanguaging, critical pedagogy, critical race theory, and teacher education in migration societies. Her published works include her monograph, *Schreibend werden: Subjektivierungsprozesse in der Migrationsgesellschaft* (2018, "Writing and Becoming: Processes of Subjectivation in the Migration Society"), an analysis of 58 literacy narratives by monolingual and multilingual university students, and the edited volume *Sprache und Bildung in Migrationsgesellschaften* (2015, "Language and Education in Migration Societies"), co-edited with Nadja Thoma.

Yvonne Lee earned her Ph.D. in Rhetoric and Composition from Kent State University and now serves as the inaugural Director of Graduate Writing Support at Lehigh University. Her current research focuses on the intersections between graduate writers, graduate advisors, and writing center practices. Lee has also published work on such topics as sensemaking in the writing center environment and service learning in a healthcare-focused sophomore writing course.

Jeff Naftzinger is Assistant Professor of Rhetoric, Composition & Writing at Sacred Heart University, where he teaches undergraduate courses on everyday writing, academic writing, and digital rhetoric. His research focuses on understanding how and why people write in both academic and non-academic contexts. He is also a member of the Writing Through the Lifespan Collaboration and is currently serving on the conference committee.

Talinn Phillips is Associate Professor of English at Ohio University where she also directs the Graduate Writing and Research Center. In addition to the lifespan, her research has investigated international graduate student writing development, liminal writing program administrators, and various intersections of graduate students and writing center support. She is co-editor of *Supporting Graduate Student Writers: Research, Curriculum, and Program Design* (University of Michigan Press, 2016), co-author of *Teaching with a Global Perspective: Practical Strategies from Course Design to Assessment* (Routledge, 2018), and co-creator of the tutor training film, *Becoming an Ally: Tutoring Multilingual Writers* (2017). She is a co-founder of the Writing Through the Lifespan Collaboration.

Contributors

Apryl L. Poch is Assistant Professor of Special Education in the Department of Counseling, Psychology, and Special Education at Duquesne University in Pittsburgh, PA. Her research is focused on understanding the components of adolescent writing by modeling the components of the Simple View of Writing (i.e., transcription, text generation, memory, and self-regulatory executive functions) at the high school level, the writing development of school-age students with learning disabilities, adolescent students' knowledge of writing, and pre- and in-service general and special educators' knowledge and beliefs about teaching writing to students with disabilities. She is currently the editor of *LD Forum*, the newsletter for the Council for Learning Disabilities.

Kevin Roozen is Professor of Writing and Rhetoric at the University of Central Florida. Kevin's research examines the development of people's literate lives along expansive histories that stretch across their multiple textual engagements. Co-authored with Joe Erickson, Kevin's book *Expanding Literate Landscapes: Persons, Practices, and Sociohistoric Perspectives of Disciplinary Development* (Computers & Composition Digital Press, 2017) presents longitudinal case studies of disciplinary writing, learning, and socialization that argue for a richer, fuller understanding of the developmental trajectories people and literate practices trace throughout the world. Kevin's research has appeared in journals including *Written Communication*, *Research in the Teaching of English*, *College Composition and Communication*, the *Journal of Basic Writing*, and in a number of edited collections as well.

Lauren Rosenberg is the author of *The Desire for Literacy: Writing in the Lives of Adult Learners* as well as a follow-up essay ("'Still Learning': One Couple's Literacy Development in Older Adulthood") and book chapter ("Following Participants as Leaders in Long Research," forthcoming in *Telling Stories: Perspectives on Longitudinal Writing Research*) that explore the ongoing literacy activities of the participants in her original study. Her research focuses on the writing practices of adult populations that are underrepresented in composition studies, community literacy studies, and feminist research ethics. She is Associate Professor of Rhetoric and Writing Studies and Director of First-Year Composition at the University of Texas-El Paso.

Anna Smith received her Ph.D. at New York University. She is currently Assistant Professor of Secondary Education at Illinois State University, following an IES Postdoctoral Fellowship in Writing and New Learning Ecologies at University of Illinois, Urbana-Champaign. She is co-author of *Developing Writers: Teaching and Learning in the Digital Age* and co-editor of the *Handbook of Writing, Literacies, and Education in Digital Cultures*. Her recent research on writing development, transliteracies, and the intersection of teaching and learning can be found in journals such as *Learning, Culture and Social Interaction*, *Theory into Practice*, *Journal of Literacy Research*, and *Literacy*.

Erin Workman is Assistant Professor in the Writing, Rhetoric & Discourse (WRD) Department at DePaul University, where she directs the First-Year Writing Program, teaches undergraduate courses in the WRD major and graduate courses in the Teaching Writing and Language concentration, and leads the Teaching Apprenticeship Practicum. Her research focuses on lifelong and lifewide writing development, employing methods of visual and lifespan mapping to study writers' perspectives of their conceptual writing knowledge. Her work has appeared in *The WAC Journal, College Composition and Communication*, and *South Atlantic Review* and is forthcoming in the *Journal of Business and Technical Communication*.

Matthew C. Zajic is Assistant Professor in the Intellectual Disabilities/Autism Program in the Health & Behavior Studies Department at Teachers College, Columbia University. Prior to this position, he was a National Center for Special Education Research Postdoctoral Training Fellow in Education and Autism Spectrum Disorders at the Curry School of Education and Human Development at the University of Virginia. His research focuses on understanding and supporting the writing development of individuals with autism spectrum disorder, with specific interests in theory, assessment, and instruction. He has collaborated on interdisciplinary research projects examining reading, writing, and broader academic skill development in young, school-age, and postsecondary students with autism spectrum disorder. He recently co-edited a special issue for *Topics in Language Disorders* focused on writing development and autism spectrum disorders.

James T. Zebroski has—happily—taught college composition since 1978, most recently at University of Houston, where he is now Professor Emeritus and where he founded the Ph.D. in rhetoric, composition, and pedagogy. For nearly forty years his research has focused on Marxism and the critical theory of composition. His book *Thinking Through Theory: Vygotskian Perspectives on the Teaching of Writing* introduced the discipline to the theoretical and pedagogical implications of Lev Vygotsky's Marxist theory. He has published more than 50 articles, chapters, and essays on critical theory and innovative teaching practices. He currently is working on two books, *Ideology and Academic Labor in College English Departments* and *Vygotsky in the Twenty-first Century*.

www.ingramcontent.com/pod-product-compliance
Lightning Source LLC
Chambersburg PA
CBHW071335080526
44587CB00017B/2851